W9-DII-828

RIVAL PLAYWRIGHTS: MARLOWE, JONSON, SHAKESPEARE

Shakespeare and His Contemporaries
James Faed Sr. (1821–1911) after John Faed (1820–1902)

Rival Playwrights:
MARLOWE,
JONSON,
SHAKESPEARE

JAMES
SHAPIRO

COLUMBIA UNIVERSITY PRESS
NEW YORK

COLUMBIA UNIVERSITY PRESS

NEW YORK, OXFORD

© 1991 Columbia University Press

All Rights Reserved

Library of Congress Cataloging-in-Publication Data

Shapiro, James S., 1955–
    Rival playwrights : Marlowe, Jonson,
Shakespeare / James Shapiro.
        p. cm.
    Includes bibliographical references and
index.
    ISBN 0-231-07540-5
    1. English   drama—Early   modern
and Elizabethan, 1500–1600—History
and   criticism.   2. English   drama—
17th   century—History   and   criticism.   3. Influence (Literary, artistic,
etc.) 4. Marlowe, Christopher, 1564–
1593—Influence.   5. Jonson,   Ben,
1573?–1637—Influence.   6. Shakespeare,   William,   1564–1616—Influence.
    I. Title.
PR651.S53   1991
822'.309—dc20   90-28933
                                               CIP

Casebound editions of
Columbia University Press Books
are Smyth-sewn and printed on
permanent and durable acid-free paper

Book design by Teresa Bonner
Printed in the United States of America

C 10 9 8 7 6 5 4 3 2 1

CONTENTS

PREFACE

THIS BOOK IS ABOUT the influence that Christopher Marlowe, Ben Jonson, and William Shakespeare had on each other's work and legacies. It emerged out of an attempt to explain why so popular and celebrated an author as Marlowe mysteriously disappeared from print, stage, and canon by the mid-seventeenth century. Paradoxically, Marlowe's extensive influence proved his undoing, as contemporary writers imitated, contained, and parodied his work, thereby rendering it anachronistic. In addressing the psychological and historical factors governing these practices, this study soon expanded to include the mutual influence of Marlowe's two great heirs, Shakespeare and Jonson; this, in turn, led to a consideration of the ways in which the accidents of influence among these three writers profoundly affected the emerging canon of English Renaissance drama.

The voices of both the living and the dead echo—and are challenged—throughout the drama of this period. No doubt the formative experience of actors-turned-playwrights like Shakespeare and Jonson, who literally mouthed Marlowe's and Kyd's words, could only have heightened their awareness of the distance separating their rivals' styles from their own. Though few would deny the pervasiveness of imitation in the Elizabethan theater, the nature of that collaborative and competitive enterprise poses all sorts of theoretical obstacles to a study of influence, not least of which is understanding how much the unusual working conditions of the Elizabethan theater shaped these rivalries and how much should be attributed to the habits of mind of the playwrights themselves.

Textual difficulties need to be faced as well: late sixteenth- and early seventeenth century plays that were not lost or quietly suppressed bear the scars of censors, scriveners, playhouse prompters, compositors, printers, and editors. In addition, given the repertorial practices of the public theaters, the chronology of plays is often difficult to establish. Moreover, the financial disincentive of making theatrical property available to competitors meant that few Elizabethan plays were published immediately after they were first staged; those that appeared in print were often subject to extensive revision (and, of course, plays were often revived long after those that imitated or parodied them had vanished).

Theories of influence readily at hand—such as Harold Bloom's notion of the "anxiety of influence" and Thomas M. Greene's description of Renaissance poets' "dialectical imitation" of classical predecessors—ultimately prove procrustean when applied to these complex collaborative encounters, especially in their emphasis on chronologically and textually stable lyric poems. Yet at many points their insights are illuminating: rivalry among Elizabethan playwrights was, after all, characterized by a version of Bloomian intergenerational strife; we need only recall Thomas Nashe's nervous insistence that "I call no man in England father but myself." And, insofar as many (if not all) of the playwrights were schooled in a tradition of imitation based on surpassing classical predecessors, Greene's ideas about Renaissance emulation are germane.

At points where these theories overlap with the historically specific conditions governing imitation among Elizabethan playwrights, they prove invaluable and are drawn on freely in the pages that follow. The same holds true for the theory of intertextuality recently advanced by Linda Hutcheon in her work on parody in postmodernist art, which focuses upon recollections that simultaneously pay tribute to rivals while rendering their work anachronistic. Hutcheon's theory is especially helpful in providing a way of talking about how confrontations between individual artists, as well as larger canonical struggles, are waged through parody.

The model of influence that informs this book is therefore eclectic. And the three main chapters—"Marlowe and Jonson," "Shakespeare and Marlowe," and "Jonson and Shakespeare"—are offered as case studies in influence that illustrate the range of intertextual concerns and strategies that came into play among these rivals. If there is one constant throughout these pages it is that rivalry and parody are conceived of as social practices, as ways of leasing and building upon the intellectual and stylistic property of other writers, ways that have much to teach us about our own collaborative enterprise.

ACKNOWLEDGMENTS

WHEN WRITING A BOOK about influence you never lose sight of just how much you owe to others. My formal debt to generations of scholars is recorded in footnotes; my informal one is more substantial, though not so easily noted. I cannot adequately calculate what I owe to those who introduced me to the study of English Renaissance drama, though I know how fortunate I have been to have studied under Bernard Beckerman, S. F. Johnson, Janel Mueller, Michael Murrin, William Ringler, John Wallace, and David Bevington.

My greatest debt is to the friends and colleagues who patiently read my work, asked tough questions, and gave good advice: James Bednarz, Thomas Cartelli, Maurice Charney, Robert Griffin, Laurie Kaplan, Stuart Kurland, Claire McEachern, John McGavin, James V. Mirollo, William Monroe, Peter Rudnytsky, William Sherman, Edward Tayler, and especially Alvin Snider. To David Scott Kastan I owe the most; what I have learned about generosity, influence, and collaboration in the scholarly world I have learned from him. I am also grateful for the feedback I received when portions of this book were read at meetings of the Marlowe Society of America, the Shakespeare Society of America, the Renaissance Society of America, and the New York Shakespeare Society.

My institutional debts are substantial: to the Huntington Library, which provided a summer grant and an ideal place to read, write, and talk things through; to the National Endowment for the Humanities, for the summer stipend that allowed me to begin this project; and to Columbia University, for providing research funds and time off that enabled me to complete the book. I would also like to thank Mary Beth Rose of *Renaissance Drama*, Arthur Marotti of *Criticism*, and Leeds Barroll of *Shakespeare Studies* for their encouragement and for allowing me to include parts of previously published articles. Lastly, I would like to thank my excellent editor at Columbia University Press, Jennifer Crewe.

A NOTE ON TEXTS

UNLESS OTHERWISE NOTED, I have quoted from modern spelling editions. Shakespeare's plays and poems are cited from David Bevington, ed., *The Complete Works of Shakespeare,* 3d ed. (Glenview, Ill.: Scott, Foresman, 1980). Marlowe's plays are cited from J. B. Steane, ed., *Christopher Marlowe: The Complete Plays* (Harmondsworth, Middlesex: Penguin Books, 1969). Marlowe's poems, along with the imitations of George Chapman, Sir Walter Raleigh, Henry Petowe, John Donne, and J. Guilpin, are cited from Stephen Orgel, ed., *The Complete Poems of Christopher Marlowe* (Harmondsworth, Middlesex: Penguin Books, 1971). Jonson's work is cited from the standard and outstanding edition, C. H. Herford and Percy and Evelyn Simpson, eds., *Ben Jonson,* 11 vols. (Oxford: Clarendon Press, 1925–52) (H&S). In the interest of consistency I have modernized quotations from Jonson and from other sixteenth-, seventeenth-, and eighteenth-century authors so that their words do not appear unnecessarily archaic in comparison with those quoted from modern spelling texts.

RIVAL PLAYWRIGHTS:
MARLOWE,
JONSON,
SHAKESPEARE

I

INTRODUCTION

IN THE FALL OF 1598, William Shakespeare, Ben Jonson, and the ghost of Christopher Marlowe crossed paths. Their encounter was, perhaps, inevitable. Five years after Marlowe's death the shards of his influence were beginning to emerge. Shakespeare, long silent on the subject of his rival, had challenged *The Jew of Malta* in *The Merchant of Venice* and had also echoed Marlowe's words in two of his most recent plays—*2 Henry IV* and *The Merry Wives of Windsor*—through the garbled parodies of Ancient Pistol and Sir Hugh Evans. He would allude to Marlowe himself a year later in *As You Like It*, where he quotes a "saw of might" from the "dead Shepherd" (3.5.81–82). It was the closest Shakespeare would come to naming a rival in his plays. Jonson's collaborative work at this time is suppressed and lost, though fragments that appear in the contemporary anthology *England's Parnassus,* and his unfinished *Mortimer His Fall,* influenced by Marlowe's *Edward II,* indicate the extent of his early indebtedness to Marlowe.

Their recollections should not be construed simply as tributes to the fading memory of a fellow poet cut off in the prime of life. In death, Marlowe was proving a greater threat to his rivals than he had been in his lifetime, as his plays and poems continued to flourish both onstage and in print.[1] Philip Henslowe's account in his *Diary* of the Admiral's Men's performances and stage properties indicates that Marlowe's plays were still regular fare at the Rose Theater as the century drew to a close. Meanwhile, two editions of "Hero and Leander" were published in 1598; the second edition of *Edward II* had just been published as had the third edition of the two parts of *Tamburlaine;* Marlowe's erotic *Elegies* were in circulation and soon to be banned and burned; his translation of *Lucan* was at the printers; and "The Passionate Shepherd," which had circulated in manuscript for some time, would soon be anthologized. Thomas Thorpe would shortly write to fellow publisher Edward Blount that Marlowe's "ghost or genius is to be seen walk[ing] the churchyard in (at the least) three or four sheets" (*Poems,* 187). Like another and more famous ghost, Marlowe's insisted: *"Remember me"* (*Hamlet,* 1.5.112). It was a ghost that continued to haunt both Shakespeare and Jonson.

The belated confrontation among the three authors took place in *Every Man in His Humour:* written (and extensively revised) by Jonson, acted in by Shakespeare (and reputedly purchased by the Chamberlain's Men at his insistence), the play quotes, then comments upon, an extended quotation from Marlowe's "Hero and Leander." What, we can only wonder, were Shakespeare's thoughts, when in Act 3 the poetaster Don Matheo attempts to pass off Marlowe's celebrated verse as his own invention:

> Rare creature, let me speak without offence,
> Would God my rude words had the influence
> To rule thy thoughts, as thy fair looks do mine,
> Then shouldst thou be his prisoner, who is thine.
>
> .   .   .
>
> Be not unkind and fair, misshapen stuff
> Is of behavior boisterous and rough:
>
> .   .   .
>
> And I in duty will exceed all other,
> As you in beauty do excel love's mother.
>
> (Q1, H&S 3:249)

Lorenzo Junior identifies the passage—"S'heart, this is in 'Hero and Leander' "—and when his friend Prospero asks him not to interrupt, he responds in frustration that Matheo "utters nothing but stolen remnants," and is unforgiving: "A pox on him, hang him filching rogue, steal from the dead? It's worse than sacrilege" (H&S 3:249). It is a curious intertextual moment: Jonson quotes Marlowe on the power that words have to influence another's thoughts at the very moment that he tries to deflect attention from his own indebtedness to Marlowe by placing the burden of unacknowledged influence upon his poetaster, Matheo.

Examples like this are what this book is about. All too little survives about the personal and professional rivalries of these authors, and only at intertextual moments like this are we offered a glimpse into the complex personal and professional dynamics of their interrelations. The scene also pinpoints some of the most contested and contradictory aspects of imitation in the Renaissance. At what point does imitation become theft? Do the same conditions apply to those who borrow from classical sources as those who imitate contemporary ones? What rights does a writer have over his words? Who is to protect the dead writer from the living? And who the living from the oppressive influence of the dead? To what extent do these theoretical distinctions apply to the collaborative productions of the English Renaissance stage?

Every Man in His Humour also contains the first recorded use of the word "parody" in English, but only in the version Jonson revised for inclusion in the 1616 Folio. The differences between the 1601 Quarto and the subsequent Folio version of the play are instructive, for they provide insight into a significant development in the understanding and practice of influence among English playwrights in the late sixteenth and early seventeenth centuries.

In the final scene of the Quarto version, the plagiarizing poetaster Matheo is exposed by Doctor Clement, who seizes the "commonwealth of paper" stuffed in Matheo's hose and reads from the confiscated scraps the following lines, taken from a sonnet by Samuel Daniel:

> Unto the boundless ocean of thy beauty,
> Runs this poor river, charged with streams of zeal,
> Returning thee the tribute of my duty:
> Which here my youth, my plaints, my love reveal.

(H&S 3:284)

When asked if this is his "own invention" Matheo admits that he has "translated that out of a book, called *Delia*" (H&S 3:284). Translated is used here in the sense applied by schoolboys: literally copied out, the most basic kind of imitation possible.

When Jonson revised this scene for inclusion in the Folio (probably some time around 1612) he altered the quotation from *Delia* to:

> Unto the boundless ocean of thy face,
> Runs this poor river charged with streams of eyes.

(H&S 3:400)

With the substitution of a couple of words, Daniel's hyperbolic Petrarchan conceit is stretched past the breaking point. Just in case audiences failed to catch the allusion (since *Delia* is not named in the Folio), Clement condemningly adds that "this is stolen." Ed Knowell then takes the attack one step further:

> A parody! A parody! With a kind of miraculous gift, to
> make it absurder than it was.
>
> (H&S 3:400)

The miraculous gift to alter and make absurd a rival's words is, of course, Jonson's own.

The poetaster's limitations are conflated first with Daniel's poetic defects, then with those of the entire "commonwealth" of English poets, as Clement executes summary justice by setting fire to the unbound anthology of English love poetry that he has seized:

> See, see how our poets glory shines! Brighter and brighter! Still it
> increases! O, now it's at the highest. And, now, it declines as fast.
> You may see. *Sic transit gloria mundi.*
>
> (H&S 3:400)

Jonson leaves ambiguous whether the ironic phrase "our poets glory" is collective or singular—that is, whether it is only the poetaster or all of the English poets whose verse is found upon him that are punished in this effort to "cleanse the air" (H&S 3:400). In performance, and in the absence of an apostrophe in the published texts, "our poets glory" remains indeterminate. In either case Jonson's own poetry survives the conflagration, outliving that of the commonwealth of English poets.[2]

Two related revisions in the final scene of *Every Man in His Humour* also register an evolving sense of imitation and canonization in the drama at this time and point to how parodic recollections are inextricably bound to emerging reconceptualizations of authorship and the canon. The first is Jonson's decision to omit Lorenzo Junior's long, earnest defense of poetry ("I can refell opinion, and approve/ The state of poesie, such as it is,/ Blessed, eternal, and most true divine" (H&S 3:285). This thirty-two line celebration of the true poet is replaced in the Folio by Lorenzo Junior's mere seconding of Clement's remark that poets are born, not made;

Clement saves Lorenzo "the labor of a defence" (3:400). The nervous urgency that characterizes the cut speech may well have made the professionally established Jonson cringe in retrospect when he came to revise his earlier work.

The second change has to do with Kitely, the possessive husband, who acknowledges his jealousy by reciting some verse on the dangers of being obsessed with his wife's fidelity. In the Folio he offers an abbreviated version of the same speech ("Oh, what a plenteous world of this will come!/ When air rains horns, all may be sure of some"), before adding: "I ha' learned so much verse out of a jealous man's part, in a play" (H&S 3:401). A jealous husband's stock response is acknowledged as purely conventional, something learned at the playhouse. When stage verse is so familiar that people use lines out of plays in their daily lives, poetry no longer needs the kind of strenuous defense once offered by Lorenzo Junior. At such a point we are dealing with a firmly established tradition, one with a history and social function, and one subject to acts of recollection that are both canonical and dismissive, or, in short, parodic.

I am not suggesting that dramatic parody begins in 1612. Far from it. By this late date, however, it has become fully implicated in the emerging practices of the public theater. Perhaps the most celebrated example of parody appeared twenty years earlier: Robert Greene's warning to Marlowe and his fellow tragedians concerning that "upstart crow," that "Shake-scene," who with his "player's heart wrapped in a tiger's hide," thinks he can write as good a bombastic line as they.[3] The lines parody York's words to the vindictive Queen Margaret in Shakespeare's *3 Henry VI:* "O tiger's heart wrapt in a woman's hide" (1.4.137). By altering a couple of key words Greene personalizes his attack on the ambitious actor-turned-playwright while at the same time demonstrating his own mastery over Shakespeare's style. Though intended as invective, Greene's parody (which depends on his readers' familiarity with Shakespeare's popular histories) also acknowledges how great a threat the young actor was becoming to the leading dramatists of the day. In this respect, Greene's parody of Shakespeare's imitation of what Jonson would later call the "furious vociferation" (H&S 8:587) of tragedians like Marlowe nicely illustrates the way in which parodic attempts to contain a rival can boomerang, serving instead to confirm and legitimate the target of the parody.

I do not mean parodic in the narrow sense of burlesque or travesty, or even in the *Oxford English Dictionary* definition of "an imitation of a work more or less closely modelled on the original, but so turned as to produce a ridiculous effect."[4] Rather, following Linda Hutcheon, I am interested in parody in the double sense implied in its etymological roots as a song, *odos,* that is *para,* a prefix that means both "against" and "beside."[5] Parodic recollections are potentially intimate, as well as oppositional, paying homage to a rival's work while at the same time displacing it, revealing its outdatedness and conventionality. Parody, then, unlike other kinds of intertextuality, is necessarily a product of authorial intention: it is a self-conscious and critical act of recollection that insists on the difference between texts and depends upon audiences or readers to recognize the signaled historical or formal distance between works of art. Finally, parody is a historicizing act: in Hutcheon's words, parody "historicizes by placing art within the history of art."[6]

In practical terms parody covers a range of artistic responses: some parody borders on the combative; some on this side of idolatry. The most interesting examples are somewhere in between and reveal the considerable tensions that come into play when writers have to come to terms with each other's styles and confront each other's influence. Hutcheon suggests that perhaps "parodists only hurry up what is a natural procedure: the changing of aesthetic forms through time."[7] I would modify this only to the extent that literary change is anything but natural; parody, is, however, a vital instrument in the making of change and in making that change seem both natural and inevitable. As such, it functions as what Hutcheon rightly labels "a form of serious art criticism," the major one employed by Renaissance dramatists, who surely had much to say about the works of their contemporaries. Parody, Hutcheon adds, is "the custodian of the artistic legacy, defining not only where art is, but where it has come from." In this capacity, parody "manages to inscribe continuity while permitting critical distance and change."[8]

I want to work from this definition of parody because it is one that is self-consciously recognized—and in *Every Man in His Humour* named —in Elizabethan drama and because, unlike many theories of influence in circulation today, it is historically and culturally specific.[9] While not denying the propriety of Hutcheon's theory of parody to her subject, the practices of post-modernist artists, I see parody as a phenomenon no less characteristic of the Elizabethan era, where many of the fundamental issues of contemporary art—including authorship, collaboration, commercialism, and canonization—had their roots.[10] Other art forms of the Renaissance—notably the visual arts and music—offer analogues (and perhaps models) for an emergence of parody as a dominant form of artistic response.

The stage provided an ideal setting for parodic encounters. First, because drama is what Mikhail Bakhtin would call polyglottal, perfect for an interplay—or clash—of different voices and styles. Second, because the drama affords the possibility of visual recollections as well. A notorious contemporary example is the familiar sight of actors imitating the hunchback gait of Laurence Olivier as Richard III while reciting "Now is the winter of our discontent," imitations that are both playful and pay homage to Olivier's tremendous influence. Although most of the visual recollections from the Elizabethan stage are lost to us, in a theatrical world in which props were reused and, as Hamlet reminds us, gestures often highly stylized,[11] it is easy to imagine that audiences were treated by the rival traditions to just these kinds of visual parodies.

Perhaps the most problematic and difficult precondition for parody is a notion of authorship and individuality, since artists almost always allude in their parodies to specific texts by specific authors. This may explain the absence of parody in the comparatively anonymous Medieval drama, where the pressure to assert the primacy of one's own voice appears far less pronounced than in Renaissance drama. Much recent work in Renaissance studies has focused on the issue of authorship, and it remains a hotly contested topic, bound up with related conceptions of originality, individualism, and ownership and control of one's work.[12] Setting aside the more problematic question of subjectivity, there appears to be a steady trend late in Elizabeth's reign towards acknowledging (and soon advertising) the authorship of plays. Certainly, the evidence of the title pages to printed plays in the 1590s indicates that authors were acknowledged by name with increasing frequency. By the close of the decade, with the appearance of Francis Meres's *Palladis Tamia* (1598) and anthologies in which authors were identified alongside poems, we have evidence of a movement towards canonizing the leading English writers. By the early seventeenth century, prefaces and dedications in Jacobean plays that acknowledge the influence of other dramatists confirm this pattern.[13] Finally, we do well to remember that while plays were the product of various cultural forces rather than autonomous creations, when the authorities sought out those responsible for politically seditious drama (which occurred, for example, with Jonson, Chapman, and Dekker's *Eastward Ho*) it was the authors themselves who were singled out and arrested.[14]

This increasing effort to distinguish authorship might appear all the more surprising since about half of the plays written from the late 1580s until the closing of the theaters in 1642 were the product of multiple authorship.[15] Even playwrights like Marlowe, Jonson, and Shakespeare, all of whom were exceptional in having produced many more plays alone than in collaboration, each worked at one time or another with one or more fellow playwrights. This brings us to a central paradox: the very frequency of collaboration in the public theater appears to have heightened sensitivity to the distinctive voices of individual dramatists.

Collaboration therefore proved to be a vital condition for the extensive use of parody on the Elizabethan stage. Collaboration also bred an unprecedented familiarity, as playwrights in the public theaters worked alongside each other, learning each other's strengths and weaknesses (who was good at comedy, who at a love scene, who best at exposition, who at bombast), learning, too, how to stitch these group efforts together seamlessly. They were also adept at imitating each other's styles when paid to do so, since older plays frequently underwent revision before being reintroduced into the company's repertory. A good instance of this is the additions Jonson provided for Kyd's popular *Spanish Tragedy*. There are few today who would see much overlap between Jonson's drama in 1602, at this point masterful prose comedy, and the Kyddian rant of the late 1580s. But given Jonson's experience as an actor playing Hieronimo in the provinces, and his early collaborative work with Henslowe's journeymen, it can come as no surprise that Henslowe would commission the additions from him and that Jonson would contribute material that is hard to distinguish stylistically from Kyd's original. The working conditions could only have reinforced a familiarity with rivals' styles that made clearer to playwrights what set their styles apart. Surely, the parodic cut and thrust of the Poets' War in the early years of the seventeenth century could not have been possible without the unprecedented degree of familiarity among playwrights. In some cases the intimacy of writers extended so far that their influence prevented works from being completed. One of the more striking (though unverifiable) examples appears in Kyd's torture-induced letter to the Lord Keeper, Sir John Puckering, where he relates that an atheistic Marlowe had dissuaded him from attempting "a poem on St. Paul's conversion" that Kyd had been "determined" to write.[16]

The repertorial practices of the commercial theaters also provided a powerful spur to parodic recollections. Commercialism in and of itself is not a precondition for parody, as evidenced by the commercial basis of the Medieval cycle drama, or early morality plays like *The Castle of Perseverance* or *Mankind.* What distinguished the Elizabethan theaters after the mid-1580s was a commercial enterprise grounded in rivalry between permanent resident companies in year-round playhouses. These circumstances gave rise to a demand for many plays, since there was no extensive repertory available. Along with these developments came the emergence of an increasingly sophisticated playgoing audience, hungry for new plays, quick to judge, and soon capable of identifying and enjoying the ways in which authors recalled and parodied predecessors and rivals, out-Heroding Herod.

By 1600 the public theaters included the Globe, the Rose, the Fortune, the Curtain, the Swan, and the Boar's Head Inn, with capacities as high as 3000 or so at the Globe.[17] A conservative guess would be that on a given day as many as 5000 spectators could have witnessed plays, and in a good week, upward of 25,000, well over ten percent of London's population (not even accounting for the very young and the infirm). Competition for audiences was fierce, and in a given week it is conceivable that ten different plays, perhaps one or two that were new, could be staged in the environs of the city. The rivalry between the two leading companies—the Admiral's and Chamberlain's Men—could be felt in the production of rival plays (the Admiral's *Sir John Oldcastle,* which counters the depiction of Falstaff offered in the Chamberlain's repertory, offers a striking instance of this). And with the emergence of the child actors in the private theaters at this time—where their diminutive stature and high voices proved ideal for parodying the styles of the adult players and the concerns of the popular theater—the possibilities of parody were multiplied. Given these institutional practices, parody proved an enormously useful device for prematurely aging a rival's work and confirming the novelty of one's own.

One result of this competitive and commercial system was the collapsing of literary generations. Where well into the sixteenth century Corpus Christi cycles could still represent (with minor revisions) the same plays year in and year out, and where Tudor morality plays offered variations on a fairly limited set of thematic concerns, the unprecedented demand for new plays and styles on the late Elizabethan stage meant that one kind of revenge drama, or romantic comedy, or heroical history, was driven out by another in rapid succession. Here, more than anywhere else, parody proved most useful, for it depends upon an acknowledgment of temporal distance and difference. Dramatists recalled predecessors, and that very act of recollection potentially signaled the datedness of what came before. Sometimes such recollections could be aggressive, sometimes nostalgic. By the reign of Charles I, Michael Drayton could consign Marlowe to an earlier literary epoch, though he himself had been part of the same generation, born the year before Marlowe.[18] No doubt the proclivity of Elizabethans to recall previous social, religious, and political orders nostalgically, especially after the death of Elizabeth, contributed to the deeply felt sense of the pastness of the recent past.[19]

Curiously, the Renaissance practice of imitation of classical authors contributed to this foreshortening of literary generations. Thomas M. Greene's magisterial study, *The Light in Troy*, traces the development in the Renaissance of imitative strategies for engaging the ancients that ranged from "sacramental" translation (of the kind exibited by Matheo) up through more complex engagements, "eclectic" and "heuristic," culminating in that most complex form of imitation, "dialectical." These dialectical acts of imitation "had to prove [their] historical courage and artistic good faith by leaving room for a two-way current of mutual criticism between authors and between eras."[20] Greene's theory of Renaissance imitation of classical authors can be extended to the public theaters, where the strategy of identifying historical distance and juxtaposing two worlds or "*significans mundi*" was appropriated by dramatists having to confront twenty-year-old rivals rather than ancients from previous millenia. For Renaissance authors dealing with the burden of the past, anachronism was key.

What made this strategy even more urgent for Elizabethan dramatists was a chronological and textual instability that never muddies Greene's scheme, based as it is upon a lyric tradition: there is no question of the pastness of Virgil or Seneca. However, given the repertorial practices of the English Renaissance stage, authors constantly ran the risk of parodically exposing as anachronistic plays that would continue to be staged before appreciative audiences long after the parodist's work had faded from the public eye.

Parody also depends upon (or tries to create the impression of) anachronism. Greene himself begs the question of how much time must pass for a sense of anachronism to be felt, and I think this is exactly the point. Parody, by exaggerating certain stylistic features, suggests that a work is more out of fashion than we might at first consider. Given the grounding of most playwrights in the grammar school (and for some, university) in which this notion of imitation or emulation was practiced, it is not surprising to see this appropriated in rivalries with near contemporaries. The trick was to distort or exaggerate historical distance. Sometimes this was accomplished by simply reminding audiences of the fact that one's rival was dead while one was still alive and writing—hence, Jonson's allusion to stealing from the dead in *Every Man in,* or Shakespeare's recollection of Marlowe as "dead shepherd." Sometimes the datedness of the work, rather than the author, would be emphasized, as in the Induction to *Bartholomew Fair,* where Jonson's ancient stagekeeper remembers old chestnuts like *Titus Andronicus* (c. 1591) and *The Spanish Tragedy* (c. 1587) as even older than they really were. By having the plays exaggeratedly dated back "five and twenty, or thirty years" (H&S 6:16) Jonson places them at the outer limits of a theatrical culture's living memory.

These repertorial practices of the Elizabethan stage also overlap at certain points with the conditions for another dominant conception of emulation, Harold Bloom's theory of the anxiety of influence, though for Bloom this anxiety is a post-Enlightenment phenomenon, and one that Shakespeare, remarkably, escapes from completely, and from which Jonson (whom Bloom argues saw imitation as simply "hard work") was immune.[21] While in the chapters that follow I call into question both of these judgments, Bloom's theory proves invaluable to the extent that some of the writers (especially Jonson and his "sons") thought in these oedipal terms and would seize upon this model of male intergenerational strife in confronting certain rivals. While Bloom's theory is fundamentally ahistorical in its universalizing psychology, nonetheless, its textually specific claims (especially its insight into the ways of creative misprision or misreading) powerfully illuminate the parodic practices of Elizabethan authors.

Conditions in the literary world of Elizabethan England were well suited for the kind of oedipal contention at the heart of Bloom's model of influence. As noted above, Thomas Nashe insisted that he could call no man father in England but himself.[22] And the theater was overwhelmingly a male world, and an aggressively competitive one at that, with rival companies, rival traditions, rival playhouses, rival actors, even a war of the theaters and war of the poets. Jonson would cultivate not only the sons of Ben but a whole tribe of followers. In addition, apprenticeship in the playhouse could only have reinforced a model of familial succession in the theaters. Finally, some of these playwrights were quite violent, Marlowe and Jonson notoriously so. So that Bloom's idea of intergenerational male strife readily offers itself as an appropriatable model for literary relations. Its limitations are that these were not really fathers and sons—

generations are crunched—and the dead authors that are recalled might have still been been alive (and in their twenties) a year or two before. Parody helped memorialize them prematurely. To the extent, then, that Greene's and Bloom's theories dovetail with Elizabethan social and institutional practices, they prove extremely useful.

One other major condition for parody existed as a result of all these developments: the formation not only of repertories but also of literary canons that rank and preserve authors and their works. Parody is perfectly suited to this task, since it acts as a kind of canonizing device in miniature, paying homage to and preserving the memory of older works while attempting to dislodge, revise, or replace them. Parody, then, is both an agent that helps produce and constantly revise the canon and, at the same time, a product of the canonizing impulse, through which writers struggled to locate themselves relationally. In an age of rapid cultural and literary change, parody proved invaluable in forming and redefining the canon.

As a way of enabling authors to imitate each other, parody, as an essentially literary strategy, takes its place alongside other cultural and institutional practices relating to literary reputation and rivalry—personal, artistic, economic. These could range in the early seventeenth century from burial at Poets' Corner at Westminster Abbey, to the publication of revised plays as collected works, to the pairing of poems (like "The Passionate Shepherd" and the "Nymph's Reply") in anthologies. Each relationship between writers obviously had its own dynamics, though in some instances there was something in an author's work that attracted a certain kind of response from a good many of his fellow writers.

With Marlowe this was certainly the case, especially with his nondramatic poems, as rival after rival imitated or tried to complete his "unfinished" works. Marlowe's early death at twenty-nine, with many of his works as yet unpublished though circulating in manuscript or on stage, no doubt made conditions ripe for such a response. These responses are parodic in the sense that they offer alternative versions of Marlowe's poems or plays, creative misprisions that offer a sense of stability and closure that had been lacking in Marlowe's profoundly ambiguous writing.

Successful imitation in the theater depended upon one's ability to delimit the popularity or even subversiveness of a predecessor's work. Perhaps the most famous example of complete containment is offered by

Hamlet, which virtually erases its model, the "ur-Hamlet," only traces of which survive in the interstices of Shakespeare's play. Containing a source meant, in part, supplanting or redirecting its course, much as Hotspur insists on containing a literal source, the River Trent, in *1 Henry IV:*

> I'll have the current in this place dammed up,
> And here the smug and silver Trent shall run
> In a new channel, fair and evenly.

> (3.1.98–100)

When Glendower responds in exasperation that you cannot redirect a source: "Not wind? It shall, it must! You see it doth" (103), Hotspur insists: "I'll have it so. A little charge will do it" (111). To redirect a source—for Hotspur as for the belated poet, "but a little charge will trench him here" (108)—is to demonstrate one's capacity to challenge and change that which is perceived as natural and inviolable. Containment, then, is the key to appropriation, to asserting one's authority and power over influential sources.

When a dramatist could parodically embed within his own work a rival's language or style or artistic vision, he could show that his rival lacked a sufficiently inclusive perspective. Thus, when Jonson recalls the romantic vision of Marlowe's "Hero and Leander" within the colloquial rhythms of his own prose comedy in *Every Man in His Humour,* he is able, through this kind of juxtaposition, to draw attention to how unrealistic and far-fetched Marlowe's world—ripped out of its context—could appear. To contain parodically a rival's work necessarily meant to acknowledge it as well—to give it definition and limits, spatial and temporal. Granting a rival's accomplishment a local habitation and a name also meant reducing that work to a set of readily definable features. The ability to imitate another's style demonstrated one's command over that style, the capacity to make another's voice just one more part of one's own many-voiced universe.

It remains to say how aggressive these acts of parodic imitation were. Thomas Greene's vision of imitation in the Renaissance as something reconciliatory and recuperative is, I think, too idealized. On the other hand, Harold Bloom's nervously patricidal scheme is too rigidly combative. My own view tends to be more flexible. Some acts of imitative appropriation—say, Shakespeare's use of *The Troublesome Raigne*—evince no anxiety or particular aggressiveness at all; others, like Jonson's abuse

of Marston in his comical satires, might be said to border on the patholog-
ical. We do well to remember that the drama of this period witnessed
both a fellowship of poets and a Poets' War. It was probably neither as
malicious nor as golden as some literary historians have made the age
sound. Poetic rivalries (then, as now) were anything but static: writers
died, others rose and declined in prominence, economic conditions within
the institutions of the theater and the playing companies changed, and
playwrights who were at blows one week could undertake a successful
collaboration the next. In spite of these ups and downs the writing of
plays remained a commercial and therefore inescapably competitive enterprise, and the competitive nature of imitation meant that imitation was
meant to displace and self-promote, to seal off the other, to contain its
popularity, and to advance one's own.

The sense of emulation I am describing here would have been
familiar, I think, to a Shakespeare who would conceive of his competition
with a rival poet in quite similar terms:

> Was it the proud full sail of his great verse
> Bound for the prize of all too precious you,
> That did my ripe thoughts in my brain inhearse,
> Making their tomb the womb wherein they grew?
> Was it his spirit, by spirit taught to write
> Above a mortal pitch, that struck me dead?
>
> ("SONNET 86," lines 1–6)

The image of the merchant ship in the opening lines of this sonnet on the
unnamed "rival poet" suggests how readily literary competition was identified with comparable commercial enterprises. The pressure of this rivalry
was sufficient to contain ("inhearse") and bury alive the creative powers of
a rival. Yet a sense of playfulness is registered here as well, for the very
act of completing the sonnet confirms the poet's capacity to transcend the
temporary threat posed by emulation. There is also the unspoken but
powerful assumption here that poets depend on rivalry and on contestation
(real or imagined) to define themselves and their successes. In the section
that follows I try to provide a context and perspective for understanding
Shakespeare's and Jonson's appropriations of Marlowe's art by first turning
to the kinds of parodic strategies that Marlowe's other contemporaries
adopted in attempting to "inhearse" the ghostly presence of their rival.

ᕦ

Sometimes a literary imitation or parody is so successful that we can never read the imitated work the same way again. Usually, though, it is only in a figurative sense that the imitation rewrites its precursor. In the case of Marlowe's "The Passionate Shepherd" and "Hero and Leander," however, the imitative responses of Sir Walter Raleigh and George Chapman proved so influential that Marlowe's originals were literally altered to accommodate his successors' "reply" and "continuation." These are extreme but by no means isolated instances of how rivals sought to appropriate and capitalize on Marlowe's achievements. Again and again his imitators acknowledged Marlowe as a force to be reckoned with. Henry Petowe, whose continuation, "Hero and Leander's Further Fortunes," was published in 1598, no doubt spoke for many when he wrote that "had that king of poets breathed longer,"

> No bastard eaglet's quill the world throughout
> Had been of force to mar what he had made,
> For why they were not expert in that trade:
> What mortal soul with Marlowe might contend,
> That could 'gainst reason force him stoop or bend?
> Whose silver charming tongue moved such delight
> That men would shun their sleep in still dark night
> To meditate upon his golden lines,
> His rare conceits and sweet according rhymes.

> (*POEMS*, 94–95)

Petowe's tribute suggests how compelling contemporary writers found Marlowe's work and how this engagement translated into a poetic contestation in which the rival sought to "contend" with and subdue Marlowe, in Tamburlainian fashion "forc[ing] him [to] stoop or bend." Apparently, there was something in Marlowe's work that seems to have invited such emulation. And though it is not possible to analyze all these poetic responses — Marlowe must surely have been subject to more contemporary imitations than any English poet before or since — in the discussion that follows I turn to a number of examples from Elizabethan poetry and drama (temporarily setting aside Jonson and Shakespeare) in order to offer a better sense of what I mean by parodic containment and how Marlowe invited it.

Of all Marlowe's work, the most imitated has been the brief lyric

"The Passionate Shepherd." R. S. Forsythe, who has traced dozens of imitations of the poem written over the past four centuries, has suggested that the influence of Marlowe's original was so pervasive that its many imitations, taken together, constitute a new genre: the invitation to love.[23] The many extant manuscript and printed versions of Marlowe's poem bear witness to a complicated history of elaborations, misattributions, imitations, and responses, so much so that it is not easy to agree upon exactly what we refer to when we speak of the "Passionate Shepherd." The original apparently circulated in manuscript for some time before appearing posthumously in print in a four-stanza version in *The Passionate Pilgrim* (1599), a collection of poems attributed to Shakespeare. Only when it reappeared the following year in the anthology *England's Helicon* (1600) was it attributed to Marlowe. This time, however, it was printed in an expanded six-stanza version. Other variations proliferated: a different six-stanza form in the popular ballad "The Lover's Promises to his Beloved" (1603); a seven-stanza version in the *Thornborough Commonplace Book* manuscript (c. 1580–1630); a five-stanza version in the collected poems of Raleigh (1813); and in the 1653 and 1655 editions of Izaak Walton's *The Compleat Angler* six and seven stanzas, respectively. There are, it goes without saying, dizzying variants between each of these versions of the poem.[24]

In a painstaking reconstruction of this textual history, Fredson Bowers has shown that much of this rich variation is a result of the interpenetration of Marlowe's poem with Raleigh's response, "The Nymph's Reply to the Shepherd," which first appeared in 1600 in *England's Helicon*. Over time, changes in the "Nymph's Reply" resulted in what Bowers terms "reverse influence."[25] In order to maintain the neat metrical and rhetorical symmetry of the Nymph's point-by-point and stanza-by-stanza refutation of the Shepherd, Marlowe's version was altered and expanded. Subsequent alterations in Marlowe's poem caused in turn further changes in Raleigh's, and so on. Bowers offers the following reconstruction of Marlowe's original version:

> Come live with me, and be my love,
> And we will all the pleasures prove,
> That valleys, groves, hills and fields,
> Woods, or steepy mountain yields.
>
> And we will sit upon the rocks,
> Seeing the shepherds feed their flocks,

By shallow rivers, to whose falls,
Melodious birds sing madrigals.

And I will make thee beds of roses,
And a thousand fragrant posies,
A cap of flowers, and a kirtle,
Embroidered all with leaves of myrtle.

A belt of straw, and ivy buds,
With coral clasps and amber studs,
And if these things thy mind may move,
Then live with me, and be my love.[26]

The poem is not only an invitation to love but also an invitation for poets to tamper with Marlowe's invention.[27] Most obviously, the list of temptations—straw belts, ivy buds, caps and kirtles—can easily be extended or varied without major damage to either meter or sense. Some, like the anonymous author of "Another of the Same Nature, Made Since" (published alongside Raleigh's response in the *England's Helicon*), were content to substitute new images, altering the landscape while leaving untouched the basic premise of Marlowe's poem:

Come live with me and be my dear,
And we will revel all the year,
In plains and groves, on hills and dales,
Where fragrant air breeds sweetest gales.

There shall you have the beauteous pine,
The cedar and the spreading vine,
And all the woods to be a screen,
Lest Phoebus kiss my summer's queen.

(*POEMS*, 213)

Others elaborated upon Marlowe's original by adding stanzas, such as the one that first appeared in 1603 in the *Roxburge Ballads* and was frequently reprinted:

Thy silver dishes filled with meat,
As precious as the Gods do eat,

Shall on an ivory table be
Prepared each day for thee and me.[28]

While Marlowe's shepherd's pastoral vision is extraordinarily tempting, it is also extremely vulnerable. Much of the attraction of the poem
derives from its capacity to conjure up an imaginary world free of mortality and social restraint; but the amount of pressure needed to puncture
this precarious vision is slight. In fact, this pressure is very near the
surface of Marlowe's original. Scratch that surface, question too deeply,
and a flood of questions follow: How urbane is this Shepherd, or for that
matter, his beloved Nymph? Are the lovers merely to observe voyeuristi-
cally the pastoral landscape, or are they to become part of it? In this
seduction poem, how genuine is the promised escape from a world of
plague, work, and devouring time?

The success of Raleigh's imitation depends upon his exploitation of
these barely suppressed features of Marlowe's poem, and his supplying the
unspoken (but also implicit) response of the Nymph herself:

If all the world and love were young,
And truth in every shepherd's tongue,
These pretty pleasure might me move
To live with thee and be thy love.

But Time drives flocks from field to fold,
When rivers rage and rocks grow cold,
And Philomel becometh dumb;
The rest complains of cares to come.

The flowers do fade, and wanton fields
To wayward winter reckoning yields;
A honey tongue, a heart of gall
Is fancy's spring, but sorrow's fall.

Thy gowns, thy shoes, thy beds of roses,
Thy cap, thy kirtle, and thy posies,
Soon break, soon wither, soon forgotten,
In folly ripe, in reason rotton.

(*POEMS,* 212)

The Nymph's jarring allusion to Philomel's rape and mutilation reminds us of the darker side of some invitations to love, as does her insistence on mortality, aging, forgetting, and lies. What Raleigh's reply seizes upon is the inevitable answer, silently skirted over in the poem, to this idealized conception of love. By turning the interrogative into the conditional, he exposes the limitations of the pastoral vision, expanding its boundaries wide enough to reintroduce the inescapable realities that pastoral would seem to exclude, except that they are not excluded as much as temporarily occluded in Marlowe's poem.

The seductive invitation to love, as Raleigh's Nymph recognizes, is simply bait, a trap. So, too, was Marlowe's invitation to other poets to tamper with his lyric, because almost all of these attempts fell short of the mark, losing the delicate balance that Marlowe achieves, either by omitting (or, alternatively, making too specific) the world that belonged outside the bounds of pastoral. It was bait that few could resist, and so it was imitated again and again, in poems and in plays. It may be that John Donne entitled his own imitation of Marlowe's poem "The Bait" for this very reason. Rather than fall into Marlowe's trap—in which efforts to contain the original poem are themselves exposed as failures—Donne chooses to transform Marlowe's naive Shepherd into a metaphysical wit, recasting Marlowe's vision as he had previously done with Marlowe's Ovidian translations in his elegies. The first two stanzas are indicative; Donne depends upon the established conventionality of the original in offering "new pleasures":

> Come live with me and be my love,
> And we will some new pleasures prove,
> Of golden sands and crystal brooks,
> With silken lines and silver hooks.
>
> There will the river whispering run,
> Warmed by thine eyes more than the sun,
> And there th'enamoured fish will stay,
> Begging themselves they may betray.

(*POEMS*, 214)

Others, like the Caroline poet J. Paulin, have the lovers abandon their natural pleasures in favor of political ones. Paulin, like Donne, depends upon his readers' familiarity with Marlowe's poem so that he can rapidly move beyond the scope and premises of the original. By the 1630s Marlowe's enormously popular poem stood as a kind of shorthand for an invitation to erotic love, and Paulin could dismiss the sensual temptations of his predecessors in favor of cerebral ones:

> Come, my Clarinda, we'll consume
> Our joys no more at this low rate;
> More glorious titles let's assume
> And love according to our state.

> For if contentment wears a crown
> Which never tyrant could assail,
> How many monarchs put we down
> In our utopian commonweal.

> (*POEMS*, 215)

By midcentury Marlowe's poem stood in relation to the "invitation" poem as Petrarch's sonnets to Petrarchanism. The pressure of the original, the sense of rivalry, is lost, and with it the possibility of real parody. The incredible success and influence of "The Passionate Shepherd" resulted in its being reduced to little more than a conventionalized poetic form.

Perhaps the best indication of the ease with which its pastoral fantasy could be parodically exploited appears in Marlowe's own parodic version of his lyric in *The Jew of Malta*. The self-parody occurs in the scene in which the slave Ithamore and the whore Bellamira reenact a debased stage version of Marlowe's shepherd's invitation to love. Bellamira and her villainous sidekick Pilia-Borza plot to manipulate Ithamore into blackmailing Barabas for his gold. Bellamira aggressively seduces Ithamore, inviting him to lie in her lap, and offers to marry him. At this point the smitten Ithamore shifts from his colloquial and hardbitten prose to heroic couplets and finally to the familiar ballad rhythm of "The Passionate Shepherd." By the end of his speech he even slips into the famous refrain of the original lyric:

> Content: but we will leave this paltry land,
> And sail from hence to Greece, to lovely Greece.
> I'll be thy Jason, thou my golden fleece;

Where painted carpets o'er the meads are hurled,
And Bacchus' vineyards overspread the world;
Where woods and forests go in goodly green;
I'll be Adonis, thou shalt be Love's Queen;
The meads, the orchards, and the primrose-lanes,
Instead of sedge and reed, bear sugar-canes:
Thou in those groves, by Dis above,
Shalt live with me, and be my love.

(4.2.106–16) (italics mine)

Ithamore badly misconstrues the meaning of the original. Through him Marlowe anticipates those who would appropriate the surface features of his poem. In his attempt to impress Bellamira, the inexperienced Ithamore offers a costlier version of the shepherd's homely invitation. And though he retains the "groves" and "woods" of the original, a "golden fleece" replaces the "gown made of the finest wool," and "painted carpets" now cover the natural landscape, in a parodic twist on the urbanized view of nature dangerously close to the surface in Marlowe's original. Ithamore's classical allusions are unintentionally ironic: Adonis and Jason are punished and destroyed through their relationships with the women they love, Venus and Medea. And, finally, he gets the world upside down: Dis is not above but the Hell below. Like Bellamira's matrimonial offer, the lyrical invitation "Come live with me and be my love" is a trap—easily imitated yet not so easy to get right. As early as 1589 Marlowe anticipates and subverts the weak imitator, parodying the imitator by parodying himself.[29]

Much like "The Passionate Shepherd," "Hero and Leander" hovers precariously on the verge of self-parody, both anticipating and preempting parodic imitation. Ezra Pound identifies just this quality as a defining feature of the poem: "I suspect that Marlowe started to parody himself in 'Hero and Leander.' He had begun with serious intentions. I recognize that this suspicion may be an error."[30] And, like "The Passionate Shepherd," "Hero and Leander" invited a spate of imitations, especially continuations, and became recognized as a mark by which poets measured their prowess. In 1653, for example, in Richard Brome's *Mad Couple Well Matched,* we are told that only an untimely interruption forestalls what would have been a collaborative victory over Marlowe's achievement: "Had not this horn-head come, we had writ lines together should have put down 'Hero and Leander.' "[31] Marlowe's poem had served as the basis for comparison two years earlier, in the critical analysis prefacing Bosworth's *Chast and Lost Lovers* (1651), by one "R. C.," who acknowledges the extent to which Bosworth's poetry is "everywhere in . . . imitation" of Marlowe.[32] He offers as an example Bosworth's debt in couplets like

> Some say fair Cupid unto her inclined,
> Mourned as he went, and thinking on her pined.

and

> As she went, casting her eyes aside,
> Many admiring at her beauty died.

to Marlowe's:

> And mighty Princes of her love denied
> Pined as they went, and thinking on her died.[33]

Until the middle of the seventeenth century, then, Marlowe's poem would be seen as the object of imitation that a struggling poet worked through to overcome. But, as R. C. notes, such ventures were risky. He quotes Ben Jonson as his authority in this regard: "The strength of his fancy, and shadowing of it in words [Bosworth] taketh from Mr. Marlowe in his *Hero and Leander,* whose mighty lines Mr. Benjamin Jonson (a man sensible enough of his own abilities) was often heard to say, that they were examples fitter for admiration than for parallel."[34]

The first and perhaps most influential attempt to contain Marlowe's effort in "Hero and Leander" (by claiming that it was incomplete) was the printer's note at the close of the poem's first edition in 1598: *"desunt nonnulla"*: 'some things are missing' (*Poems,* 40). It is not clear, however, that what is missing is missing at the end (if that were so the editorial intervention might have read "left unfinished"). C. S. Lewis, in his justification of Chapman's continuation, cites the poem's problematic closure as a major reason for reading the two authors works as complementary: "A story cannot properly end with the two chief characters dancing on the edge of a cliff."[35] But in Marlowe's works they do, and do so repeatedly. So pervasive is this conception of Marlowe's incompleteness (rather than allowing for the possibility that Marlowe stops his works at these points for a reason) that "Hero and Leander" does not even appear in the standard edition of Marlowe's *Works* independent of Chapman's continuation. Fredson Bowers argues in circular fashion that "Chapman's work has become so identified with this poem as to make an edition of the *complete* poem desirable here." [36]

Twenty years after writing his continuation of Marlowe's poem, Chapman still spoke of "Hero and Leander" as "that partly excellent poem of Master Marlowe's." [37] Chapman clearly read Marlowe's poem carefully, and his continuation amounts to a folding or rolling back, a reversal of Marlowe's course. Perhaps the greatest transformation is Chapman's translation of Marlowe's erotic and ironic poem into something moral, instructive, and something that takes itself (and its narrator) quite seriously. Despite C. S. Lewis's urgings, the two works do not form a unified whole, nor are the artists' sensibilities complementary. While Chapman wishes that his Muse let Marlowe's departed soul know "how much his late desires I tender/ (If yet it know not)" (*Poems*, 48), his poem nonetheless stands as a sustained and coherent challenge to Marlowe's artistic vision.

Chapman's first step in containing Marlovian excess and lack of "form" (for Chapman, a key generic and philosophical concept) was to divide Marlowe's narrative roughly in half and preface those halves with clarifying "Arguments" (though with such an uncomplicated narrative it is not at all clear why an argument is needed in the first place). These "Sestiads" summarize the narrative selectively; it is as if Chapman were describing what he wishes were in the poem. It is not that his summaries are incorrect. Rather, they repackage Marlowe's effort into something that appears to be linear, causal, and therefore incomplete.

Before reading a line of Marlowe's, then, one's expectations are shaped by Chapman:

> Hero's description and her love's;
> The fane of Venus, where he moves
> His worthy love-suit, and attains;
> Whose bliss the wrath of Fates restrains
> For Cupid's grace to Mercury:
> Which tale the author doth imply.
>
> (*POEMS*, 17)

Chapman's emphasis from the outset upon the "wrath of Fates" takes a minor and digressive point in Marlowe's narrative and reformulates it as the cause of Leander's loss of "bliss." It seems to have carried over from his efforts at describing the "wrath of Achilles" in his roughly contemporaneous translation of the *Iliad*. This is a remarkable misreading, since Cupid only asked that the lovers enjoy each other and be blessed; the wrath of the Fates is directed not against Hero and Leander, but against Cupid; and finally, the whole digression turns into an explanation for why scholars are poor, not why Hero and Leander were fated to a tragic and deserved end. As Louis Martz and others have noted, it is a universe in which all forces—the Fates, and gods like Mercury and Neptune—are subject to love's unpredictable power. In such a world no stable point of reference (certainly not Providence or the gods or the Fates) exists from which to condemn the lovers. If gods are lovestruck and foolish, how can mortals escape?[38]

Chapman's account in the "Argument" prefacing the second "Sestiad" continues this pattern of selective, moralizing reconstruction:

> Hero of love takes deeper sense
> And doth her love more recompense;
> Their first night's meeting, where sweet kisses
> Are th'only crowns of both their blisses;
> He swims t'Abydos, and returns;
> Cold Neptune with his beauty burns,
> Whose suit he shuns, and doth aspire
> Hero's fair tower and his desire.
>
> (*POEMS*, 31)

There are two misleading statements here and a factual error. Hero does not take "deeper sense" of her lover in the way Chapman implies—that is, thinking deeply and guiltily about what is in store for her. Her emotions, like Leander's, remain at the surface in Marlowe's poem; moral constraints are quickly overwhelmed by powerful sexual feelings. And the sweet kisses are the only crowns because the lovers are so innocent they do not know any better. Leander sails, not swims, to Abydos. Even more surprising is Chapman's omission of the poem's literal and figurative climax: Hero and Leander make love. The distortions in this brief summary signal Chapman's strain in altering events to lead up to the direction taken in his continuation. Chapman's sense of the poem was a far cry from the popular perception of the poem—glimpsed at in Thomas Middleton's

A Mad World, My Masters (c. 1604–06)—as one of those aphrodisiacal "luscious marry-bone pies for a young married wife." [39]

The first line of Chapman's additional Sestiads—"New light gives new direction, fortunes new"—encapsulates his larger emulative strategy. The dawn with which Marlowe's poem ends welcomes in no Ovidian aubade but the harsh, intrusive light of day. With the change in atmosphere comes a change in genre as well—"More harsh (at least more hard) more grace and high"—and more significantly, in narrative tone. An epic, legislating narrator has replaced the elusive and ironic one. There is no self-mocking here, no emotional involvement with the protagonists based on physical attraction, and no irony.

Henry Petowe's 628-line "Hero and Leander's Further Fortunes" (1598) offers a striking contrast to Chapman's continuation. He, too, sensed something incomplete in the poem, its failure to satisfy "all men's expectation." Petowe's effort seems to have generated immediate scorn, and in his prefatory remarks he tries to defend his poetic venture:

> To make the cause manifest . . . why Envy thus barketh at me, I entreat your wisdom to consider the sequel. This history of *Hero and Leander,* penned by that admired poet Marlowe, but not yet finished (being prevented by sudden death), and the same (though not abruptly, yet contrary to all men's expectation) resting like a head separated from the body, with this harsh sentence, *Desunt nonnulla.*
>
> (*POEMS*, 91)

Since Petowe reads Marlowe's poem as historical romance, "Hero and Leander" is incomplete to the extent that it failed to bring its romantic plot to a satisfying end. In offering to enlarge upon "this history of 'Hero and Leander,' " Petowe claims to have been "enriched by a gentleman, a friend of mine, with the true Italian discourse of those lovers' further fortunes" (*Poems,* 91), apparently unaware of the Greek original and its tragic denouement. Where Chapman was disturbed by an ending that never moved towards the promiscuous lovers' doom, Petowe was struck instead by the poem's failure to offer a truly happy ending. Marlowe had left off at the crucial juncture, resting uncomfortably between marriage and death, the comic and the tragic.

The result is an equally instructive misreading. In brief, Petowe's Hero is wooed by the Duke of Sestos, who banishes Leander in hopes of winning Hero. He fails, and dies of love. His successor, the next Duke, accuses Hero of poisoning his predecessor and imprisons her, pending a trial by combat if any will defend her. This is a psuedo-Spenserian world, with lines like "Whilom yclad in darkness' black-tanned skin" (l. 506), and allusions to characters in Italian romance (e.g., to Brandimarte, from Boiardo's *Orlando Innamorata* in the reference to "Brandamour" (*Poems,* 231). Petowe focuses upon the romantic hints of Marlowe's poem to the exclusion of all else: where Marlowe mocked the gods and Chapman restored their dignity, Petowe quickly banishes them, the Fates, and other mythological trappings. Altered, too, is the ironic and intrusive narrator. The streamlining results in a narrow devotion to story-line.

Where Chapman's addition brings the harsh, moralizing "new light" of tragedy and epic, Petowe's brings wild improbability and final happiness. A disguised Leander returns, slaughters the evil Duke, and is made lord of Sestos. He reveals himself to his love, is reunited with her, and they live happily ever after:

> All sorrows fled, their joys anew begin.
> Full many years those lovers lived in fame,
> That all the word did much admire the same.

> (*POEMS,* 109–10)

The poem was a failure. Petowe himself acknowledged as much when he wrote in his next poem, the Shakespearean "Philocasander and Elanira" (1599), that while his "wandering Muse down head-long fell" in the earlier effort, "Blest may her second resurrection be." Traces of his earlier engagement linger in "Philocasander," in which both Hero and Leander are introduced only to be unfavorably compared with his new lovers. Petowe's continuation suggests how seductive Marlowe's poem was for emerging writers, yet how strenuously it resisted simple containment.

The imitation of "Hero and Leander" that appears in *Nashe's Lenten Stuffe* (1599) comes closest to capturing the spirit of Marlowe's original.[40] The work was composed during Nashe's stay at Yarmouth, the fishing port, where he fled after the *Ile of Dogs* affair in 1597. Much of the prose narrative is a mock encomium on Yarmouth's most popular haul, kippers, or red herring, and the climax of the narrative is an explanation of the origin of the herring. He introduces Marlowe's Ovidian story in order to offer his own tale of metamorphosis:

To recount *ab ovo,* or from the church-book of his birth, how the
herring first came to be a fish, and then how he came to be king of
fishes, and gradationately how from white to red he changed, would
require as massy a tome as Holinshed; but in half a pennyworth of
paper I will epitomize them. Let me see, hath anybody in Yarmouth
heard of Leander and Hero, of whome divine Musaeus sung, and a
diviner muse than him, Kit Marlowe?[41]

The mock encomium on the herring contains a true one, to his dead
friend and one-time collaborator (if we are to trust the title page of *Dido,
Queen of Carthage*), Marlowe. And the imitation that follows reveals a full
grasp of Marlowe's intentions and style:

> Two faithful lovers they were, as every apprentice in Paul's church-
> yard will tell you for your love, and sell you for your money. The
> one dwelt at Abidos in Asia, which was Leander; the other, which
> was Hero, his mistress or Delia, at Sestos in Europe, and she was a
> pretty pinckany and Venus' priest.[42]

Even as he recalls the familiar opening of Marlowe's poem (framed by an
acknowledgment that the story is familiar to any frequenter of the bookstalls of St. Paul's), Nashe makes the story even more familiar, as Hero is
compared to the mistress of Daniel's sonnets, Delia, and is described
colloquially as "a pretty pickany." G. R. Hibbard notes that "Nashe's
rendering of the story . . . rests on the same trick of reducing the rare
and exotic to the orderly and commonplace, or bringing the mythological
down to the level of everyday life."[43] This familiarization is intensified by
his substituting rambling conversational prose for rhymed couplets and
replacing the extended similes and mythological inserts of Marlowe's
poem with bits of popular culture.

Paradoxically, though, the very process of familiarization keeps
Nashe close to the spirit of the original. Like Marlowe (and in contrast to
Chapman) he does not try to penetrate the surface of the lovers' emotional
encounter or impose any moral or psychological complexity upon them.
Instead, like Marlowe, he dwells on surface details, details that inevitably
lead, as in Marlowe, to digression:

> By the sea-side of the other side stood Hero's tower, such an other
> tower as one of our Irish castles, that is not so wide as a belfry, and
> a cobbler cannot jet out his elbows in.[44]

His narrator, as a result, recalls and outdoes the dispassionate Ovidian narrator of Marlowe's poem, drawing attention to himself and his inventiveness.

Marlowe had chosen to end his poem at the point where he could no longer sustain the balance between heroic wonder and comic deflation. Chapman and Petowe, confronted with this instability and, for them, inconclusiveness, right the balance by offering, respectively, moralizing and romanticizing endings. In a brilliant stroke, Nashe has the lovers die but turns that back into the comic: Hero and Leander meet again in the end, but only on our plates (or in our guts) during Lent. The gods (petty and imperious, like Marlowe's), mourning their loss, "translated" Leander into ling, Hero into herring, and Hero's nurse (a "shrewish snappish bawd") into hot mustard, for " 'Hero and Leander,' the red herring and ling, never come to the board without mustard, their waiting maid."[45]

Nashe retains sufficient distance from his original to reproduce its effect, its resistance to taking itself too seriously, and its dispassionate Ovidian qualities (like Marlowe, he eschews a commitment to either tragedy or comedy through deflation and parody). He achieves this distance by relocating Marlowe's narrative within the markedly different terms of his prose fiction, and in so doing, hits upon a strategy for generic containment similar to the one that Shakespeare and Jonson would employ when recalling the poem in *As You Like It, Every Man in His Humour,* and *Bartholomew Fair.* One of the most effective ways of parodying Marlowe, his work reveals, was to take his poetry and resituate it in a (necessarily hostile) dramatic or prose fictional universe.

❧

For those who sought to imitate Marlowe's plays on the Elizabethan stage, the practice of embedding Marlovian features within the confines of their own dramatic design was fraught with unforeseen difficulties. More so than his poems, Marlowe's drama, especially the enormously influential *Tamburlaine* plays, invited and yet consistently undermined imitation. If *Tamburlaine, Part I* begins with a casual dismissal of Marlowe's predecessors—"From jigging veins of riming mother wits,/ And such conceits as clownage keeps in pay,/ We'll take you to the stately tents of war" (Prologue, 1–2), *Tamburlaine, Part II* concludes with what may be read as a veiled challenge to his successors. The conqueror's admonition to his sons could easily double as Marlowe's warning to his literary heirs:

> The nature of thy chariot will not bear
> A guide of baser temper than myself,
> More than heaven's coach the pride of Phaeton.
>
> (5.3.230–2)

To grasp Apollo's reins (or laurels) proved both irresistible and dangerous. In the years immediately following *Tamburlaine*'s success, many, Phaeton-like, sought to succeed Marlowe. Peter Berek notes that of the thirty-eight extant plays performed on the public stage between 1587 and 1593, ten "show clear debts to *Tamburlaine*." [46] This tally does not include lost but probably derivative plays like *Tamercham I and II* (for which only the "plot" of Part I survives). Berek calls them "Tamburlaine's Weak Sons." Attempting to imitate and capitalize on Marlowe's success, their imitative encounters rendered them vulnerable to those aspects of Marlowe's work that resisted such acts of containment. Content to appropriate what Jonson would later call the "scenical strutting and furious vociferation" (H&S 8:587) of Marlowe's plays, most failed to grasp the complex political and historical processes with which these were intertwined. Few of these plays are read, studied, or staged today. But they serve as instructive foils to Shakespeare's and Jonson's subsequent and far more successful efforts to appropriate Marlowe's work. Indeed, there is considerable evidence (from subsequent parodies) that both dramatists were attentive to how and why these imitations failed, and learned from their mistakes.

Before turning to two typical examples from this group—Robert Greene's *Alphonsus, King of Arragon* and Thomas Lodge's *The Wounds of Civil War* (both c. 1588)—it is worth observing that the first and most influential imitation of *Tamburlaine, Part I* was Marlowe's own sequel, *Tamburlaine, Part II*. There is little doubt that the second play was conceived of after the success of the first onstage, a point underscored in the play's Prologue:

> The general welcomes Tamburlaine received
> When he last arrived upon our stage
> Hath made our poet pen his Second Part.
>
> (PROLOGUE, 1–3)

Editors are quick to point out that when Marlowe sat down to write this sequel he had virtually exhausted his biographical material, though he had left his hero alive; the first play thus provided "the major 'source' " of the second.[47] In imitating his own success Marlowe was able to do what other imitators could not: repeat himself. As a result, the sequel effectively anticipates and precludes the kind of "continuation" or "further adventures" that characterized Chapman's and Petowe's imitations of "Hero and Leander." But the second play does not so much rewrite the earlier work as intensify its effects through numbing repetition of Tamburlaine's insistent self-authorizations, his increasingly meaningless conquests, and the escalating level of violence through which they are achieved. The stage becomes a treadmill. Tamburlaine's breaking faith with Cosroe in the first play is repeated when Sigismond betrays Orcanes in the second; Mycetes's fecklessness is mirrored in Almeda's; Bajazeth's torture is outdone by the abuse of the captive kings; the siege of Babylon is like the siege of Damascus; and Theridamas's wooing of Olympia recalls Tamburlaine's of Zenocrate. The list can easily be extended.[48] And while the first play concludes in marriage and the second in death, the endings have an oddly detachable (almost interchangeable) quality. It remains debatable whether the repetitions occur with sufficient difference to constitute parody. My own sense is that given the repetition compulsion that characterizes Tamburlaine's successive conquests within each of the two plays, the relative lack of difference makes the sequel even more disturbing.

Nevertheless, this kind of imitation could also make *Tamburlaine, Part I* seem partial and incomplete. This sense was reinforced when the two plays—though performed separately—were printed together three times during the 1590s. It has also affected editorial practice. Thus, for example, though the Revels editor acknowledges that "Part One was completed, it seems clear, as a self-sufficient play," he still treats the two plays as comprising a larger whole. His conclusions are typical: if Marlowe

> had not written Part Two, the first play might have seemed an evasive and short-sighted work which raised questions about tyrannical self-assertion without satisfactorily following them through; or it might have stood as a powerful enigma, ending true to itself; or as a bold invitation to admire a frighteningly capacious heroic image, rightly issuing to victory.[49]

But who is to say that Marlowe's intentions were not to offer such a powerful enigma or bold invitation? More to the point, is any of these issues decisively resolved in the second play? I would argue instead that

Part Two is, not a response in the sense that Cunningham suggests (that is, one that resolves problems raised but left unanswered in the first play), but rather a continuation and intensification along quite similar lines. The moral and political instability of the first play is, if anything, exacerbated, not resolved (Does Tamburlaine die because he cursed Mohamet? Burned the Koran? Caught a fever? Is his end just retribution or a transcendence of earthly bounds? Is any kind of normative political world restored?).

An even more extreme version of the argument that we should see the two plays as comprising a single ten-act drama is offered by Roy Battenhouse, who urges that "*Tamburlaine* should be read as a two-part play consistently shaped within a broadly Christian moral tradition."[50] For Battenhouse, *Tamburlaine, Part II* unambiguously resolves the unanswered question of the first "part": "How shall this proud atheist be brought to his deserved overthrow?"[51] The moral closure Battenhouse would impose upon Marlowe's work is a modern variation of the moralizing that characterized Chapman's completion of "Hero and Leander." Critical and imitative traditions dovetail in their attempt to resolve the disturbing and ambiguous, to render Marlowe's work morally stable by insisting upon the incompleteness of the initial work. Marlowe scholarship needs to take a long view and consider why so many scholars and poets strove to complete Marlowe's finished (and published) works.

The guilty parties are not just the moralists. Take, for example, a recent case from the opposite end of the ideological spectrum: William Empson's posthumous book on Marlowe's *Doctor Faustus*.[52] Unhappy with an ending in which Faustus is punished for his pact with the devil, Empson asserts that there was a conspiracy (whose members included both printers and censors) to betray and rewrite the original ending of *Doctor Faustus*, in which, according to Empson, Marlowe's hero had walked away at the end of the play free and clear. Empson's unpersuasive argument is nevertheless useful in showing how insistent critics have been in denying the authenticity of the shape of Marlowe's work. It is also indicative of the extent to which Marlowe's work invites and at the same time resists such acts of critical or imitative containment. Invites, because Marlowe repeatedly concluded his work at a point of instability, something that holds true not only for his lyric poems, *Doctor Faustus*, and *Tamburlaine*, but also for his translation of Lucan's *Pharsalia* (which ends with Caesar, having crossed the Rubicon, approaching Rome), for the *Massacre at Paris* (which ends with the animadversions at the court of Henry of Navarre), and for *The Jew of Malta* (which closes with yet one more reversal in the Machiavellian world of Mediterranean politics). Ironically, then, the very two features that paved the way for imitations—Marlowe's habit of parodying himself and the unstable and seemingly open-ended way in which his works come to a close—undermined the very emulative efforts they invited. Those who would render Marlowe's work anachronistic would have to tackle his work from a more oblique angle.

Robert Greene learned this the hard way. Shortly after *Alphonsus, King of Arragon* was first staged, he was ridiculed for his impoverished imitation of Marlowe's style. Greene writes in *Perimedes the Black-Smith* (1588), that, as a result, he has left writing for the stage and has returned to his "old course, to palter up some thing in prose," after "two gentlemen poets . . . had it in derision, for that I could not make my verses jet upon the stage in tragical buskins, every word filling the mouth like to fubarden of Bo-Bell, daring God out of heaven with that atheist Tamburlaine."[53] Something had gone terribly wrong in *Alphonsus*. Modern critics have seconded the judgment of the gentlemen poets: for Una Ellis-Fermor, the "subjugation of Greene's genius to Marlowe's seems in this first play to be wholly disastrous not so much because of his crude attempt to reproduce and outdo a popular figure as because his imagination is itself invaded."[54]

It must have seemed easy enough to offer at least a passable version of Tamburlainian rant and the popular stage effects of Marlowe's plays. What undermined Greene's imitation was that it misjudged the interdependence of Marlowe's politics and poetry. Thus, for example, issues carried over from *Tamburlaine,* such as disobedience to one's sovereign or what constitutes legitimate deposition, are raised but never directly confronted. In addition, Marlowe's handling of providentialist claims seems to have confused Greene. Where in Marlowe's plays providentialist assertions are made, they are left unrealized; in contrast, they are not only made but confirmed in *Alphonsus*. But this conflicts directly with Alphonsus's Tamburlainian claim that he controls the Fates. The conflict is neither resolved nor even acknowledged and may well have proved unsettling to audiences. Irving Ribner is mistaken, I think, in describing *Alphonsus* as a moral refutation of Marlowe's subversive work.[55] The evidence points instead to a Greene who entered Marlowe's dramatic universe without quite having his bearings. Heroical history is notoriously difficult to conclude satisfactorily, and Greene tripped up most in the ending. Perhaps he thought he was following Marlowe's lead by concluding with a marriage. In doing so he failed to grasp how in *Tamburlaine, Part I* Marlowe subverted this New Comic closure even as he reproduced it. In sum, Greene simply misunderstood (or nervously fled from) what constitutes the dynamic tensions of the *Tamburlaine, Part I:* the inherent conflict in the concept of honor between birth and virtue (his overreacher, in a curious reversal, has the first but almost repudiates the second); the conflict between providentialist assertions (including Zenocrate's) of the hero's downfall, and the failure of greater powers to overcome the hero; and most damningly, the failure to recognize that Marlowe's closure— the crowning and marrying of Zenocrate—is sardonically conveyed (as Zenocrate must pick her way in her coronation march through the battered and bleeding bodies of her first betrothed, Arabia, and then both Bajazeth and Zabina). Greene tries emulating Marlowe's solution to the problem of closure and achieves instead a ludicrous, confused, and self-contradictory ending that elides the many ethical and political issues his play has raised and skirted.

His engagement is not controlled, and what might have been an attempt (as Ribner would wish to see) to relocate Marlowe's tragical history within the framework of a comical history failed miserably—in fact, never reached the point where it could even articulate its difference in this way. In lieu of dramatic tension we are offered an ethical and generic seesaw. Greene's firmer grasp of history in subsequent plays— notably *Orlando Furioso, James IV,* and the collaborative *Looking Glass for London*—led away from tragical to comical history, and, ultimately, to history as fantasy. Like the weak Mycetes, he must have found himself "aggrieved/ Yet insufficient to express the same" (*Tamburlaine, Part I,* 1.1.1–2) by their common adversary, Tamburlaine. Greene's effort nevertheless pointed to a strategy better employed by subsequent imitators: securely embedding Marlowe's tragical history within the larger bounds of comedy. As we shall see in chapter III, Shakespeare's parody of Marlowe's Tamburlaine in the comic universe of Belmont in *The Merchant of Venice* may have its precedents in Greene's early struggle to contain Marlovian tragedy within a more capacious comic structure. The irony is that Greene himself would warn Marlowe to watch out for the intrusive emulation of that "upstart Crow."

Where Greene floundered and almost drowned, Thomas Lodge chose not to immerse himself so haphazardly in the treacherous undertow of *Tamburlaine* in his *The Wounds of Civil War.* He seems to have recognized how vulnerable an imitator could be; recognized, too, the political and ethical implications of closely imitating *Tamburlaine*. Unlike Greene, Lodge found in Marlowe's work not only a paradigm for depicting over-reachers but also a model of the dangers of factionalism that follows in the wake of autonomous assertions of honor, the desire for revenge, and unchecked political aspiration. Instead of trying to contain Marlovian tragedy within heroical (or comical) history, Lodge attempted instead to steamroll over the political complexity of Marlowe's work. Yet while Lodge appears to have had a better grasp of the political matrix of Marlowe's play, in the end he too fails to control the problems raised by the Marlovian political and historical processes he has introduced. His imitation is illuminating in two respects, though: first, for illustrating the kinds of visual and verbal borrowings characteristic of early imitations of Marlowe; second, for intimating how heterodoxy could serve as a valuable check upon orthodoxy, and in a more controlled imitation, create the kind of dynamic interplay of the two that would subsequently become a defining feature of both Shakespeare's dynastic histories and Jonson's major comedies. Ultimately, though, what distinguishes his imitation from Greene's is Lodge's decision to appropriate elements of Marlowe's style where he found it useful, rather than attempt a play that sought to outdo Marlowe at his own game. As a result, there appears to be a lot more of the Marlovian in Lodge's play, with a lot less at stake.

The plot of Lodge's *The Wounds of Civil War* is straightforward: angered that his rival Marius is chosen as general, Scilla, in retaliation, returns to Rome and seizes power. Most of the play depicts Marius' party's unsuccessful attempt to depose Scilla. By the end, both Marius and his son have died and Scilla is pronounced dictator. Unexpectedly, however, Scilla rejects the office, repudiates the heroic values that have heretofore governed his actions, and dies. What is fascinating is how Lodge fuels this orthodoxy by borrowing so much disturbing heterodox material from Marlowe's plays.[56]

The play draws at many points upon visual incidents in *Tamburlaine*. The elaborate stage entrance at Act 3, scene 3, recalling and perhaps outdoing Tamburlaine's chariot drawn by captive kings, offers a striking example:

> Enter Scilla in triumph in his chair triumphant of gold, drawn by
> four Moors before the chariot; his colors, his crest, his captains, his
> prisoners: Arcathius, Mithradates' son, Aristoion, Archelaus, bear-
> ing crowns of gold, and manacled (3.3.1 SD).

But a degree of moral confusion is inevitably raised by such representations: are we to celebrate Scilla's triumphant coup or expect the downfall of a man who is called "the scourge of Asia" (4.1.210)?

The episode where the vanquished Consul Carbo must prostrate himself so that Scilla may tread upon his neck (which does not appear in Lodge's sources) similarly reenacts and rivals Tamburlaine's treatment of Bajazeth. Other stage actions also appear to be modeled on Marlowe's play: the scene in which the members of the "Senate rise and cast away their gowns, having their swords by their sides" (1.1.243 SD) recalls Tamburlaine's similar gesture (*Tamburlaine, Part I* 1.2.41), while the entrances of Marius and his sons "very melancholy" (2.2.1 SD) and "all in black and wonderful melancholy" (5.2.1. SD), while drawing on a communal theatrical visual idiom, nonetheless connect them with Tamburlaine's recent and striking entrance "all in black and very melancholy" (*Tamburlaine, Part I*, 5.2.1 SD).

Turning from visual to verbal indebtedness, Tamburlaine's vaunting blank verse becomes for Lodge a shorthand for identifying political usurpers. Scilla's speech as he enters "triumphant" is typical:

> You Roman soldiers, fellow mates in arms,
> The blindfold mistress of incertain chance
> Hath turned these traitorous climbers from the top
> And seated Scilla in the chiefest place,
> The place beseeming Scilla and his mind.
> For were the throne where matchless glory sits
> Impaled with furies threat'ning blood and death,
> Begirt with famine and those fatal fears
> That dwell below amidst the dreadful vast,
> Tut, Scilla's sparkling eyes should dim with clear
> The burning brands of their consuming light,
> And master fancy with a forward mind
> And mask rapining fear with awful power.
> For men of baser metal and conceit
> Cannot conceive the beauty of my thought.
>
> (2.2.1–16)

The speech reads like a catalogue of Tamburlainian rant with its allusions to fortune's wheel, treasonous climbers, the hero's penetrating eyes, forward mind, aspiring thoughts, and disdain for those of base metal and conceit. It also imitates the syntactic features of Marlowe's verse paragraph with its end-stopped lines strung together with conjunctive clauses.

Marius, too, is inclined to Tamburlaine's style, especially to the kind of geographic sweep of which Tamburlaine is so fond. Compare his speech in Act 4, scene 1 when he is at the height of his powers—

> Th'Euxinian Sea, and fierce Sicilia Gulf
> The river Ganges and Hydaspis stream
> Shall level lie, and smooth as crystal ice,
> Whilst Fulvia and Corneila pass thereon;

—to Tamburlaine's at height of his:

> The Euxine Sea, north to Natolia;
> The Terrene, west; the Caspian, north north-east;
> And on the south, Sinus Arabicus;
> Shall all be loaden with the martial spoils
> We will convey with us to Persia.
>
> (*TAMBURLAINE*, PART TWO, 4.3.102—6)

In imitating these visual and verbal features Lodge follows Marlowe thus far and no farther. He avoids the kind of confusion that engulfs Greene, and tries to appropriate from *Tamburlaine* only what he can harness to his own orthodoxy. While we witness the exhilirating climb of not one but two aspirants, the play moves, at times shakily, but most of the time inevitably, towards Marius' expected demise and Scilla's repudiation of tyrannical power. The histrionic style turns diminuendo by Act 5, and vaunting terms are replaced by clowns, lyric passages, and moments of considered introspection. Scilla recognizes in a way inconceivable for Tamburlaine that in his rise he killed enough friends and relatives of those present to set in motion yet another round of attempted usurpation:

> Romans, some here have lost at my command
> Their fathers, mothers, brothers, and allies.
> And think you Scilla thinking these misdeeds
> Bethinks not on your grudges and mislike?
>
> (5.5.130—33)

Lodge has it both ways: he represents (then has his hero repudiate) politically destabilizing action. Audience sympathies are correctly channeled if we abide by Lodge's guiding premise: rebellion is always worse than the existing political regime. In contrast to *Tamburlaine*, in *Wounds* autonomous self-assertion and honor, when set against the public good, must give way. At the play's end, the dominant image of the triumphant hero is reversed: paradoxically, to "master fortune" (5.5.150) Scilla must now be hitched to her chariot (5.5.315–19). Audiences might well anticipate problems, though, with the political vacuum that follows Scilla's renunciation of power and his preference for a contemplative life. Once again, however, Lodge avoids potential contradiction. Thus, while Scilla chooses the contemplative life, he dies in that scene before he can live it, and is "buried" with the "great pomp" (5.5.403 SD) consistent with his heroic achievements. The expected struggle for succession never materializes in an ending that slinks away from the sharp political contestation that prevailed throughout the play. Silent on the issue of succession, Lodge backs away from the political complexities his play has raised, preferring instead the fantasy solution of having Scilla die repentant, then buried gloriously, in a final stage tableau that distracts us from Marlovian issues raised and left unresolved. It would await a dramatist with a more confident grasp of his own sense of political and historical process to take hold of the reins Marlowe had temptingly offered at the end of *Tamburlaine, Part II* and subordinate Marlowe's vision to a more comprehensive and capacious one in the three parts of *Henry VI* and, a decade later, in *Henry V*.

❧

Insofar as his plays and poems invited such extensive imitation, Marlowe served as a facilitating writer. Over time, his own efforts became increasingly identified with those of his imitators, so that, by the 1620s, Jonson could conflate the "Tamerlanes and Tamer-chams of the late age" (H&S 8:587). The ease with which lesser authors could begin to approximate the sound of his verse and the nature of his visual spectacle helped ensure his canonical demise. If the poetic language of predecessors can be imagined as a giant linguistic junkyard, Marlowe's verse was like an old car that had been stripped for parts.

When Thomas Dekker fantasized in 1607 about the Elysian fields where deceased Elizabethan dramatists convened, his pantheon still included Marlowe. Dekker describes how in this afterworld these writers could be found carousing to one another at the holy well, some of them singing paeans to Apollo, some of them hymns to the rest of the gods, whilst Marlowe, Greene, and Peele had got under the shades of a large vine, laughing to see Nashe (that was but newly come to their college) still haunted with the sharp and satirical spirit that followed him here upon earth.[57]

Less than seventy-five years later, when the young Restoration dramatist Charles Saunder in 1681 was attacked on the grounds that his *Tamerlane the Great* "was only an old play transcribed," he was able to reply that

> I hope I may easily unload my self of that calumny, when I shall testify that I never heard of any play on the same subject, until my own was acted, neither have I since seen it, though it hath been told me, there is a Cock Pit play, going under the name of the *Scythian Shepherd*, or *Tamberlain the Great*, which how good it is, any one may judge by its obscurity, being a thing, not a bookseller in London, or scarce the players themselves, who acted it formerly, could call to remembrance, as far, that I believe that whoever was the author, he might e'en keep it to himself secure from invasion, or plagiary.[58]

Marlowe had gone from unmatchable to virtually unknown, from pillaged to pilloried. Dekker's canon of University Wits would be replaced by Fuller's description of Jonson and Shakespeare holding court at the Mermaid tavern. Marlowe had disappeared. In the late seventeenth century John Aubrey would report (before dismissing) the fantastic claim that it was Ben Jonson who "killed Mr. Marlowe the poet on Bunhill, coming from the Green-curtain playhouse" (H&S 1:178). A century and a half later Clemence Dane would write a verse play called *William Shakespeare* in which Marlowe's murder is attributed to Shakespeare himself.[59] While these accusations are groundless, there is a figurative sense in which there is some truth to them. Though subject to frequent imitation in the late 1580s and early 1590s, Marlowe's work was never quite contained, fixed, rendered anachronistic. It would await, in different ways, the interventions of Shakespeare and Jonson, who, at least canonically, would apply the deathblow by the early seventeenth century. After their drama Marlowe's plays would not be taken seriously again for three centuries. How this happened, and what its implications would be for the canon of English drama, is the subject of the next three chapters.

II

MARLOWE AND JONSON

Jonson is the legitimate heir of Marlowe.
—*T. S. Eliot*[1]

ELIOT'S OBSERVATION has not been met with much enthusiasm by most Jonson scholars, who have resisted the view that Marlowe and Jonson are related, let alone that Marlowe is Jonson's poetic precursor.[2] Instead, critics have viewed Jonson's and Marlowe's poetics as fundamentally opposed: where Marlowe is father of blank verse tragedy, Jonson is master of prose comedy. Where Marlowe is heir to a native dramatic tradition, Jonson is imitator of the classics. And where Marlowe (and his works) are iconoclastic, subversive, and morally unstable, Jonson (and his works) are conservative, satiric, and corrective. The source of this polarity can be partially traced back to Jonson himself: it was he who derided the "scenicall strutting, and furious vociferation" (H&S 8:587) of plays like *Tamburlaine,* and he who "was often heard to say" that the "mighty lines" of "Mr. Marlowe" were "examples fitter for admiration than for parallel" (H&S 11:145).

The most recent generation of Jonson scholars has focused with increasing intensity on Jonson's classicism, especially in regard to his conception of imitation. While recent studies by Richard S. Peterson, Thomas M. Greene, Katherine Maus, Douglas Duncan, and others have enlarged our understanding of Jonson's dramatic (and especially nondramatic) works, they have inevitably read back into Jonson's plays a classicism Jonson only later came to advocate.[3] Concomitantly, this critical emphasis has shifted attention away from Jonson's formative involvement in the popular drama of the 1590s.[4] The result is a figure who would have been unrecognizable to Philip Henslowe when he hired Jonson in 1602 to write additions to *The Spanish Tragedy,* or to London audiences that had seen Jonson act the part of Zulziman at that converted bear-baiting pit, the Paris Garden.

I offer a revisionist reading of Jonson in response to (and in way of explanation of) Jonson's own revisionist account of his artistic development.[5] The irony is, of course, that Jonson's self-fashioning has, in Eliot's words, led to a reputation "of the most deadly kind that can be compelled upon the memory of a great poet. To be universally accepted; to be damned by the praise that quenches all desire to read the book . . . and to be read only by historians and antiquaries."[6] What needs to be addressed is what compelled Jonson to refashion his identity as a playwright, what led him to suppress (and in his collected *"Works"* efface) evidence of his extensive participation in the popular dramatic tradition.

Extending Eliot's observations, I argue that a major reason for this suppression is the pressure Jonson experienced as a popular dramatist confronted with Marlowe's legacy. This is not to say that Jonson's engagement with Marlowe excluded other poetic encounters. It did not. Kyd, we know, figured largely in Jonson's development. And we also know from his *Conversations with Drummond* and *Discoveries* that he was widely and deeply read in classical, Continental, and especially English authors, and had a vigorously emulative response to many of them. Marlowe's influence was formative, however, in a way that Dekker's, Marston's, Shakespeare's, or Kyd's was not; it would redirect the nature of Jonson's development as a popular playwright and would generate the unusual constellation of imitative strategies Jonson employed in his early dramatic output.

I have spoken of Jonson's relationship to Marlowe in terms of filial succession (as Eliot does in describing him as Marlowe's "legitimate heir") in part because Jonson understood and experienced literary succession in these patriarchal terms.[7] For Jonson, literary and filial succession follow remarkably similar patterns. In his plays and criticism they are often conflated or confused, something that should come as no surprise given Jonson's obsession with creating, not just sons of Ben, but a veritable "Tribe" of male successors.[8] The need to designate literary heirs in terms of patrilinear descent was coupled with a desire to choose a (literary) progenitor (though we cannot choose our fathers, nor, as Harold Bloom puts it, can poets choose their precursors) and to reject one whose influence was inhibiting. Tellingly, when we turn to Jonson's formative drama

—especially plays like *Every Man in His Humour* and *Poetaster*—his exploration of poetic succession becomes thematically intertwined with the oedipal struggle of young men (who are poets) attempting to escape repressive fathers (who are blocking figures not to young love but to the heir's poetic development). Jonson's concern with poetic succession calls to mind Freud's remark in "A Disturbance of Memory on the Acropolis" that it "seems as though the essence of success were to have gotten farther than one's father, and as though to excel one's father were forbidden."[9]

Jonson's response to Marlowe's influence often resembles that of a son to his father: first emulating, then rejecting, then coming to terms with and succeeding the paternal figure. Jonson was sensitive to patrilinear tensions and dangers to succession; he writes in his *Discoveries* that "[g]reatness of name, in the father, oft-times helps not forth, but o're-whelms the son: they stand too near one another." He recognizes that the "shadow kills the growth; so much, that we see the grand-child come more, and oftener to be the heir of the first, than doth the second." The immediate heir, overwhelmed by this influence, "dies between," while "the possession is the third's" (H&S 8:576). Jonson's remarks help explain his evasive maneuver of skipping a generation in tracing his artistic lineage: we need to exercise some care in taking him at face value when he tells us that Horace and Martial are his progenitors rather than Kyd and Marlowe. In this regard Jonson's strategy resembles a general Renaissance tendency to downplay connections between itself and its Medieval antecedents, preferring instead to trace its lineage to classical models; in both cases self-definition is contingent upon an assertion of independence (and difference) from immediate forebears.

Jonson's conception of the filial basis of poetic imitation is elaborated in an illuminating passage in his *Discoveries,* where he defines imitation as being able "to convert the substance or riches of another poet" to one's own use by making "choice of one excellent man above the rest," whom one must follow until one grows a "very he: or, so style him, as the copy may be mistaken for the principal" (H&S 8:638). Like a son growing in the image—and shadow—of his father, the poet grows into this "very he" before, ideally, transcending his progenitor. It may be that the hint of oedipal tension in Jonson's relationship to Marlowe gave rise to John Aubrey's report (mentioned above) that it was Jonson who killed Marlowe on Bunhill, coming from the Green-curtain playhouse (H&S 1:178). For Jonson, overcoming Marlowe would not be this easy.

To maintain that Jonson is Marlowe's legitimate heir, that his work reflects a strong anxiety about Marlowe's influence, necessarily calls for a reappraisal of Jonson's ideas of imitation and of his evolution as a poet and playwright. It has implications as well for the recurrence of parody and poetasters in Jonson's early drama, for his unusual thematic attention to the struggle between fathers and sons in his early plays, and for the ways in which his Jacobean comedies from *Volpone* through *The Devil Is an Ass* are informed by a more improvisational engagement with and appropriation of the Marlovian model.

☙

If Jonson had not escaped hanging in 1598 (after killing the actor Gabriel Spencer), he would most likely be remembered as one of Henslowe's journeymen, the author of a half dozen or so lost Elizabethan plays, mostly tragedies, along with the unusual humours play that had been staged the month of his arrest. Francis Meres, in his *Palladis Tamia,* would have offered the finest praise during the playwright's life, ranking Jonson along with Marlowe, Kyd, and Shakespeare in his list of English tragedians. Only fragments of Jonson's output would have survived: those passages (apparently from tragedies or tragical histories) anthologized in Robert Allott's *England's Parnassus* (1600). Other sources concur in depicting Jonson as a maker of popular tragedies. For John Weever, in his *Epigrammes in the Oldest Cut and Newest Fashion* (1599), he is "embuskined Jonson." [10] And Henslowe's *Diary* records payments in 1598 for the "tragedy of Benjamin's plot" and in 1599 for the collaborative tragedy of *Robert II, King of Scots.* Jonson was also paid for a tragical history *Richard Crookback* (1602), collaborated with Thomas Dekker on a domestic tragedy called *Page of Plymouth* (1599), with Henry Chettle and Henry Porter on *Hot Anger Soon Coled* (1599), and with Nashe on *The Ile of Dogs* (1597). All of these plays (and perhaps others) that Jonson wrote for Henslowe's companies are either lost or suppressed (H&S 11:307–8). Henslowe also paid him for additions to Kyd's *Spanish Tragedy,* evidently confident of Jonson's ability to write in a style compatible with Kyd's outmoded vein. Dekker tells us elsewhere that Jonson had spent some time playing Hieronimo in provincial performances, as well as performing the title role in *Zulziman,* a lost play that might have capitalized on the success of exotic Eastern tragedies generated by Marlowe's *Tamburlaine* (H&S 1:13–14). Jonson's apprenticeship in popular tragedy was apparently extensive. As for Jonson's early comedies, the only record we have is his comment to Sir William Drummond that half his comedies were not in print; it may be, as Jonson's Oxford editors speculate, that he was using the term "comedy" loosely to signify plays in general (H&S 1:283). At any rate, even this fragmentary list is enough to suggest that we need to be wary when Jonson speaks of *Every Man in His Humour* as his first fruits. He apparently labored long and hard first to master Elizabethan tragedy, then equally hard to efface any record of this enterprise.

The fragments of Jonson's verse contained in Allott's anthology offer a brief and suggestive glimpse of his dramatic style in the mid- to late 1590s. Two are rhymed couplets:

> Those that in blood such violent pleasures have,
> Seldom descend but bleeding to their grave.

and

> Wars greatest woes, and misery's increase,
> Flows from the surfeits which we take in peace.

(H&S 8:363)

For some, the formal, sententious couplets are the stuff of Elizabethan revenge tragedy,[11] though such lines would be equally at home in a history play. In either case they sound like the pronouncements of an authoritative figure in a homiletic drama; there is little sense of irony or of the playful undercutting that characterized Jonson's subsequent treatment of such "fustian."

The longest excerpt quoted by Allott is more helpful:

> Gold is a suitor never took repulse;
> It carries palm with it, (where e're it goes)
> Respect, and observation; it uncovers
> The knotty heads of the most surly grooms,
> Enforcing iron doors to yield it way,
> Were it as strong rammed up as Aetna gates.
> It bends the hams of Gossip Vigilance,
> And makes her supple feet as swift as wind.
> It thaws the frostiest, and most stiff disdain,
> Muffles the clearness of Election,
> Strains fancy unto foul Apostacy,

And strikes the quickest-sighted Judgement blind.
Then why should we despair? Despair, away:
Where Gold's the motive, women have no nay.

(H&S 8:363)

The speech appears to be a fairly conventional soliloquy, spoken by a scheming and villainous protagonist who brushes aside misgivings about his plotting, confident in his misogynistic conviction that women are ultimately swayed by gold. Stylistically, the speech resembles the generalized blank verse characteristic of much of the drama of the mid- to late 1590s, a style indebted to Marlovian tragedy: strongly end-stopped lines, joined by syntactic suspension through iteration and conjunctive clauses into a swelling verse paragraph, here capped by a syntactically strained couplet. Instead of classical allusions, Jonson invokes the emblematic figures of the homiletic tradition: "Election," "Judgement," "Vigilance," and "Apostacy."

Jonson's finest re-creation of an earlier Elizabethan mode is to be found in his additions to *The Spanish Tragedy*. Anne Barton has argued compellingly that the additions in the 1602 Quarto are by Jonson and that they are characteristic of thematic concerns—especially the relationship of father and son—that recur in his plays. Yet even in re-creating Kyd's style Jonson turns to Marlowe, according to Barton, as "a way of keeping himself in touch with other manifestations of the popular idiom he needed to invoke in writing his additions."[12] Thus, in the fifth addition, Jonson echoes a pair of famous lines from *Doctor Faustus* ("Had I as many souls as there be stars,/ I'd give them all for Mephostophilis" [1.4.102–3]) in a passage that could easily have come from *Tamburlaine:*

I tell thee, Viceroy, this day I have seen revenge,
And in that sight am grown a prouder monarch
Than ever sat under the crown of Spain.
Had I as many lives as there be stars,
As many heavens to go to, as those lives,
I'd give them all, I, and my soul to boot,
But I would see thee ride in this red pool.[13]

The infinite comparisons (as many lives as stars, as many heavens as those lives), the overwhelming pride, the disdain for life when weighed against

revenge, and the swelling and suspended verse paragraph all hark back to
the bragging blank verse of Marlowe's Scythian shepherd. Moreover, the
triumph described here is visualized in characteristically Marlovian terms
—another's humiliation—worth attaining even at the Faustian price of
one's soul.

If Jonson indirectly recalls Marlowe in these additions, he takes him
on directly in a dramatic fragment—probably written a few years before
Sejanus His Fall (1603)—entitled *Mortimer His Fall*. Little is known about
this work, other than the brief editorial note appended to it in the 1640
Folio that states the obvious: "Left unfinished."[14] It reflects a Jonson that
antedates his defensive inclusion of parody and poetasters, one that indicates an urge to move beyond the derivative tragedies of his early engagements in Henslowe's service. It also antedates the repertory of features
that would soon be associated with Jonson: colloquial prose, contemporary
settings, admonitory satire, and rambling plots and subplots filled with
gulls and humours.

The surviving outline indicates that Jonson planned a play modeled
on Marlowe's *Edward II,* which apparently was still in the Admiral's Men's
repertory as late as 1602.[15] We have here the stuff of Marlowe's tumultuous denouement: the haling away of Kent, the humiliation and torture
of the king, and the hired assassins and torturers (H&S 7:58). Jonson
appears to have sought to go beyond Marlowe with a radically new type
of tragedy, replete with choruses of "Ladies," "Courtiers," and "Country
Justices, and their Wives." What is so striking in this case is the
discrepancy between Jonson's theoretical plans and pronouncements and
the surviving fragment of the first hundred or so lines from the play. If
the outline of the plot did not signify his intention to include these
various choruses, we would never guess it from the opening soliloquy of
the play, which begins in the traditional vein of the overreacher soliloquizing on his triumph over rivals and over Fate.

Mortimer His Fall is a *de casibus* play in the popular tradition,
mingling English history and revenge drama, and as such comes closest
to the traditions Jonson repudiates elsewhere in his plays and criticism.
Its opening scenes are in blank verse (with a few rhymed couplets).
Internal evidence suggests that the scenes were written before the end of
the century.[16] There are few feminine endings, the syntax is fairly stilted,
and Jonson does not enjamb over phrase boundaries, as Jacobean and
Caroline dramatists regularly did. The dialogue is awkward and unnatural. Consider, for example, Mortimer's first encounter with the Queen:

Isabel. My Lord! Sweet Mortimer!

Mor.   My Queen! My Mistress!

  My Sovereign! nay, my Goddess! and my Juno!

  What name, or title, as a mark of power

  Upon me, should I give you?

Isabel.   Isabel,

  Your Isabel, and you my Mortimer:

  Which are the marks of parity, not power,

  And these are titles, best become our love.

Mor. Can you fall under those?

Isabel.   Yes, and be happy.

          (H&S 7:61–62)

If we encountered such wooden dialogue in a mature Jonson play we might suspect that he was engaged in burlesque. It is but a stone's throw from here to the lovers' exchange in Littlewit's puppet show in *Bartholomew Fair* ("O Leander, Leander, my dear, my dear Leander,/ I'll for ever be thy goose, so thou'lt be my gander" [H&S 6:130]).

The opening soliloquy is, however, a *tour de force* and stands in a tradition reaching back to morality Vice figures, through Marlowe's soliloquizing overreachers—Faustus, Barabas, the Guise, and Mortimer Junior. The speech looks forward to Jonson's more complex handling of the overreacher in his depiction of Volpone and Sir Epicure Mammon. The style of the passage also bears a strong resemblance to Jonson's efforts in this vein excerpted in Allott's anthology.

It is worth juxtaposing the speech with its parallel in *Edward II,* a gloating tirade that Marlowe places immediately before the play's reversal. In both passages a Machiavellian Mortimer has just overthrown the king and his brother and, having eliminated all rivals and won the love of Isabel, exults:

  This rise is made, yet! And we now stand, ranked,

  To view about us, all that were above us!

  Nought hinders now our prospect, all are even,

  We walk upon a level. Mortimer

  Is a great lord of late, and a new thing!

  A prince, an earl, and cousin to the King.

  At what a diverse price, do diverse men

Act the same things! Another might have had
Perhaps the hurdle, or at least the axe,
For what I have, this crownet, robes, and wax.
There is a Fate, that flies with towering spirits
Home to the mark, and never checks at conscience.
Poor plodding priests, and preaching friars may make
Their hollow pulpits, and the empty aisles
Of churches ring with that round word. But we
That draw the subtle, and more piercing air,
In that sublimed region of court,
Know all is good, we make so, and go on,
Secured by the prosperity of our crimes.
Today, is Mortimer made Earl of March. . . .

(H&S 7:60)

And now Marlowe's:

The prince I rule, the queen do I command,
And with a lowly congé to the ground,
The proudest lords salute me as I pass;
I seal, I cancel, I do what I will.
Feared am I more than loved;—let me be feared,
And when I frown, make all the court look pale.
I view the prince with Aristarchus' eyes,
Whose looks were as a breeching to a boy.
They thrust upon me the protectorship,
And sue to me for that that I desire;
While at the council table, grave enough,
And not unlike a bashful puritan,
First I complain of imbecility,
Saying it is *onus quam gravissimum*,
Till being interrupted by my friends,
Suscepi that *provinciam,* as they term it,
And to conclude I am Protector now.
Now all is sure, the Queen and Mortimer
Shall rule the realm, the king, and none rule us. . . .

(5.4.46–64)

Jonson here challenges Marlowe at his strength: the Machiavellian over-reacher assured of his control over Fate and Fortune, enthralled with his own villainy, disdainful of rivals or threats, proud especially of his skill in duplicity. The passage surely refutes the claims of those who glibly assert that Jonson could not write tragedy. Apparently, he could pen tragedies too easily, though he could not yet discover his own, original voice in this genre.

Yet Jonson must have also realized that something was missing: Marlowe's handling of history must have struck him as more slippery, more subversive, than a cursory experience of *Edward II* would suggest. While a providential history is consistently recalled (one thinks here of Mortimer's speech on cruel Fortune's wheel), it is simultaneously exposed as a construct no less fictional than the other generic constructs Marlowe resurrects and undermines in his plays. I am suggesting here that Jonson, in the act of imitating *Edward II,* became aware of this tension or subversion underlying his model—and broke off his attempt, unwilling or unable to appropriate or work around this Marlovian characteristic. To imitate the surface stylistic features was not to capture the essence of what made Marlowe's art so compelling and disturbing. Jonson may well have sensed that Marlowe's more complex and cynical handling of historical process offered a powerful critique of his own and revealed it as inadequate if not anachronistic. If so, he understood this better than Marlowe's more derivative heirs, like Robert Greene and George Peele, who, while appro-priating Marlowe's visual and verbal style in works like *Selimus* and *The Battle of Alcazar,* often appear oblivious to the subversive features of Marlowe's plays. Possibly, in response to this tension with his precursor, Jonson saw the implications of the historical relativism underlying his Marlovian model and tried to wrest the story into a more providentialist historical framework by introducing such moral signposts as the classical choruses and the Nuncius.

Despite the difficulties Jonson faced in confronting his Marlovian model in *Mortimer,* he would nonetheless try, one last time, to yoke Marlowe's style to his own brand of tragical history, this time in *Sejanus.* Not surprisingly, the same tensions between classical pronouncements and an underlying anachronistic model of heroical history recur. Insofar as *Sejanus* offered classical history, however, Jonson was able to mask his debt to the Elizabethan heroical history somewhat more effectively. He went to considerable lengths to do so, providing for example, extensive classicizing details such as marginal notes that indicate which editions of classical texts he consulted. [17] Nonetheless, despite this insistence on the play's classicism, the presence and pressure of Marlovian heroical drama remains strong. For Herford and Simpson, Sejanus' speeches hark "back to Barabas" and at other moments have "touches of Tamburlaine"; his "colossal brag belongs to the Marlowesque phase of tragedy" (H&S 2:21–2). This is nowhere more apparent than in Sejanus' soliloquy at the outset of Act 5. Tacitus is set aside in favor of Barabas and Mortimer Junior:

> Swell, swell, my joys, and faint not to declare
> Your selves, as ample, as your causes are.
> I did not live, till now; this my first hour:
> Wherein I see my thoughts reached by my power.
> But this, and gripe my wishes. Great, and high,
> The world knows only two, that's Rome and I.
> My roof receives me not; 'tis air I tread:
> And, at each step, I feel my advanced head
> Knock out a star in heaven! Reared to this height,
> All my desires seem modest, poor and slight,
> That did before sound impudent: 'Tis place,
> Not blood, discerns the noble, and the base.
>
> (H&S 4:436)

By the climax of the speech Sejanus is squarely in the tradition of Marlowe's Tamburlaine, who, bored with earthly conquest, threatens to strive with the gods themselves:

> Is there not something more, than to be Caesar?
> Must we rest there? It irks, t'have come so far,
> To be so near a stay.
>
> .   .   .
>
> It is our grief, and will be our loss, to know
> Our power shall want opposites; unless
> The gods, by mixing in the cause, would bless
> Our fortune with their conquest. That were worth
> Sejanus' strife: durst fates but bring it forth.
>
> (H&S 4:437)

His fate is characteristically Marlovian: like Faustus, he is dismembered: with "violent rage" his body is ripped "limb, from limb," then "torn, and scattered":

> this [one] hath cut off his hands;
> And this his feet; these fingers, and those toes;
> That hath his liver; he his heart.
>
> (H&S 4:468)

Even more than recalling Faustus or Tamburlaine or Mortimer, *Sejanus* hearkens back to Barabas (whose fate is equally horrible) and to *The Jew of Malta*. Like Ferneze's Malta, Tiberius' Rome is a city of appalling sexual and political corruption, so much so that, for Anne Barton, tragedy "in *Sejanus* is really an anachronism, the property of the past." [18] While Barton does not pursue the possibility of *Sejanus* as a version of Marlovian "tragic farce," she does suggest that the play marks a turning point in Jonson's development as dramatist, arguing that it pointed the way towards his major, Aristophanic, Jacobean comedies, notably *Volpone:*

> Both *Sejanus* and *Volpone* concern themselves with the relation be-
> tween a master and his parasite, one in which patron and dependent
> work together for a time with devastating efficiency and success, in
> a partnership which allows them a seemingly effortless control over
> other people, until it is destroyed by a mutual violation of trust.
> Institutionalized justice in both plays . . . is a farce. [19]

The Jew of Malta could easily be substitued for *Volpone* here. If *Sejanus* can be said to anticipate *Volpone* in this way, it does so because both plays look back to a Marlovian past: the central pairing of master and servant, the highly theatrical scheming to achieve political, sexual, and financial ends, the series of betrayals, and the overreaching ambition (and the attendant gloating) that ends in poetically just (though cruel) punishment.

Insofar as *Sejanus* is a decisive, though flawed, transitional work for Jonson, it is so because it pointed the way for Jonson to transpose Marlowe's tragical history into his inimitable Jacobean comedy. The play's acknowledged failure in the public theater should not be attributed to its off-putting classicism as much as to its representation of tragical history that proved too anachronistic for audiences at the Globe in 1603; the play lingers somewhere between *Edward II* and *The Jew of Malta*, but while Marlowe's plays somehow managed to straddle tragedy and farce, *Sejanus* fails to do so and may have come across to audiences as either mildly confused or simply old-fashioned political history. After *Sejanus* (with the exception of *Cataline* in 1611), Jonson abandoned both history and tragedy, though he did not repudiate the Marlovian elements in his work; instead, he found a place for them within a different genre. In doing so Jonson would come to acknowledge that poets' "eminence appears but in their own way. Virgil's felicity left him in prose, as Tully's forsook him in verse." "Each," Jonson acknowledged, "hath his way of strength" (H&S 8:589). Before examining the ways in which the Marlovian is refigured in Jonson's four mature Jacobean comedies—*Volpone, The Alchemist, Bartholomew Fair,* and *The Devil Is an Ass*—I want to return to his late Elizabethan plays to explore the decisive role they played in enabling Jonson to come to terms with Marlowe's legacy.

⌘

In his efforts at writing a new kind of drama—the humours plays and comical satires of 1598 through 1602, including *Every Man in, Every Man out,* and *Poetaster*—Jonson would find newer and more successful strategies for confronting Marlowe. In his response to Marlowe, Jonson exemplifies Harold Bloom's definition of the poet who "is not so much a man speaking to men as a man rebelling against being spoken to by a dead man (the precursor) outrageously more alive than himself." [20] For Jonson, this rebellion took the form of parody.

Marlowe's premature death exacerbated the problem of his influence for many, and for Jonson, eight years his junior, in particular. Throughout his life Jonson's rivalries were characterized by direct, unmediated confrontation: his man-to-man combat in the Low Countries, in which he slew his rival before both camps and took *"opima spolia* from him" (H&S 1:139), is representative of this attitude. A similar impulse can be detected in his role in the Poets' War, his fatal encounter with Gabriel Spencer, and his struggles with Marston, Dekker, Daniel, Inigo Jones, and others. But Marlowe's death made this kind of aggressive, unmediated confrontation impossible. One way of understanding Jonson's recourse to parody, then, is to see his parodic quotations as acts of exorcism —in this case exorcising the anxiety of stealing from the dead; the

German word for quoting (*zitieren*) conveys just this in its secondary meaning as "the calling up of ghosts."[21] Jonson, through imitative quotation, can simultaneously evoke and set to rest, exorcise and thereby come to terms with the troubling (not least because dead) precursor.

Great parody—like great forgery—depends upon an artist's absolute mastery of a predecessor's style. One of Jonson's finest attributes, exemplified in his drama between 1598 and 1602, and apparent throughout his career, is his superb skill at imitating the verse styles of his predecessors. Critical interest in Jonson as master of prose comedy has obscured this. We should wonder instead why a metrist with such a fine ear for distinctive verse rhythms should relinquish the medium in favor of prose. It may well be that Jonson mastered this skill in his early collaborative years in the theater. He subsequently showed delight in displaying this mimetic capacity: in the self-consciously anachronistic but delicious poulter's measure of the Vice Iniquity in *The Devil Is an Ass;* the Skeltonics of *The Fortunate Isles;* the Kyddian rhetoric of his additions to *The Spanish Tragedy;* the highly wrought Elizabethan love poetry of *A Tale of a Tub;* and the jingling rhymes of the puppet show in *Bartholomew Fair,* which grafts Marlowe's rhymed couplets to the clumsier rhythm of Richard Edward's *Damon and Pithias.* The list—and with it Jonson's range—could easily be extended: despite Jonson's harsh judgments of Donne's metrical style, his facility at imitating Donne's elegies (elegies themselves indebted to Marlowe's earlier translations) was such that critics still dispute which one of them wrote the "The Expostulation." When Jonson wanted to approximate—or parody—the stylistic features of rivals and predecessors he could do so masterfully. Father to prose comedy, he was heir to the great experimental age of Elizabethan versification.

His urge to display this talent borders on the compulsive in some of the plays of the late 1590s. He seems to need to pause to reassert for himself and for his audience his ability to mimic, to display his control over the style of precursors, which he feels he has fully digested. Consider the wonderfully irrelevant battle of bombastic blank verse in *Every Man in,* where Jonson, through Clement, displays his technical virtuosity at reproducing the modulations of Elizabethan end-stopped pentameter, quite close to what he was the first to describe as "Marlowe's mighty line." Clement, in what Prospero refers to as the "height of style," recites,

Mount thee my Phlegon muse, and testify,
How Saturn sitting in an Ebon cloud,

Disrobed his podex, white as ivory,
And through the welkin thundered all aloud.

(H&S 3:283)

The lines are probably a parodic recollection of Tamburlaine's vaunting account of his capture of Bajazeth:

As when a fiery exhalation,
Wrapt in the bowels of a freezing cloud,
Fighting for passage, makes the welkin crack,
And casts a flash of lightning to the earth.

(TAMBURLAINE, PART ONE, 4.2.43–6)

Jonson, while demonstrating his mastery of iambic pentameter (here emphasizing the lines' artificiality through rhyme), also suggests that— despite classical allusions, ornate vocabulary, suspended and elaborate syntax, metrical regularity, and high astounding terms characteristic of Marlovian verse—the style is as obnoxious and as windy as what Clement actually describes: a flatulent father of the gods, or rather, tellingly, son to the father of the gods, Ops, overthrown by his aspiring son.

Jonson cannot seem to resist showing (with an almost child-like delight and crudity) his expertise in imitating this style. He next takes it "a step or two lower" with a triple rhyme that accentuates the unnaturalness of the verse even further:

From Catadupa and the banks of Nile,
Where only breeds your monstrous crocodile:
Now are we purposed for to fetch our style,

(H&S 3:284)

here recalling antecedents like Tamburlaine's exotic peregrinations through Africa:

From thence to Nubia near Borno Lake,
And so along the AEthiopian sea,
Cutting the Tropic line of Capricorn,
I conquered all as far as Zanzibar.

(TAMBURLAINE, PART TWO 5.3.137–40)

When revising the play for the Folio edition Jonson omitted this poetic exchange, perhaps recognizing in retrospect how revealing this was of his emulative anxiety. Even Wellbred found the last example "too far-fetched." For Jonson, the style remained not only flatulent and monstrous but also foreign, a claim that accords with his later criticism that Marlowe's language fled "from all humanity" (H&S 8:587).

The unmasking that is central to these plays works on several levels: just as the Buffones, Matthews, and Littlewits are unmasked, so too are the outmoded, artificial, and unnatural styles of Jonson's predecessors. For Jonson, the process of revision is a gauge of self-correction (which is, I suppose, why he could not fathom a Shakespeare who never blotted a line). Jonson is obsessed with revision, with identifying and unmasking the vestigial elements of his native progenitors, then parodying, demystifying, and casting them out. Freud's comment on this process in his *Jokes and Their Relation to the Unconscious* offers an explanation for this behavior: "*Parody* and *travesty* achieve the degradation of something exalted in another way: by destroying the unity that exists between people's characters as we know them and their speeches and actions, by replacing either the exalted figures or their utterances by inferior ones . . . . The same mechanism is also used for *unmasking,* which only applies where someone has seized dignity and authority by a deception and these have to be taken from him in reality."[22] The deceiver here is Marlowe, whose style, for Jonson, had "nothing in [it] but the scenical strutting, and furious vociferation, to warrant [it] to the ignorant gapers" (H&S 8:587).

Jonson's meticulous revision of *Every Man in* for inclusion in the Folio[23] provides a striking example of the process of unmasking and casting out, here directed at his own earlier dramatic output, his first acknowledged and legitimate offspring. Jonson thus effectively buries remaining traces of tension; as Jonas Barish puts it, the "presence of tension in Jonson reveals itself most obviously in his insistent claim to be without tension."[24] Far more than "[d]ramatic probability and stylistic consistency" (H&S 1:366), as Herford and the Simpsons would have it, account for Jonson's revisions of *Every Man in.* A comparison of the Quarto and Folio texts suggests the intentions underlying Jonson's revision and testifies to his ongoing struggle to efface the influence of native progenitors. The allusion to Tamburlaine in the 1601 Quarto, subsequently deleted along with the contest over bombastic blank verse, provides a case in point. In the earlier version Knowell speaks of his servant Musco disguising himself "with so special and exquisite a grace," as a strutting, swaggering soldier, "that (had'st thou seen him) thou wouldst have sworn he might have been the Tamburlaine, or the Agamemnon of the rout" (H&S 3:239). In the revised version of the play the servant is demoted to one of the "decayed, ruinous, worm-eaten gentlemen of the round": a "Serjeant-Major, if not a Lieutenant-Coronel," but assuredly not a Tamburlaine (H&S 3:353).

A more significant and far-reaching revision is the deletion of Knowell Junior's rejoinder to his father, an impassioned defense of originality in poetry:

> Opinion, Oh God, let gross opinion
> Sink and be damned as deep as Barathrum.
> If it may stand with your most wished content,
> I can refell opinion, and approve
> The state of poesie, such as it is,
> Blessed, eternal, and most true divine:
> Indeed if you will look on poesie,
> As she appears in many, poor and lame,
> Patched up in remnants and old worn rags,
> Half-starved for want of her peculiar food,
> Sacred invention, then I must confirm,
> Both your conceit and censure of her merit. . . .

> (H&S3:285)

The speech, which continues for another twenty lines, rehearses by now familiar arguments: the weak poet is "half-starved for want of her peculiar food/Sacred invention," terms recalling those used earlier in describing Matheo's theft from Marlowe. Jonson also attacks "brainless gulls" who "utter their stolen wares/With such applauses in our vulgar ears" and an audience that sets "no difference twixt these empty spirits,/ And a true poet." Jonson here invokes the New Comic situation so familiar to Shakespearean comedy and gives it a twist: the source of tension between father and son is not a woman but Poetry herself, described by the young male lover in terms usually reserved for his beloved. But the unification toward which the play drives is not the creation of a new family structure through the marriage of man and woman but a new poetic order that follows a true poet's union with Poetry herself. As Jonson himself struggled to overcome and circumvent forbidding poetic models like Marlowe during the years in which he forged his style, his plays often appropriate this intergenerational conflict inherent in New Comedy and reformulate this strife as an interpoetic one. That the speech is directed at a father figure possibly played by Shakespeare (in the Chamberlain's Men production of 1598) adds another dimension to the complexities of interpoetic relations. In the revised version this confrontation between aspiring son and repressive father (who admits to having once dreamt "on naught but idle poetry" [H&S 3:197]) is omitted, replaced by Justice Clement's cheery observation that poets "are not born every year, as an alderman." Knowell Junior's reply is now brief: "Sir, you have saved me the labor of a defence" (H&S 3:400). Herford and Simpson's claim that "Few Elizabethan plays owed less, in fact, to the stimulus or guidance of previous literature than *Every Man in His Humour*" (1:345) needs to be reversed: few Elizabethan plays evince so earnest and desperate a struggle to repudiate the stimulus of poetic precursors.[25]

Jonson, through the juxtaposition of poetaster and true poet, reiterates the belief, repeated in his critical writings, that imitation that never goes beyond mere mimicry is fatal to all but the strongest of poets. He writes in *Discoveries* that "we so insist in imitating others, as we cannot (when it is necessary) return to our selves" (H&S 8:597). The feared loss of poetic identity, the possibility of being consumed (rather than having a "[s]tomach to concoct, divide, and turn all into nourishment" [H&S 8:638], that is, consume another's poetic authority) dogged Jonson. He returned to it in his next play, *Every Man out of His Humour*, where weak poets become fixed at the level of mimicry. The play is about literary indigestion: the play's many imitators, lacking the necessary "stomach to concoct, divide, and turn all to nourishment," swallow what they take in "crude, raw, or indigested" (H&S 8:638). In the end either they are purged or their lips are sealed; the result is essentially the same. The imitators who fill the play take on the characteristics Jonson ascribes in *Discoveries* to derivative poets who are "like children, that imitate the vice of stammerers so long, till at last they become such; and make the habit to another nature, as it is never forgotten" (H&S 8:597).

Every Man out, which has the notoriety of being the longest extant English Renaissance play, is virtually unactable in the form that has come down to us (and it has not been acted professionally since the Restoration [H&S 9:185–88]), since Jonson chose to add material for the printed version, the first of his works that he saw into print. The result, as one critic puts it, is "a book about a play about literature."[26] The unusual features of the play can partly be accounted for in terms of Jonson's confrontation with and exploration of his relationship to native predecessors, his increasing conviction of independence from them, and his use of parody and poetasters in triumphing over them. It also suggests the extent to which Jonson was nervously aware of the dangers that awaited those who imitated too servilely for too long. Characteristically, in asserting (with no irony) that 'he follows in no poet's footsteps,' Jonson quotes from Horace on the title pages of the Quarto and Folio: *"Non aliena meo pressi pede"* (H&S 3:419).

Each of Jonson's humorous characters in *Every Man out* chooses a literary style (and the attendant world implied by this style) and attempts both to inhabit that world entirely and to impose that world upon others. In Anne Barton's terms, the output of Jonson's contemporaries and forebears becomes "a kind of barometer to the folly of those characters who read and quote from it." [27] Terrance Dunford takes this argument a step farther in his "Consumption of the World: Reading, Eating, and Imitation in *Every Man out of His Humour,"* where he argues that the inhabitants of the play "'read' their world and consume it in their readings by attempting to project them upon reality." Ultimately, each character "claims that his book (and its literary form) is the only true articulation of reality," while "all other texts are relegated to the category of 'art.' " [28] It is but a short step from here to the larger submerged claim that Jonson, casting out and exposing these gulls, effectively undermines the mimetic claims of the Elizabethan models consumed by these humours and thereby claims greater fidelity to reality and life for his own art. Saviolina peppers her discourse with phrases borrowed from Sidney and Greene ("from whence she may steal with more security"). Fungoso lounges about, reading from Sidney's *Arcadia,* while his sister Fallace prefers Lyly's Euphuistic prose. Puntavolo is enamored of the conventions of romance, Brisk with Daniel, Clove with Marston. While there is no imitator of Marlowe, Clove urges Orange to "talk fustian a little," and Buffone tosses out odd bits of hyperbolic blank verse reminiscent of Tamburlaine's histrionic gestures:

> With that, the moody squire thumped his breast,
> And reared his eyen to heaven, for revenge.

> (H&S 3:508)

One gull can praise another for the manner in which he "doth so peerlessly imitate any manner of person for gesture, action, passion, or whatever," while another acknowledges that only by consuming others can growth occur: "if we fed upon another, we should shoot up a great deal faster, and thrive much better" (H&S 3:581). All are punished, in a play that "is a parody of literature and the ease with which literary forms are imitated," [29] and whose structure provides an ideal medium for Jonson to repudiate poetic precursors, asserting his emergent originality and independence, and measure the distance that separates the true poet, who can properly digest and absorb a (by now outmoded) poetic tradition, from those amateurish imitators who merely choke on it.

As these examples show, central to the *Every Man* plays (and to *Poetaster*) is Jonson's imposition of a poetaster between himself and the object of parody. Poetasters are useful, perhaps necessary intermediaries for Jonson, through which he can confront precursors. In their faithful and woefully unoriginal mimicry they resemble the children who cannot shake the habit of imitating the stutterer. Transferring his criticism to the mimic and not the object of imitation, Jonson can mock the weak while indirectly confronting the strong, simultaneously admiring and rejecting poetic models. The poetasters are thus scapegoats, bearing Jonson's anxiety more justifiably directed at the authority of poetic precursors. By heaping scorn upon their ignorant delight in the very models he wants to repress and reject, and by inviting and exhorting us to scorn these characters, their values, and their poetic preferences, Jonson indirectly corrects and revises the work of his predecessors.

Intrinsic to Jonson's inclusion of parody and poetasters is his juxtaposition of styles. We might think here of Shakespeare's response to Marlowe in *The Merchant of Venice* (not just in relation to *The Jew of Malta* but in its depiction of the Prince of Morocco as a debased Tamburlaine whose hyperbolic and bombastic blank verse is set off against the conversational stage prose spoken by other characters).[30] It is a technique especially attractive to writers of comedy, more so for writers of realistic social comedy, whose aim is the representation of love and life and the problems of social relation. For such authors, parodic juxtaposition becomes a useful device for foregrounding an unrealistic—Jonson might say untruthful—mode of life and love and language. If the aim of the comic dramatist is the creation of a meaningful comic world, then one of his first tasks is to challenge (by juxtaposition or by parodic subversion) the inadequate dramatic worlds offered by previous artists. Untimely ripped from their world by poetasters, the conventionality of older comic worlds cannot help but reinforce for audiences the illusion (and thereby the inadequacy) of older poetic visions, while presumably recommending the comic world, in Jonson's case the prose world, in which they are embedded.

Jonson foregrounds filial strife, parody, poetasters, plagiarism, and especially revision yet again in *Poetaster,* the last of his "comical satyres" and a play which marks a "turn" in his engagement with Marlowe. In *Poetaster* the problem of Marlowe's influence surfaces in Act 1, scene 1, when a poet-dramatist (and, confusingly, *not* the poetaster of the title) enters reciting the closing lines of "the hasty errors of our morning muse":

> Then, when this body falls in funeral fire,
> My name shall live, and my best part aspire.
>
> (H&S 4:206)

The poet is Ovid, the poem the fifteenth elegy of Book I of his *Amores.* And in the ensuing scene he must confront a repressive father, Ovid Senior, intent on blocking his poetic career. The elegy he recites is about envy—which pains the living poet, not the dead one. Significantly, it is also about canonization and the making of a male literary historical tradition. After a brief digression, Ovid proceeds to read the forty-four-line elegy in its entirety, an unusual dramatic strategy for Jonson, especially so early on in a play. The first eight lines read:

> Envy, why twitst thou me, my time's spent ill?
> And call'st my verse, fruit of an idle quill?
> Or that (unlike the line from whence I sprung)
> War's dusty honors I pursue not young?
> Or that I study not the tedious laws;
> And prostitute my voice in every cause?
> Thy scope is mortal; mine, eternal fame:
> Which through the world shall ever chant my name.
>
> (H&S 4:207)

By the third or fourth couplet attentive listeners might have remembered where they had heard those lines before: Marlowe's notorious and recently banned (and burned) translations of Ovid's *Elegies:*

> Envy, why carpest thou my time is spent so ill,
> And terms my works fruits of an idle quill?

Or that unlike the line from whence I sprung,
War's dusty honors are refused being young?
Nor that I study not the brawling laws,
Nor set my voice to sale in every cause?
Thy scope is mortal, mine eternal fame,
That all the world might ever chant my name.

(*POEMS*, 134)

There is no Lorenzo here to cry foul, no critic exclaiming "steal from the dead? it's worse than sacrilege." In light of the subject of the poem — the paradox that only in death the poet most triumphs and most lives — it is hard to believe that Jonson could have included this Marlovian imitation with no sense of the irony involved. Yet, despite the similarities between the passages, Jonson no doubt saw his version as a substantial revision of Marlowe and made no objection when his translation was included in editions of Marlowe's elegies after 1602, with the words "The same by B.J."[31]

The alterations range from factual to stylistic. Jonson, for instance, corrects Marlowe's mistaken rendering of Accius (Lucius Accius) as Plautus (a fine point of classical scholarship that had only recently been set right), no doubt experiencing the kind of self-satisfaction evident in the marginal notes to his copy of Chapman's *Homer* (e.g., "*O quam inepte haec omnia, et sequentia!*" [(H&S 11:594) [Oh, how inept is all this and that which follows!]). J. B. Steane, comparing the two versions, stresses Jonson's regularization, his smoothing out of Marlowe's rougher edges.[32] Marlowe's "brawling" laws become Jonson's "tedious" ones; "bond-men cheat" is changed to "slaves be false." More tellingly, Marlowe's

Therefore when flint and iron wear away,
Verse is immortal, and shall ne'er decay,

(*POEMS*, 135)

is bled dry in Jonson's

The suffering ploughshare or the flint may wear:
But heavenly poesy no death can fear.

(*POEMS*, 136)

Jonson, however, more closely approximates Marlowe's vein when he alters

> Let base-conceited wits admire vile things,
> Fair Phoebus lead me to the Muses' springs,
>
> *(POEMS, 135)*

to a vivid and forceful

> Kneel hinds to trash: me let bright Phoebus swell,
> With cups full flowing from the Muses' well.
>
> *(POEMS, 136)*

As Steane observes, the greatest difference in their sensibilities is apparent in their translations of Ovid's final couplet.[33] Jonson writes,

> Then when this body falls in funeral fire,
> My name shall live, and my best part aspire.
>
> *(POEMS, 136)*

His couplet's balance and closure differ sharply from Marlowe's:

> Then though death rakes my bones in funeral fire,
> I'll live, and as he pulls me down, mount higher.
>
> *(POEMS, 135)*

This closing couplet neatly encapsulates what sets Marlowe apart: the violence, the paradoxical and continuous struggle, and, above all, the defiant assertion of autonomy, even in the face of death. In his precise, sure-handed reworking of Marlowe's translation we can locate Jonson's parting of ways. His revision reflects an increasing self-confidence in his poetic choices, one that acknowledges (and literally copies) Marlowe's strengths while with equal ease departs freely from what it finds remiss or defective in this precursor's style. For it is to Marlowe's verse style, above all, that the early Jonson responded to most powerfully, a style that could charm not only the "innocent gapers" in the theater but aspiring poets, too.

❧

Jonson's mature comedies, especially *Volpone,* mark a "counter-turn" in his development as dramatist. Critics like Barton have attributed this to his construction of a drama built upon the principles of Aristophanic Old Comedy, with its limited interest in love and romance; its political topicality; its satiric bite and harsh, often violent, humor; and its exposure of vice and unregenerate behavior.[34] But for Jonson "*Comedia Vetus*" was not Aristophanic but the native homiletic tradition of the Vice play,[35] a dramatic form, as David Bevington, Bernard Spivack, and others have shown, that powerfully informed Marlowe's drama (especially *The Jew of Malta* and *Doctor Faustus*) and that provided a model much closer at hand than Aristophanes for the savage farce, ambivalent closure, structural repetition, and sympathetic villains that recur in Jonson's mature comedies.[36]

In *Volpone* Jonson moves full circle: Marlowe's influence, once threatening, proves beneficent, as Jonson returns to *The Jew of Malta* in creating his most powerful and memorable play. With this receptive imitative response Jonson's absorption of Marlowe is nearly total, any anxiety of influence replaced by a mimesis that completes and ultimately begins to exhaust Marlowe's art. Jonson is able here to contain and control the Marlovian tone and the Marlovian overreacher within the confines of his own comic design. Critical attempts to label *Volpone* as a corrective, Aristophanic, or satiric comedy undervalue the extent to which the work is informed by Jonson's appropriation and transformation of Marlowe's dramatic form. In terms of Thomas M. Greene's taxonomy of imitation, Jonson here exhibits the most sophisticated kind of imitation—"dialectical" or "improvisational"—in which the artist moves through imitation to originality.[37]

Jonson responds in *Volpone* to what was proleptically Jacobean in Marlowe's play: the radical skepticism, slippery moral center, Machiavellianism, and Italianate intrigue anticipate the spirit and concerns that would inform so many Jacobean tragedies. When revived at the court of Charles I by Heywood forty years after its inception, *The Jew of Malta* must have seemed remarkably modern in its cynical social and political vision. Jonson recognized and exploited this quality: he found in Marlowe's play a world in which money's corruptive power could sever master from servant, husband from wife, and perhaps most disturbingly, parent from child (though Jonson characteristically replaces father/daughter with father/son). Marlowe's *The Jew of Malta* also served as a paradigm for a world of repeated play-acting and dissembling, one irremediably corrupt politically and judicially, where the execution of authority remains problematic. In this respect, yet another effect of Marlowe's play is felt in the troubling conclusion of Jonson's comedy, a feature that had earlier figured in the unsettling closure of Shakespeare's emulative encounter with *The Jew of Malta* in *The Merchant of Venice*.

From the outset, as T. S. Eliot first observed, *Volpone* immerses us in a Marlovian universe—stylistically, visually, and thematically:

> Good morning to the day; and, next, my gold:
> Open the shrine, that I may see my saint.
> Hail the world's soul, and mine. More glad then is
> The teeming earth, to see the longed-for sun
> Peep through the horns of the celestial ram,
> Am I, to view thy splendor, darkening his:
> That, lying here, amongst my other hordes,
> Show'st like a flame, by night; or like the day
> Strook out of chaos, when all darkness fled
> Unto the center.

> (H&S 5:24–25)

The speech—for Eliot "in the manner of Marlowe, more deliberate, more mature, but without Marlowe's inspiration"[38]—conflates Faustus's aspiring soliloquy with Barabas's opening speech. Recalling Faustus in his study and Barabas in his counting house, the play opens with the overreacher, isolated, declaring his devotion to his object of desire. At the same time, as with Faustus and Barabas, we sense in Volpone's chambers a stifling feeling of enclosure heightened by the protagonist's restlessness, his desire for play, and his desire, simply, for more. Volpone's opening speech also invokes a Marlovian restructuring of values and the playful undermining of theological and ethical claims.

Structurally, too, *Volpone* owes much to Marlowe's work, most notably in Jonson's creation of a plot based on repeated, virtually interchangeable episodes. Thus, Volpone's gulling of Voltore, Corbaccio, and Corvino, in the second, third, and fourth scenes of Act 1, follows a dramatic pattern Marlowe had employed in representing Tamburlaine's successive and ultimately numbing conquests of Mycetes, Cosroe, Bajazeth, and Calapine; in Faustus's repeated and eventually demeaning demonstration of his powers with Benvolio, Frederick, Martino, the Carter, the Horse-courser, and the Hostess; and in Barabas's murderous schemes against Lodowick, Mathias, Jacomo, Barnadino, and Calymath. We have here a dramatic unfolding radically different from the kind developed by Shakespeare. Intrinsic to this almost compulsive repetition is the protagonist's reiterated assertions of self, paradoxically coupled with his insistence on role-playing, masking, and self-fashioning, as that self is shown to be a fictional, pliable construct. Volpone's disguise as a mountebank likewise harks back to Barabas's playing the part of another professional entertainer, a French musician.

In comparing *Volpone* with *The Jew of Malta* Eliot justly argues that Jonson, like Marlowe, should be considered as a master of farce and caricature, a creator of a drama of great and terrifying directness, a creator, too, of a drama that intentionally lacks the third dimension, depth, that we have come to associate with Shakespeare and Shakespearean drama. Eliot is instructive in setting Marlowe and Jonson together against Shakespeare: the feature "which distinguishes Barabas from Shylock, Epicure Mammon from Falstaff, Faustus from . . . Macbeth" is an animating power, an artistic wholeness and dramatic universe.[39] Jonson, like Marlowe—and to a great extent through Marlowe—discovered the possibilities generated by what Eliot describes as two dimensionality, or alternatively, of caricature. Put another way, where language is subordinated to character in Shakespeare's play, character is virtually an extension, a creation of language, in the works of Marlowe and Jonson. The search for depth or coherence of character in Jonson (as in Marlowe) is a search for identity, and that identity is attained when a voice or language is found. Marlowe's drama can thus be seen as helping to liberate Jonson from the dominant Elizabethan comic form—Shakespearean New Comedy—allowing for a remarkable release of creativity and originality in the mature comedies that followed.

If *Volpone* reaches back to *The Jew of Malta*, *The Alchemist*, written seven years later, finds in Marlowe's *Doctor Faustus* a powerful stimulus. Acted frequently during Jonson's formative years in the theater (c. 1595–97), revised by William Birde and Samuel Rowley in 1602, *Faustus* continued to be performed up through the Caroline period.[40] It was also frequently reprinted: the "A" text for the third time the year that *The Alchemist* was written, the "B" text five times more during Jonson's lifetime, including the years in which both his 1616 and 1631 Folios were produced. How chagrined was Jonson, one wonders, to find his

Works jostled (and perhaps outsold) by Marlowe's old-fashioned fare at London's bookstalls?

The Marlovian subtext is explicitly recalled in Act 4 of the *Alchemist,* when the outraged Surly accuses Subtle of being

> the Faustus,
> That casteth figures, and can conjure, cures
> Plagues, piles, and pox, by the Ephemerides,
> And holds intelligence with all the bawds,
> And midwives of three shires?
>
> (H&S 4:381)

It is not Subtle, however, but Sir Epicure Mammon, who is, in Barton's words, "the real Faustus of the play.[41]" Like Marlowe's Faustus, Mammon had first desired to use his powers to better mankind. Where Faustus had dreamt of girding Germany with a wall of brass, and curing plague, so, from the outset, Mammon dwells on public service: he'll "undertake . . . to fright the plague /Out o'the kingdom, in three months," and will "give away so much . . . Shall serve the whole city, with preservative" (H&S 5:316). For Mammon, the alchemical power enables its possessor to

> confer honor love, respect, long life,
> Give safety, valor; yea, and victory,
> To whom he will.
>
> (H&S 5:315)

When the confidence game is finally uncovered, Mammon informs Love-Wit that the "great loss in hope" was not so much his own but the "commonwealth's." Face parodically recalls Faustus's civic plans when describing how Mammon

> would ha' built
> The city new; and made a ditch about it
> Of silver, should have run with cream from Hogden,
> That, every Sunday in More-fields, the younkers
> And tits, and tom-boys should have fed on, gratis.
>
> (H&S 5:404)

But, as Barton notes, just as in Marlowe's play, there is a rapid and disappointing falling away in the protagonist's dream. Interest in the public good is quickly transformed into desire for egoistical gratification. Doctor Faustus's great plans for knowledge and power ultimately manifest themselves in little more than globetrotting, Pope-baiting, arousal at the sight of Helen of Troy, and pranks not much more elevated than those "parodied" by his servant Wagner.

Jonson capitalizes on just this diminution and its attendant self-deception, and in constructing *The Alchemist* along these lines Jonson did not have to change all that much. He simply had to relocate Faustus, remove him from the scholarly world of Wittenburg, strip the play of its larger theological overtones, and place the aspiring overreacher within a comic London world, where the great deceivers of mankind do not wear horns or throw squibs. Mammon is a secular Faustus. And he proves to be more than Faustus, for he is an overreacher whose monumental greed exceeds Barabas's and whose fantasies make those of the Passionate Shepherd seem tame. In Mammon's great speech in Act 2, scene 2, Jonson neatly conflates the desires of all three of these Marlovian prototypes:

> I will have all my beds, blown up; not stuffed:
> Down is too hard. And then, mine oval room,
> Filled with such pictures, as Tiberias took
> From Elephantis: and dull Arentine
> But coldly imitated. Then my glasses
> Cut in more subtle angles, to disperse,
> And multiply the figures, as I walk
> Naked between my succubae.
>
> .   .   .
>
> My meat, shall all come in, in Indian shells,
> Dishes of agate, set in gold, and studded
> With emeralds, sapphires, hiacynths, and rubies.
> The tongues of carps, dormice, and camels' heels,
> Boiled i'the spirit of Sol, and dissolved pearl,
> (Apicius' diet, 'gainst the epilepsy)
> And I will eat these broths, with spoons of amber,
> Headed with diamond, and carbuncle.
> My footboy shall eat pheasants, calvered salmons,
> Knots, godwits, lampreys.

(H&S 5:319–20)

Mammon extends the culinary fantasy of "The Passionate Shepherd"—

> Thy silver dishes filled with meat,
> As precious as the Gods do eat,
> Shall on an ivory table be
> Prepared each day for thee and me.[42]

—to ludicrously extravagant dimensions; even the Shepherd's offer of "Coral claps and amber studs" are echoed and outdone in Mammon's amber spoons and studded dishes of agate.

At the same time, Mammon's account of "emeralds, sapphires, hiacynths, and rubies" recalls and surpasses Barabas's description of gems of fantastic value:

> Bags of fiery opals, sapphires, amethysts,
> Jacinths, hard topaz, grass-green emeralds,
> Beautious rubies, sparkling diamonds,
> And seldseen costly stones of so great price . . .
>
> (*JEW OF MALTA,* 1.1.25–28)

And Mammon's desire to "walk/ Naked between my succubae" calls to mind the climactic moment in Marlowe's play when Faustus summons the most famous succuba of the Elizabethan stage and wonders:

> Is this the face that launched a thousand ships
> And burned the topless towers of Ilium?
>
> (*FAUSTUS,* 5.1.97–98)

Mammon's speech is a *tour de force,* bringing together of the many faces of Marlovian desire for financial, sexual, and magical power. By inflating the desires of Marlowe's tragic heroes to comic proportions Jonson is able to harness one of the defining features of Marlowe's work to his own ends. Once transported into Jonson's universe of comic self-deception, Marlowe's overreachers provide an energy and dynamism that fuel Jonson's plot and characterization. By 1611 Jonson can, in Carew's words, "overcome/A knotty writer" to "bring the booty home" and no longer "think it theft."[43]

Marlowe makes an appearance in Jonson's next, and, for some, greatest comedy, *Bartholomew Fair* (1614), though here he takes his place alongside other Elizabethan authors who are acknowledged in the course of the play, including Chaucer, Shakespeare, Sidney, and Fletcher.[44] The presence of Marlowe is much less pronounced than it had been in either *Volpone* or *The Alchemist* and is limited to Littlewit's revision of "Hero and Leander" for the puppet show at the Fair.

Jonson was busy at this time with revising his previous plays for inclusion in the 1616 Folio, and, as I argue in the final chapter, a substantial part of this revision had to do with retrospectively ironing out his relationship with Shakespeare and clarifying the critical positions he identified with his own work. One of the most important of these principles—recounted in the Prologue to *Every Man in* (c. 1612–14)—had to do with mimesis and with

> deeds, and language, such as men do use:
> And persons, such as Comedy would choose,
> When she would show an image of the times.
>
> (H&S 3:303)

The immediate target of this Prologue is Shakespearean drama. But the same criteria served equally well against a Marlowe whose plays' "scenical strutting and furious vociferation" embodied a dramatic world opposite to the kind Jonson was coming to advocate, at least in his critical remarks.

Bartholomew Fair also marks a return to Jonson's use of poetasters in his engagement with Marlowe, though by 1614 it is Shakespeare (and his late Romances), far more than Marlowe, that engages Jonson's attention. The poetaster is more of a vestige of an earlier practice than a signal of a sustained, anxious literary engagement.

When Bartholomew Cokes discovers that Leatherhead is about to perform Marlowe's "Hero and Leander" and asks if he plays "it according to the printed book?" (which he assures us he has read), Leatherhead answers "By no means, sir," and goes on to explain that he offers a "better way." Marlowe's original

> is too learned, and poetical for our audience; what do they
> know what Hellespont is? Guilty of True loves blood? Or
> what Abidos is? Or the other Sestos hight?
>
> (H&S 6:120)

And Cokes agrees: "Th'art i'the right, I do not know my self." Torn from their original context, Marlowe's syntax (and geography) seem absurd and foreign. Jonson distinguishes (and embeds) Marlowe's "poetical" language from his own, "familiar" conversational prose, that is, "language, such as men do use." Leatherhead explains that he has "entreated Master Little-wit, to take a little pains to reduce it to a more familiar strain for our people," and Littlewit modestly acknowledges that he has

> only made it a little easy, and modern for the times, Sir, that's all;
> As for the Hellespont I imagine our Thames here; and then Leander,
> I make a dyer's son, about Puddle Wharf: and Hero a wench o'the
> Bankside, who going over one morning, to old Fish Street; Leander
> spies her land at Trig-stairs, and falls in love with her. Now I
> introduce Cupid, having metamorphosed himself into a drawer, and
> he strikes Hero in love with a pint of sherry, and other pretty
> passages there are, o'the friendship, that will delight you, Sir, and
> please you of judgment.
>
> (H&S 6:120–21)

While we can smile at the poetaster's disastrous revision of Marlowe's narrative, Littlewit's procedures are not all that different from Jonson's own; he merely exaggerates them and handles this imitation as a poetaster, not a poet. Like Jonson, though, he topples incipient tragedy into farce by transforming the strange into the (over)familiar. Moreover, like Jonson, Littlewit recognizes the mimetic limitations of Marlowe's dated poem, its failure to speak to the experience of contemporary Londoners.

A number of things are therefore going on at once in this passage, and it is crucial to distinguish Jonson's recollection of Marlowe from his critical concerns about language and mimesis, and both of these from Jonson's habitual attacks on bad poets and dramatists (like Littlewit and Lanternhead) and misunderstanding audiences. In this sense, Edmund Wilson's assertion that an "anal" Jonson's "filthy travesty of Marlowe's *Hero and Leander* in terms of bankside muck has an ugliness which makes one suspect that Jonson took an ugly delight in defiling a beautiful poem which he could not hope to rival"[45] is misdirected and fails to do justice to Jonson's obvious admiration for a poem he was reputed to have found fitter for admiration than imitation. On the other hand, Jonas Barish's suggestion that "*Hero and Leander* [is] only very roughly after Marlowe" and that "from the looseness of the imitation of Marlowe, it can be assumed that Jonson is burlesquing the theme rather than any particular version of it"[46] does not adequately recognize the extent to which Jonson's parody takes its place within an extended engagement with Marlowe's work; this struggle was rarely on a thematic level.

Where Jonson had quoted from "Hero and Leander" verbatim in *Every Man in,* in the puppet show at Bartholomew Fair he chooses to conflate Marlowe's verse with the antiquated poulter's measure of Richard Edwards's *Damon and Pithias* (1565), making Marlowe's verse seem even more anachronistic. When this strategy is joined to ones in which Hero and Leander (played by puppets!) are found in comfortable London surroundings, and their endearing naivete replaced by salaciousness, the effect of Marlowe's romantic narrative is completely undermined:

> Gentles, that no longer your expectations may wander,
> Behold our chief actor, amorous Leander,
> With a great deal of cloth, lapped about him like a scarf,
> For he yet serves his father, a dyer at Puddle Wharf,
> Which place we'll make bold with, to call it our Abidos,
> As the Bankside is out Sestos, and let it not be denied us.
> Now, as he is beating, to make the dye take the fuller,
> Who chances to come by, but fair Hero, in a sculler;
> And seeing Leander's naked leg, and goodly calf,
> Cast at him, from the boat, a sheep's eye, and a half.
>
> (H&S 6:125)

The recollection of Marlowe resembles Shakespeare's metadramatic allusion to Marlowe in the Player's speech in *Hamlet,* which was Shakespeare's last great (and parodic) testament to a formative influence who had, at long last, been absorbed and who no longer provided the same kind of threat or set off creative sparks. As in the Player's speech, Marlowe's verse (juxtaposed by both Shakespeare and Jonson with conversational prose) stands as the embodiment of an anachronistic, mimetically unsatisfying voice, poetry that no longer spoke to what Jonson called a "modern" sensibility. The Marlovian vein, for Jonson, was almost tapped out.

This did not preclude one last attempted evocation, in *The Devil Is an Ass,* Jonson's last Jacobean comedy, and one in which he turns even further back to his Elizabethan roots in finding his way towards renewed creativity. By 1616 the Elizabethan tradition in which Jonson placed Marlowe had become virtually synonymous with "anachronistic." Where Jonson had underscored the datedness of Marlowe's verse in *Bartholomew Fair* by yoking it to what Marlowe would no doubt have referred to as "jigging veins of rhyming mother-wits," in *The Devil Is an Ass* Jonson takes the extraordinary step of specifying both when his play is written and how much time has elapsed since the dramatic world his play both evokes and replaces. When the minor devil Pug asks that Iniquity the Vice be allowed to accompany him to London he is quickly reprimanded by the Devil himself:

> To choose
> This, for a Vice to'advance the cause of Hell,
> Now? As Vice stands this present year? Remember,
> What number it is. Six hundred and sixteen.
> Had it been five hundred, though some sixty
> Above; that's fifty years agone, and six,
> (When every great man had his Vice stand by him,
> In his long coat, shaking his wooden dagger)
> I could consent, that, then this your grave choice
> Might have done that, with his lord chief, the which
> Most of his chamber can do now.
>
> (H&S 6:166–67)

The days of the Morality tradition are long gone, so out of fashion that *Faustus* can provide, not creative stimulus (as it had in *The Alchemist*), but simply the basis of a weak joke upon which to base the plot. The play takes belatedness as its subject, as Jonson, searching for new terrain and for inspiration, returns more or less explicitly and ironically to a popular dramatic mode that had been implicit in many of his plays of the previous twenty years. But instead of Faustus we get Fitz-dottrell, who does not know a Devil when he sees one. And rather than provide a direct engagement with Marlowe's reconceptualization of the morality (or devil) play in *Faustus,* we are offered instead a fairly tame replaying of the kinds of gulling typical of Jonson's earlier Jacobean plays. Times had changed so much that by 1616 Marlowe's transgressive world no longer exerted quite enough pressure in an England in which contemporary excesses seemed worse than imaginary ones in hell and where practices like the exorcist

John "Darrell's tricks" (H&S 6:265) proved more deadly than those of Mephistopheles. For Jonson, long after he had been for Shakespeare, Marlowe was exhausted.

If we pause and look retrospectively over the course of Jonson's long career as public dramatist, his imitative encounter with Marlowe can be seen to offer a double completion, a double act of caricature: the first kind in the caricatured types in the *Every Man* plays (characters who become associated not only with various humours but also with various literary styles); the second kind in their successors, the full-blown caricatures in *Volpone* and *The Alchemist*. Volpone and Sir Epicure Mammon are not marginalized poetasters, constantly scrutinized and criticized by onstage critics, but grand overreaching caricatures, infused with an animating spirit, holding forth unabashedly and bombastically.

When Jonson stopped putting Marlovian characters in their place, when he was no longer preoccupied with overcoming his Elizabethan precursors, he let his characters acquire sufficient enormity—of vitality and vice—and thereby allowed for what Eliot, I think rightly, finds a beautiful, serious, and somber poetic vision. It is a richly imaginative and exuberant world, one that insists that we not approach Jonson as archeologists, mining his works for lodes of classical authority, but consider him through what Eliot calls a "knowledge of Jonson," which I understand to mean a knowledge of how he came to be what he is remembered for, and the relationship of his talent to a native tradition, a tradition he reshaped by translating the Marlovian overreacher to a new, comic, and unflinchingly severe universe. This Jonsonian strategy led Eliot to conclude (in terms critics have usually reserved for Marlowe) that we find in Jonson "a brutality, a lack of sentiment, a polished surface, a handling of large bold designs in brilliant colours." [47] Jonson, having fully digested his poetic forebear, plays out the dramatic possibilities cut short by Ingram Friser's fatal blow at the Inn at Deptford.

When Jonson was to turn again, nostalgically, to Elizabethan models in his late years—in plays like *The New Inn, A Tale of a Tub, The Sad Shepherd,* and *The Magnetic Lady*—he would turn to the Shakespearean world of pastoral and romance he had rejected in favor of the Marlovian. [48] Barton, in her excellent account of Jonson's nostalgia for Elizabethan dramatic forms he had once repudiated, makes too little of the distinction (emphasized by Eliot) between the Marlovian and Shakespearean impulses in Elizabethan drama. Jonson had mostly followed the Marlovian one and had exhausted it; in turning back he would explore a path not taken. In his late years, even as *Doctor Faustus* and *The Jew of Malta* were staged at court and at the public theaters, Jonson shows little interest in responding anew to their challenge. He had already transformed the tradition that he had inherited, bequeathing to his followers a dramatic tradition that, along with its major rival, Shakespeare's, left little room for what had been the infinite riches of Marlowe's style—a style that, as a result, appeared too raw, undigested, and crude for the sensibilities of subsequent generations of theatergoers, though, in fact, it had simply been a patrimony too carefully and too thoroughly consumed by Marlowe's two great heirs.

III

SHAKESPEARE AND MARLOWE

NECDOTES ABOUT Shakespeare and Jonson have fostered an image of the two as mighty opposites; those concerning Shakespeare and Marlowe often collapse distinctions, some going so far as to suggest that we are dealing, not with two minds, but a single genius. This myth is familiar enough to have motivated Woody Allen's spoof, "But Soft, Too Soft":

> [A] book I have just read . . . attempts to prove conclusively that the real author of Shakespeare's works was Christopher Marlowe. The book makes a very convincing case and when I got through reading it I was not sure if Shakespeare was Marlowe or Marlowe was Shakespeare or what. I know this, I would not have cashed checks for either of them—and I like their work. [1]

The book that inspired Woody Allen's story may well have been Calvin Hoffman's popular paperback, *The Murder of the Man Who Was "Shakespeare."* Hoffman so fervently believed that Marlowe actually was Shakespeare that upon his recent death he endowed a handsome annual prize to be awarded to the scholar who most convincingly demonstrates that Marlowe wrote Shakespeare's plays. The most far-fetched claim was advanced by Archie Webster, who argues that Marlowe not only wrote all of Shakespeare's plays but also survived long enough to revise the 1623 Folio. [2] The notion that Marlowe was Shakespeare is an oddly persistent one, and I am sure I am not the only Shakespearean who has to refute this claim every year or so when it is raised by a curious undergraduate.[3]

Two things, I think, explain its enduring appeal (besides the conviction, characteristic of a good many challenges to Shakespeare's authorship, that "nobody with only a grammar school education could have written such masterpieces"). The first is that of all Shakespeare's contemporaries, Marlowe is generally accepted as having most influenced his development. The second is that while no solid evidence survives that demonstrates that Shakespeare and Marlowe ever met, there is plenty of circumstantial evidence, some of it "dark" and ambiguous, connecting the fortunes of the two. No less than those like Hoffman who invent conspiracy theories (e.g., that Marlowe was not murdered at Deptford but whisked away to the Continent, where he wrote Shakespeare's plays), traditional scholars have had to reconstruct a narrative of the relationship of the two authors on unusually flimsy foundations. The "facts," insofar as they exist, are as follows.

Born and baptized in the same year, 1564, by the age of twenty-four or so both Shakespeare and Marlowe were living in London and working in the commercial theater. Their names are apparently linked as early as 1592, when fellow playwright Robert Greene warns "those gentlemen his quondam acquaintances, that spend their wits in making plays," of "an upstart crow, beautified with our feathers, that with his *Tiger's heart wrapt in a player's hide,* supposes he is as well able to bombast out a blank verse as the best of you: and being an absolute *Iohannes fac totum,* is in his own conceit the only Shake-scene in a country."[4] While neither Marlowe nor Shakespeare is specifically named, most scholars concur that the "famous gracer of tragedians" Greene addresses is Marlowe, while "Shake-scene" almost surely refers to Shakespeare. There is far less critical consensus, however, about what the passage means.[5]

Offense, apparently, was taken by both Marlowe and Shakespeare, but to what is unclear. Henry Chettle alludes to this reaction in his Epistle to *Kind-Harts Dreame* (1592), where he writes that Greene's letter to "diverse play-makers" (which, to complicate matters, some scholars now attribute to Chettle himself),

> is offensively by one or two of them taken. . . . With neither of
> them that take offence was I acquainted, and with one of them I care
> not if I never be. The other, whom at that time I did not so much
> spare, as since I wished I had, for that as I have moderated the heat

of living writers, and might have used my own discretion (especially
in such a case) the author being dead, that I did not, I am as sorry
as if the original fault had been my fault, because my self have seen
his demeanor no less civil than he excellent in the quality he pro-
fesses. Besides, diverse of worship have reported his uprightness of
dealing, which argues his honesty, and his facetious grace in writing,
that approves his art.[6]

Greene's and Chettle's veiled remarks offer strikingly alternative views.
Marlowe is described by Greene as a leading and influential dramatist;
Chettle would prefer not to associate with his kind. Greene's Shakespeare
is a rapacious imitator, whereas Chettle's is "upright" and "honest."

Both Shakespeare's and Marlowe's plays were in repertory at the
Rose Theater around 1592, and a year or so later Pembroke's Men were
performing history plays written by each of them. Frustratingly, we have
no further record of their interaction during Marlowe's lifetime. Their
names are not linked again until five years after Marlowe's death, when
Francis Meres listed both Shakespeare and Marlowe among notable English writers of tragedy.[7] Twenty-five years later, in a poem prefacing the
1623 Folio of Shakespeare's *Works,* Ben Jonson would note how far
Shakespeare surpassed "Marlowe's mighty line" (H&S 8:391). The only
other contemporary evidence is to be found in their plays and poems
themselves.

These, then, are the facts. And they are tantalizing, for they provide
only the briefest of glimpses into a complex personal and literary encounter. It is easy to imagine that in the intimate worlds of play production
and literary patronage in London during the early 1590s their paths
crossed at many points. For all we know they might have known each
other as neighbors (Marlowe lived in Norton Folgate, Shakespeare nearby
in Shoreditch) or collaborated on some lost (or even extant) plays. Nonetheless, outside of the evidence found in their work, nothing is known,
even secondhand, of what they thought of each other or of how they got
along.

Literary historians have therefore had to flesh out the story of their
relationship from evidence offered in what the two have written. This
path, too, has been beset with dangers, in part because the chronology of
Marlowe's and, to a lesser extent, of Shakespeare's early plays and poems
has been subject to revision and debate. Up until the mid-twentieth
century two views of their relationship predominated. One, held by

disintegrators like J. M. Robertson, maintained that the young Shakespeare was a reviser of Marlowe's work. Once these claims were shown to
be based on erroneous textual assumptions about the bad quartos of 2 and
3 *Henry VI,* critics (like F. P. Wilson) could dismiss the idea that
"Shakespeare commenced dramatist as a botcher of other men's plays." [8]
Alongside the disintegrationist school (elements of which are to be found
as late as 1940s in John Bakeless's work on Marlowe),[9] there was an
evolutionary view of the development of the Elizabethan stage that shaped
perceptions of Marlowe's relationship to Shakespeare. It had its antecedents in the antiquarian interests of early nineteenth-century editors of
Shakespeare who also collected and edited Marlowe's work. Within these
evolutionary terms Shakespeare's plays were seen to have emerged from
less highly developed species in Kyd, Lyly, and Marlowe. To shift metaphors (and to oversimplify matters), the development of the drama was
imagined as a kind of relay race, with Kyd (who provided Senecan
rhetoric) passing the baton to Lyly (who contributed courtly comedy),
who passed it on in turn to Marlowe ("father of English tragedy"), while
Shakespeare ran the victorious anchor leg of the race. As reductive and
inadequate as this conception of literary history sounds, it probably has
had much to do with the recanonization or and renewed interest in
Marlowe in this century.

Perhaps the most significant (and influential) break with earlier
critical traditions occurred in Nicholas Brooke's essay on "Marlowe as
Provocative Agent in Shakespeare's Early Plays." [10] Brooke moves beyond
the Tillyardian assumptions governing F. P. Wilson's account (in which
Marlovian heterodoxy is juxtaposed with Shakespearean orthodoxy) and
argues that Marlovian subversiveness penetrated Shakespeare's early plays.
Ultimately, though, the "Marlovian figure subserves a purpose in the
moral-historical pattern, and his most potentially disturbing aspects are
not allowed to develop." [11] This is a Shakespeare in control, one who early
on steers dangerously close to the Marlovian heterodoxy with characters
like Aaron the Moor in *Titus Andronicus,* but who, by the time of *Richard
II,* can parody this subversive ethos, simultaneously offering a "radical
criticism of the Marlovian ethos" and at the same time putting Marlowe
"in his place." [12] For Shakespeare, then, Marlowe was "the creator of
something initially alien which he could only assimilate with difficulty,
through a process of imitative recreation merging into critical parody." [13]
Brooke tells of temptation resisted: this close brush with Marlowe's
heterodoxy not only confirmed Shakespeare's moral vision (and provided a

readily identifiable style and ethos for audiences to condemn), but also taught him never to treat order "with simple confidence" again.

Far more so than his critical predecessors, Brooke put special emphasis on those moments of intertextual recollection and struggle. This perspective was subsequently (though all too briefly) refined and developed by Marjorie Garber, who invites us to imagine Marlowe and Shakespeare "busy playing what looks to be a game of cards":

> But when we get a a little closer we can see that instead of cards, they're using plays—each has a handful of quartos, octavos, and on Shakespeare's part, some sheets of Folio. Marlowe plays first, and he puts down *The Jew of Malta. The Merchant of Venice*, Shakespeare replies, laying down a quarto from his own hand. *Dido Queen of Carthage*, says Marlowe. *Antony and Cleopatra*, Shakespeare answers. Now Marlowe, considering, puts down *Edward II*, and Shakespeare counters immediately with *Richard II. Doctor Faustus*, offers Marlowe, in some desparation, but with a half-smile of triumph. A pause—and then Shakespeare says softly, *Macbeth*. Marlowe takes a deep breath, and looks through his depleted hand. Finally he speaks. *Tamburlaine the Great Parts I and II*. And Shakespeare, with an apologetic smile, lays down his cards. *Henry IV Part I*, he says, deliberately, *Henry IV Part II*, and *Henry V!*[14]

For Garber, like Brooke before her, in the end, the triumph is Shakespeare's: with *1 Henry IV* "Hal's victory over Hotspur [becomes] a metaphor for Shakespeare's dramatic victory over Marlowe, a subversion of Marlovian sublime into a tempered mold of revision and balanced complexity."[15] Just as Hal completes the dying Hotspur's words, so too does Shakespeare Marlowe's. The victory enables Shakespeare to juxtapose "two schools of drama and two patterns of heroism," while simultaneously exposing the failure of vision (and inevitable exclusion or downfall) of his own characters. Like Brooke, Garber emphasizes Shakespeare's parodic response and his characteristic identification of Marlovian ethos and style, though her concerns move from Brooke's somewhat reductive dichotomy of order/disorder to an exploration of the playwrights' representations of "heroism, kingship, and drama itself."[16]

Several other scholars have redirected the narrative of this literary rivalry in crucial ways. Harold Brooks has argued that Shakespeare's early plays influenced Marlowe more than most scholars have acknowledged.

Brooks puts considerable emphasis on Marlowe's borrowings in *Edward II* from *Richard III* (which he dates as early as 1591), most notably on Marlowe's modelling elements of the "bashful-puritan" Mortimer upon Shakespeare's hypocritical Gloucester.[17] And M. C. Bradbrook, whose work on the relationship of the two authors has extended over many decades, has argued for a response on Shakespeare's part that is deeply personal: "Shakespeare reacted to Marlowe in a selective way, and as a person; that is to say, there is an emotional train of association in his borrowings."[18] For Bradbrook, Shakespeare's relation to Marlowe differs from his response to other contemporaries in that he learned from Marlowe in reaction rather than in the assimilative mode that characterized his reponse to Lyly, Kyd, and others. As in an earlier essay,"[19] she views the relationship in terms of a personal rivalry (for Bradbrook, Marlowe figuratively and perhaps literally, though she hedges on this, is *the* rival poet), a rivalry that lost its edge after Marlowe's death.

In a parenthetical aside, Bradbrook suggests a possible resemblance to Marlowe in "Mercutio's bawdy wit" and sudden death "in a futile brawl."[20] Joseph Porter, in the most ambitious biographical argument to date about Shakespeare's response to Marlowe, goes well beyond Bradbrook's hint, arguing that through Mercutio, "Shakespeare carries out a major and hitherto largely unremarked phase of his negotiations with the memory of Marlowe,"[21] converting "Marlovian homosexuality into phallocentric male friendship charged with erotic overtones and undertones."[22] For Porter, Shakespeare's reaction to Marlowe is "at once a containment of subversiveness and a creation of subtle new subersiveness,"[23] as Shakespeare confronts the "challenge presented by Marlowe's sexuality" by inviting "Marlowe into the realm of the canonical heterosexual, not only to give him some free rein but also to kill him off."[24]

Porter's provocative reading signals both the dangers and the possibilities of locating a discussion of influence upon assumptions about the authors' attitudes towards sexuality, attitudes difficult to substantiate. Porter himself acknowledges that at times he is on pretty shaky ground, and I am not ultimately persuaded by his more sweeping claims about Shakespeare's acts of "incorporation," and "transmission of Marlovian corporeality."[25] The real value of Porter's study depends upon his insights into the unusually mediated ways in which Shakespeare confronted Marlowe and his legacy several years after Marlowe's death. Something is going on in *Romeo and Juliet,* something suppressed and uneasy, something difficult to identify with any confidence. What is striking is that, for all the richness and complexity of Shakespeare's confrontation with the pressure of Marlovian subversion in *Romeo and Juliet,* he never deals with Marlowe's words. Perhaps this stage was a necessary prelude to the period of parodic recollection that was to follow. In this sense, Porter's work— grounded in psycho-biography, and focusing on Shakespeare's handling of character—is complementary to my own and may help explain what my emphasis on verbal recollection cannot: where was the relationship being played out in the mid-1590s, before the period marked by extensive parodic engagement and nostalgic tribute?

My own version of Marlowe and Shakespeare's relationship departs from Porter's and from other accounts in several fundamental ways. First, I am interested in the trajectory of Shakespeare's response over time, particularly from his early writings in the late 1580s up until his engagement with Marlowe appears to come to an end, around the turn of the century. Second, I am interested in why Shakespeare returned to Marlowe —that is, what combination of personal, cultural, and historical forces shaped his responses to his dead rival. I pursue a historicized approach to influence, though one rooted in the intertextual recollections that signal key moments in their literary encounter.

In following this approach I part company with those, like Harold Bloom, whose claim that Shakespeare remained free of the pressure of Marlowe's influence is misdirected to the extent that they have accepted Shakespeare's own reconstructed and retrospective version of his debt to Marlowe.[26] The central argument of the pages that follow is that only years after Marlowe's death (after Shakespeare had at last appropriated and contained Marlowe's art) is this debt acknowledged, and the shards of Marlowe's influence slowly emerge. Not surprisingly, it is a "gentle" and generous Shakespeare who pays tribute to his rival.

The defining feature of Shakespeare's parodic response to Marlowe, then, is its belatedness. During the early years of the 1590s when the two were in closest competition, Shakespeare (who may have been reciting Marlowe's lines at this time as an actor) generally avoids recalling Marlowe's style in his own works, parodically or otherwise. What had begun in plays like *Titus Andronicus* as the kind of assimilative imitation that characterized his response to writers like Kyd, Greene, Lodge, and Peele emerged years later in works like *The Merchant of Venice* as a riskier attempt to transcend a voice that proved difficult to control. The parodic recollections of Marlowe that began to appear in the plays that Shakespeare wrote between 1597 and 1600—including, 2 *Henry IV*, *Henry V*, *The Merry Wives of Windsor*, *As You Like It*, and *Hamlet*—signal the complexity and extent of the earlier rivalry. This brief period witnessed a concentrated exploration—and, through parodic recollections, an exorcism—of Marlowe's legacy that culminated by the century's end in generous acknowledgments of the extent of his debt to Marlowe's art that neatly erase any sign of the long and intense artistic struggle.

I would like to work backward, then, from these late nostalgic tributes, retracing the patterns of imitation, repudiation, rapprochement, experimentation, followed by successful appropriation and finally parody, that characterized Shakespeare's responses to Marlowe's art in his histories, comedies, and tragedies. I have devoted a long section to each of these genres, in part because Shakespeare's reaction to Marlowe is closely related to his reconceptualization of these genres. I also try to locate the shifts in their relationship in light of emerging theatrical and historical concerns that colored Shakespeare's reaction to Marlowe. What follows is an exploratory, rather than a comprehensive, march through their plays and poems. My main interest in this chapter is to show how, when, and why Shakespeare recalled and parodied Marlowe, what he found unassimilable in Marlowe's art and what he was able to contain, and what, after this literary engagement came to a close around 1600, the effects of this rivalry were upon their respective reputations.

<hr />

HISTORY

In *HENRY V*, written in the spring or early summer of 1599, Shakespeare returned a final time to the kind of drama he had begun writing in the late 1580s in his *Henry VI* plays: heroical history. The genre had emerged in large measure in response to the threat posed by the Spanish Armada of 1588, and its great exemplar was Marlowe's *Tamburlaine* (a play that, though written and first staged shortly before the attempted Spanish invasion, would retrospectively be viewed as an Armada play to the extent that it was, and became, a touchstone for the social and political reconfigurations England experienced in light of the Armada victory). A major reason for this identification, besides its striking political and historical concerns, was that so many of the heroical plays that followed in wake of the Spanish defeat (and which further defined the genre) closely modeled themselves upon Marlowe's heroical history. It would be left to these imitations, though, like George Peele's *The Battle of Alacazar,* to seize upon and exploit the more jingoistic aspects of the post-Armada national- ism.[27] That Marlowe was aware of the political ramifications of the Armada there can be little doubt. His *Massacre at Paris,* for instance, includes in Henry IV's account of the Guise's crimes the international destabilization created by the Armada:

> Did he not cause the king of Spain's huge fleet
> To threaten England, and to menace me?

> (5.2.112–13)

In *Tamburlaine,* however, this kind of overt historical allusion is sub- merged within a generalized exploration of contemporary politics and nationalism.

Ten years after the early flourishing of the genre, in the spring of 1599, Shakespeare must have been struck by the return of two threatening forces, one literary, the other military: Marlowe and the Armada. In the closing years of the decade, six years after his death, Marlowe had resur- faced as a powerful presence: his works remained in circulation onstage and in print, and a new generation of contemporary writers, including Jonson, Chapman, Dekker, Petowe, Donne, and Raleigh, were busily responding to the stimulus of his poems and plays.

Of late, Marlowe had been on Shakespeare's mind as well. Shake- speare, that same year, would quote from and pay tribute to the "dead shepherd" in *As You Like It* and had recalled Marlowe's other shepherd, the Scythian Tamburlaine, in his most recent history play, *2 Henry IV,* where the kind of parodic recollection of *Tamburlaine* we search for in vain in the first tetralogy appears almost ten years later in Pistol's bombastic outburst:

> Shall pack-horses
> And hollow pamper'd jades of Asia,
> Which cannot go but thirty mile a day,
> Compare with Caesars, and with Cannibals,
> And Trioant Greeks?

> (2 HENRY IV, 2.4.162–66)

Pistol's speech hearkens back deliberately and in exaggerated fashion (twenty now swollen to thirty) to Tamburlaine's resounding cry:

> Holla, ye pampered jades of Asia!
> What, can ye draw but twenty miles a day,
> And have so proud a chariot at your heels,
> And such a coachman as great Tamburlaine.

(TAMBURLAINE, PART TWO, 4.3.1–4)

Marlowe's "Holla" rings "hollow," but only from the vantage of a decade's experience. With such belated and parodic recollections (made even more damning by the contamination of Marlowe's lines with those of his weak imitator, Greene), Shakespeare, as Anne Barton has observed, once again attempted to lay the ghost of Marlowe's historical and heroical visions to rest.[28]

With *Richard II*, Shakespeare had set his second tetralogy in motion by responding to Marlowe's late English history, *Edward II*, a play that was itself influenced by Shakespeare's earlier histories, especially *2* and *3 Henry VI*. As I argue below, Shakespeare's appropriation of *Edward II* in *Richard II* proved thorough, and with Pistol's parody in *2 Henry IV* we see how, as the tetralogy progressed, Shakespeare began to fix his attention once again on his unresolved relationship with Marlowe's earliest histories, *Tamburlaine, Parts One and Two.*

Coinciding with the return of Marlowe was the renewal of the Spanish threat (neither, really, had quite disappeared in the course of the 1590s).[29] When Thomas Phillipes wrote from the Continent in July of 1599 warning of the danger of a new Spanish Armada, he spoke in terms borrowed from Shakespeare's recent *1 Henry IV*, describing the Spanish commanders Count Fuentes and the Adelantado as "the Hotspurs of Spain," rash seekers after honor who "may carry the young King [Phillip III] into some action contrary to all probability." Phillipes goes on to suggest a causal relation between the Spanish threat and the recent departure of the Earl of Essex for Ireland ("whereunto the absence of the most and best of our soldiers, as [the Spanish] conceive . . . might give encouragement").[30] Essex's departure and his anticipated return are also alluded to in *Henry V*, where in an unusual break from his practice of keeping topical political allusions out of his drama, Shakespeare invites us to imagine the victorious return from Ireland of "the general of our

gracious Empress . . . [with] "rebellion broached on his sword" (5.Prol.32).
As in Phillipes's account, Shakespeare here blurs the division between
history and drama. *Henry V*, like *Tamburlaine* before it, was very much
rooted in topical interest in war and nationalism.

In considering the creative processes that led to the making of *Henry*
V I would like to locate the culmination of Shakespeare's response to
Marlowe's histories—in particular to the two parts of *Tamburlaine*—
within the context of the political climate in London during the threat of
a new Spanish Armada in 1599. I am interested in how this led Shakespeare to return to Marlowe's dramatic universe of 1588 and re-present it,
offering his own conqueror drama in 1599. My central claim here is that
not until *Henry V* does Shakespeare conclusively resolve his engagement
with early Marlovian history. He does so by writing a *Tamburlaine* play
that indicated what had changed politically and poetically between the
Armada threats of 1588 and 1599.

Before returning to this belated and conclusive imitation in *Henry*
V, I first explore, in a necessarily rapid overview, what has been called the
ricochet of the earlier histories that led up to this, focusing on Shakespeare's response in the *Henry VI* plays to *Tamburlaine;* Marlowe's response
to Shakespearean history in *Edward II;* and, more briefly, since this is
familiar terrain, Shakespeare's alternative reactions to Marlowe in *Richard*
III and *Richard II*. Much fine scholarship has been produced—and will no
doubt continue to be written—comparing Shakespeare's and Marlowe's
histories. The discussion that follows does not, however, attempt such a
comparison. It is limited to their mutual influence, is constrained even
further by dwelling only on those moments of intertextual recollection
that occur in these plays, and is motivated by the conviction that the
history of their histories is inseparable from the complex history of their
rivalry.

At the very moment that Shakespeare concludes his cycle of national
history plays he also points back to its beginnings, as the final Chorus of
Henry V invites us to recall the subject of the *Henry VI* plays:

> Henry the Sixth, in infant bands crowned King
> Of France and England, did this king succeed;
> Whose state so many had the managing,
> That they lost France and made our England bleed,
> Which oft our stage hath shown.

(epilogue, 9–13)

We might expect to find in Shakespeare's earliest histories a young dramatist at the outset of his career following the path that more experienced playwrights had taken in imitating Marlowe's popular model. The opposite occurs. Where Lodge, Greene, and a host of lesser worthies scrambled to write plays replete with high astounding terms, human footstools, and chariots drawn across the stage by captive kings, Shakespeare's *Henry VI* plays resist offering this version of heroical history. In this sense, the earlier plays are appropriately invoked at the end of *Henry V* insofar as their repudiation of heroical history corresponds to the ironic representation of the conqueror in *Henry V*. It is almost as if the Epilogue to *Henry V* seeks to validate an ironic reading by appealing to the dark political vision of the earliest histories (a strategy that would not make much sense in a nationalistic or patriotic reading of *Henry V*, which may explain why productions that favor this interpretation frequently cut these final lines).

From the outset, *1 Henry VI* (which, as I argue below, probably followed *2* and *3 Henry VI*),[31] challenges the historical vision and essentialized notion of honor that Marlowe ironically depicts (an irony apparently lost on many of his derivative imitators) and offers at the outset a kind of *Tamburlaine, Part Three:* what happens when the conquering hero is interred, leaving his ill-equipped successors behind.[32] Thus *1 Henry VI* begins with a "dead march," the passage of Henry's "hearse" (1.1.104) recalling the "doleful march" of that omnipresent prop of *Tamburlaine, Part Two*. Since *1 Henry VI* was performed at Henslowe's Rose, there is the additional possibility that Henry's hearse was the same one used in *Tamburlaine*, enhancing the visual correspondence between the two plays. Bedford's expression of grief—

> Hung be the heavens with black, yield day to night!
> Comets, importing change of times and states,
> Brandish your crystal tresses in the sky
> And with them scourge the bad revolting stars
> That have consented unto Henry's death
>
> (*1 HENRY VI*, 1.1.1–5)

—recalls the words of an earlier "scourge," Tamburlaine, in his own remonstrance against nature for Zenocrate's death:

Raise cavalieros higher than the clouds,
And with the cannon break the frame of heaven;
Batter the shining palace of the sun,
And shiver all the starry firmament,
For amorous Jove hath snatched my love from hence.

(*TAMBURLAINE, PART TWO*, 2.4.103–7)

Visually and verbally, then, the play begins then in high Marlovian style. Gloucester's hyperbolic elegy, which follows Bedford's, recasts Henry as a Tamburlaine-like conqueror for whom conquest was an effortless extension of his will: "He never lifted up his hand but conquered." His description recalls Menaphon's vivid depiction of Tamburlaine as "So large of limbs . . . Such breadth of shoulders as might mainly bear Old Atlas' burden," whose eyes are "piercing instruments of sight,/Whose fiery circles bear encompassed/ A heaven of heavenly bodies in their spheres" (*Tamburlaine, Part One*, 2.1.9–11, 14–16):

Virtue he had, deserving to command.
His brandished sword did blind men with his beams;
His arms spread wider than a dragon's wings;
His sparkling eyes, replete with wrathful fire,
More dazzled and drove back his enemies
Than midday sun fierce bent against their faces.

(*I HENRY VI*, 1.1.9–14)

The pattern of Marlovian recollection is continued in the next speech, where Exeter's words recall the terrifying stage image of Tamburlaine in his chariot drawn by captive kings. The Marlovian echoes continue to gain in intensity:

Upon a wooden coffin we attend,
And death's dishonorable victory
We with our stately presence glorify,
Like captives bound to a triumphant car.

(*I HENRY VI*, 1.1.19–22)

The king's death is viewed, not in any providentialist framework, but as a conspiracy of the heavens, a dishonorable victory, and their "stately presense" glorifies death's victory much as Tamburlaine's captive kings glorified his.

The elevated and ritualized ceremonial with which the play begins, typical of Marlovian heroical history, is quickly and devastatingly undermined by what follows. The lyrical, suspended verse paragraphs are punctuated by the bickering and infighting of the funeral participants. Gloucester accuses Winchester of liking none but "an effeminate prince" that he "may overawe" (1.1.35–36), while Winchester counters that Gloucester should mind his ambitious wife before criticizing others. The funeral ceremony continues to disintegrate. A messenger interrupts Bedford in midsentence as he tries to return to the abandoned hyperbolic mode, followed by another messenger and then a third, each bringing news of English losses. It is not even clear what happens to the hearse itself. The Arden editor nervously slips it offstage at line 45,[33] but there is no textual evidence for this. We are left, I think, with an uncomfortable feeling of Henry's hearse unceremoniously abandoned, first by Bedford, then Gloucester, then Exeter, leaving only Winchester to oversee Henry's rites.

In the first scene of the play Shakespeare thus effects a transition from the world and language of heroic drama to one in which its ceremonials have no place, where the complex political interactions leave little room for the celebration of the heroic. Put another way, in *1 Henry VI,* performed in repertory with Marlowe's plays at the Rose, Shakespeare takes *Tamburlaine* one step farther, playing out in this continuation a transposition of the heroic world to one of acute political realities. To do this indicates an understanding and command not only of Marlowe's stylistic features and habits but also of the political and historical vision they convey. Such a maneuver on Shakespeare's part was exceptionally daring and marks off his imitation sharply from those of Greene, Lodge, and the other weak sons of *Tamburlaine.* David Riggs has written that Shakespeare "reshaped Marlowe's heroic values to the point where they could be accommodated within a portrayal of fifteenth century English history on the Elizabethan stage."[34] I would put it somewhat differently: by relocating a Marlovian ethos—especially regarding concepts of honor, legitimacy, and kingship—Shakespeare embarks upon his own potentially radical drama, in which not only Marlovian drama but also these issues themselves are subject to often withering scrutiny. In elaborating upon the hint from Marlowe, Shakespeare's histories expose how explosively political the idea of honor could be: it could justify rebellion; raise the issue of the role of religious, royal, and educational institutions in the construction of timeless values; and extend the tension between "blood" and "deeds" as the constitutive features of honor until in political terms the tension emerges as one of "old legitimacy" versus "new efficiency," as figured in the struggle between Richard II and Bolingbroke (and refigured in Marlowe's adversarial Edward II and Young Mortimer).

The heroical and domestic histories of the late 1580s and early 1590s were no longer the same once Shakespeare unhitched the problems of honor, legitimacy, and kingship from their abstract moorings in exotic locales and distant times and set them loose in the recent English past. The representation of honor, in particular, became a particularly volatile political concern. To the extent that *Tamburlaine* celebrates the rise of a lowly shepherd to absolute rule, predicated on and authorized by his unquestioned heroical qualities, it is fantasy—though undoubtedly it spoke powerfully to a culture that was experiencing unprecedented transformations in social order and mobility. In *Tamburlaine,* honor, as defined by heroic deeds (and words to match), is invoked as an essentialized attribute: Tamburlaine, who is described by the virgins of Damascus as the "Image of honor and nobility" (I:5.1.76), has it; the feckless Mycetes, at the other extreme, does not. Honor is assumed to be intrinsic: it cannot be faked nor (like Richard III or even Henry V) can one fashion oneself to accord with this code of behavior. One cannot just seem honorable or initially act honorably (as the Governor of Babylon learns). Above all, this idea of honor is free from conditions of obedience, especially to one's sovereign.[35]

Such a vision of honor quickly becomes problematic when Shakespeare transfers it to an English landscape of the fifteenth century. Talbot, in *1 Henry VI,* comes closest to it: his valor recalls the prowess and "terror" of Tamburlaine. He describes himself to the French Countess as one who "Razeth your cities, and subverts your towns,/ And in a moment makes them desolate" (*1 Henry VI,* 2.3.64–5), and is later seen disgustedly stripping the cowardly Sir John Falstaff of his Garter, "this ornament of knighthood," for "usurp[ing] the sacred name of knight" (4.1.29, 40). But unlike Tamburlaine, he finds himself in a world of snipers and witches, where women and boys can kill. With Talbot's death, such a hero, and such an unqualified code of honor, disappear from Shakespeare's histories until the far more ambiguous examples of Hotspur and Henry the Fifth.[36]

Because Marlowe is less interested in highlighting the tension between old and new forms of honor and legitimation, his drama does not develop, as Shakespeare's does, as a series of explorations of these dynamics (and ultimately of their underlying fiction or constructedness). This perhaps is the most significant difference in the directions taken by their histories. To the extent that it is a function of influence, it seems likely that Marlowe uncovered this explosive and potential tension in *Tamburlaine* but was diverted to equally compelling social, sexual, religious, and economic dislocations, while Shakespeare focused more steadily upon its ramifications within the English political landscape in his *Henry VI* plays.

We are now in a better position to assess Shakespeare's earlier engagment with Marlowe in 2 and 3 *Henry VI*, given the evidence that Shakespeare tends to efface or obscure signs of Marlowe's influence until he had gained sufficient mastery over his rival's style. A few main points emerge. The two plays were probably written earlier than *1 Henry VI* and may have been initially designed—in the tradition of *Tamburlaine* and its imitators—as a two-part series.[37] They are also Shakespeare's most Marlovian drama, though they do not borrow either structually or verbally from Marlowe's plays, and they avoid the kind of parodic recollection of Marlowe we saw in in the opening of *1 Henry VI*. Although there is no conclusive proof that *1 Henry VI* followed the second and third parts, the sophisticated response to Marlowe in that play would seem to suggest that it emerged from Shakespeare's previous engagement in his two-play sequence to *Tamburlaine*. The Marlovian "feel" of *2 and 3 Henry VI* has led critics from Malone and Dyce to Brooke and Bakeless to insist that Shakespeare's 2 and 3 *Henry VI* were simply revisions of Marlowe's earlier work.[38] Moreover, *2 and 3 Henry VI* are Shakespeare's darkest histories, lacking the possibility of accommodation and even the fiction of politically satisfying closure. The humor, when it emerges at all, is the savage and violent kind characteristic of Marlowe's work. One reason for this dark vision is that when Shakespeare boldly relocates Marlowe's heroic idiom onto native English soil (though gradually, via France), he may not yet have fully recognized what naturalized heroic drama led to. For Herbert Howarth, the plays reveal that "heroes are butchers, nobles are ignoble" and "ideal heroism . . . a delusive name."[39] If he did see these implications, then the Shakespeare of his midtwenties viewed nationalism even more dimly than some recent critics suppose.

It is tempting to read these early histories as in some sense incomplete (as many, following Tillyard's lead, have) until the harmonious vision of a successful Richmond at the end of *Richard III* securely brings to a close the first tetralogy. To do so, however, is to efface what is experimental and to some extent provisional in these plays and to obscure a crucial stage in Shakespeare's development as dramatist and historian. Shakespeare in these two plays is subversive in a more Marlovian vein, for there is no fiction of accommodation in the atrocities of the houses of York or Lancaster. To the extent that Marlowe is what Nicholas Brooke has called a "provocative agent," this is nowhere more so than in the human and political dynamics of these earliest histories.

Perhaps the greatest indication of the success of Shakespeare's challenge to Marlovian history in 2 and 3 *Henry VI* is that Marlowe, who seems oblivious to the myriad other imitations or responses, sat up and took notice of Shakespeare in his next history, *Edward II*.[40] It is perhaps the only time in his career as dramatist that he shows how powerfully a rival had influenced him. For Anne Barton, Marlowe "seems to have felt impelled to imitate Shakespeare's new style of history play, much in the way that Raphael, painting in the Vatican Stanza della Segnatura, suddenly was led to create figures patently Michaelangelesque after he had been shown the unfinished Sistine ceiling."[41] *Edward II* begins with the strong intimation of "Shakespearean" history. The distance from *Tamburlaine* is great: we are no longer on foreign soil, no longer in an abstract social and political universe, rather, as in 2 and 3 *Henry VI*, the scene is a factious English court.

And as in the *Henry VI* plays the major tension, from the start, is decidedly political: the barons, claiming that their aristocratic rights have been abused by Edward's favoring of his minion Gaveston, seem justifiably rankled. In *Edward II* one can almost sense Marlowe playing at Shakespearean drama, and the pressure of his model perhaps explains the occurrence of verbal parallels at this early point in the play. When Mortimer complains that Gaveston

> wears a lord's revenue on his back
> And, Midas-like, he jets it in the court,
> With base outlandish cullions at his heels,
>
> (*EDWARD II*, 1.4.409–11)

his words apparently echo the Queen's attack in 2 *Henry VI* on "that proud dame, the Lord Protector's wife" who "sweeps it through the court with troops of ladies," and "bears a duke's revenue on her back" in (2 *Henry VI*, 1.3.76–77, 80).[42]

Another, slighter echo occurs two scenes earlier, when Mortimer, when urged by Isabel not "to levy arms against the king," responds "Ay, if words will serve; if not I must" (1.2.82–83), which recalls the tense moment of rebellion in 2 *Henry VI* when the sons of the captured, aspiring York offer their father their support:

> *Edw.* Ay noble father, if our words will serve.
> *Rich.* And if words will not, then our weapons shall.
>
> (5.1.139–40)

While such phrases may merely be commonplace stage idiom, the lines of the general argument remain strong: at the outset, at least, Marlowe is writing a lot like Shakespeare, not only in the historical and political point of view, but also in the verse style (there is a notable shift away from high astounding terms, set speeches, and even a greater percentage of run-on lines that break down the Marlovian verse paragraph).[43]

What is so fascinating about Marlowe's experimentation with Shakespearean history in *Edward II* is that midway through the play this vision is abandoned. Marlowe at that point redirects the play towards his proven strategy of radically juxtaposing overreaching ambition and the human propensity to abuse power with the formal and "conservative" closure critics like Wilbur Sanders and Walter Cohen identify.[44] With Mortimer's soliloquy in Act 5 we find ourselves back in the familiar Marlovian world of a Machiavellian usurper, one who is unaware that he has reached the zenith of his stratagems:

> The prince I rule, the queen do I command,
> And with a lowly congé to the ground,
> The proudest lords salute me as I pass;
> I seal, I cancel, I do what I will.
> Feared am I more than loved;—let me be feared,
> And when I frown, make all the court look pale.
>
> (*EDWARD II*, 5.4.46–51)

Mortimer's self-absorbed speech is worlds apart from the acute social criticism that typified his earlier speeches. His initial condemnation of Edward in Act 2 offers a strong contrast:

> The idle triumphs, masks, lascivious shows,
> And prodigal gifts bestowed on Gaveston,

Have drawn the treasury dry and made thee weak;
The murmering commons overstreched hath.

. . .

Thy court is naked, being bereft of those
That make a king seem glorious to the world;
I mean the peers, whom thou shouldst dearly love.
Libels are cast against thee in the street:
Ballads and rhymes made of thy overthrow.

(2.2.157–60; 172–76)

In following Shakespeare's 2 *and* 3 *Henry VI,* Marlowe chose to dramatize
the "weak king dilemma." But what finally distinguishes him from
Shakespeare is that his interest is drawn to the dramatic possibilities of
the "*weak* king" rather than the "weak *king.*"

One result is that Shakespeare's 2 and 3 *Henry VI* (at least from the
perspective of political censorship or self-censorship) appear more transgressive than *Edward II.* Marlowe's borrowing from Shakespeare in Act 2,
scene 2, where the Barons castigate the King, offers a good example:

The wild O'Neill, with swarms of Irish kerns,
Lives uncontrolled within the English pale.

(2.2.164–65)

If we look at the corresponding passage in 2 *Henry VI* (from the 1623
Folio) the similarities are unremarkable, at best:

Great lords, from Ireland am I come amain,
To signify that rebels there are up,
And put the Englishmen unto the sword.

(3.1.282–3)

However, when we turn to *The Contention* (the "bad" Quarto of 1594), we
find what may have been closer to Shakespeare's uncensored original:

The wild O'Neill my lords, is up in arms
With troops of Irish kernes that uncontrolled,
Doth plant themselves within the English pale.

(*THE CONTENTION,* 9.134–6)

Cairncross, who edited the Arden edition, persuasively argues that in instances like this the Folio version of 2 Henry VI has undergone censorship sometime between 1593 and 1623, most likely during Elizabeth's last years, when the Queen intensified efforts to subdue the rebellious Irish.[45] Strikingly, Marlowe's play, though reprinted, did not undergo similar censorship, and I suspect that this was so because its trangressive concerns were not narrowly political or historical ones, easily detectable by censors like Tilney, but were more diffuse, here and elsewhere in his canon, and included sexual, economic, and especially religious transgressions that continue to trouble orthodox readers today.[46]

There is little doubt that in the "O'Neill" passage Marlowe is borrowing from Shakespeare[47]: the allusion comes from Robert Fabyan's New Chronicles of England and France (1516) where "the great O'Neill" (created Earl of Tyrone in 1543) who "thrice invaded the Pale" is mentioned. Thus, the incident fits with the time period that Shakespeare, not Marlowe, is concerned with. In addition, while we know that Shakespeare elsewhere consulted Fabyan's Chronicles for 2 Henry VI,[48] there is no evidence that Marlowe did. My point here is that at this crucial political moment in the play, Marlowe's allusion is anything but germane, topical, or even consistent with his historical materials. Apparently, he picked up and used the snippet from Shakespeare that without the survival of the bad Quarto of 2 Henry VI would have gone unobserved, perhaps like other examples now lost to us. The same lack of historical and therefore political specificity holds true for another borrowed phrase, four lines later in Edward II, when Mortimer charges that "The haughty Dane commands the narrow seas" (2.2.166), a claim that sounds a lot like the one Queen Margaret advances in chastising her weak husband: "Stern Falconbridge commands the narrow seas" (3 Henry VI, 1.1.246). As in the earlier example, Shakespeare's claim has historical validity (he gets the point from Hall), while there is no evidence of Danish interference at all in Edward II's reign; Marlowe just lifts this, presumably for effect. But it is precisely this kind of example that distinguishes their relative interest in and commitment to political history. Whereas critics have identified connections to topical military concerns in Henry VI (especially to the events of 1590–91), the same does not hold true for Edward II.

It is fascinating to consider at what point it dawned upon Marlowe, as he wrote in a Shakespearean vein, how different the strength and source of Shakespeare's political history were from his own. Walter Cohen is surely correct in locating the power of Marlowe's play in its privatization of public concerns (though unfair in holding this against Marlowe).[49]

Apparently, intraclass and interclass conflict were, for Marlowe, less dramatically compelling—or perhaps simply less engaging—than others kinds of transgressive concerns (his next history, *The Massacre at Paris,* locates the political struggle within a bloody religious conflict during a period of sustained Catholic threats to Elizabeth). Care must therefore be exercised not to judge Marlowe by Shakespearean standards. In veering away from a drama of national and political concerns, Marlowe retains, as Philip Edwards has recognized, a sense of the sacredness of kingship, one that Shakespeare's plays deconstruct so effectively.[50] This very sacredness, however, intensifies the power of the destructive impulses: the echo of Edward's horrid scream at Kenilworth lasts long after the production ends.

While this appears to be the only time Marlowe responds to this extraordinary extent to a rival's work, Shakespeare continued to appropriate Marlovian history—both heroical and tragical—in subsequent plays. *Richard III* and *Richard II* offer an interesting contrast in this respect. In the latter we find a repoliticization of the "weak king" dilemma Marlowe had appropriated in *Edward II,* as Shakespeare redirects the deposition in a disturbing political direction (which may help explain why its deposition scene was never published during Elizabeth's reign, while the notorious Marlowe's never underwent similar censorship). The sexual and religious tensions that dominate Marlowe's *Massacre at Paris* and *Edward II* seem not to have been particularly influential upon Shakespeare's national history plays. Suffice it to say that Shakespeare takes as his point of departure the "Shakespearean" drift of Marlowe's *Edward II* to the kind of realization that Marlowe had avoided, while steering clear of Marlowe's shift to an overreaching ironically providentialist closure (replete with allusions to Fortune's wheel) at the close of *Edward II.*

In *Richard III,* however, this is precisely what characterizes for critics like Muriel Bradbrook the Marlovian dynamics of this tragical-history. The governing Tudor myth, in which Richmond must triumph over an evil Richard at Bosworth Field, made the rise and fall of a Marlovian overreacher an attractive model for representing Gloucester. In *3 Henry VI* he had been identified with the heroic aspirations of a Tamburlaine—going so far as to echo Tamburlaine's desire for "the sweet fruition of an earthly crown":

How sweet a thing it is to wear a crown
Within whose circuit is Elysium.

(*3 HENRY VI*, 1.2.30)

By *Richard III,* though, he is recast in a different Marlovian pattern, that of a Marlovian overreacher ultimately overthrown. The tension in the play is thus generated by the attractiveness of the overreaching hero set against the inevitabiity of the providential scheme that brings him low. This is the stuff of Mortimer's fall, of the Guise's, of Faustus's, too. Following Marlowe, then, Shakespeare juxtaposes heterodox behavior with moral closure. To the extent that it is an uncomfortable fit it serves to underscore the fictionality and inadequacy of the predictable (but not entirely persuasive) providential conclusion to *Richard III.*[51]

Insofar as both *Richard II* and *Richard III* rework the familiar patterns of Marlowe's tragical histories, they have been grouped by critics among Shakespeare's early "tragedies."[52] His command of this Marlovian material is thorough, to the extent that details are drawn from the most overreaching of Marlowe's heroes, Faustus, in the deposed Richard II's self-reproving lament, where Faustus's famous expostulation upon Helen of Troy—"Was this the face that launched a thousand ships" (5.1.97)— is echoed and transformed into:

> Was this face the face
> That every day under his household roof
> Did keep ten thousand men? Was this the face
> That, like the sun, did make beholders wink?
> Is this the face which faced so many follies,
> And was at last out-faced by Bolingbroke?
>
> (*RICHARD II,* 4.1.282–87)

Shakespeare, who avoided writing tragedies in the decade between the heavily imitative *Titus Andronicus* and *Julius Caesar* (with the exception of the romantic tragedy *Romeo and Juliet*) may well have been avoiding confronting the "famous gracer of tragedians," in the genre in which his rival had excelled. If so, we can locate in tragical-histories, especially *Richard III,* his successful appropriation of these elements of Marlovian tragedy (so that in the Faustian moments of *Macbeth* or *The Tempest* we find no verbal recollections, or parodies, of Marlowe's play). It would await *Henry V,* however, for the successful containment of Marlowe's early heroical history, *Tamburlaine.*

❧

Having rejected the possibility of heroical history in 1589, what would have led Shakespeare to write a play modeled on this paradigm a decade later? The answer is bound up with the issue of belatedness, what has transpired in the course of those intervening years. Shakespeare must have been struck with a sense of déjà vu when viewing English soldiers in 1599 training once again in and around London as they had in 1588 in preparation for the Spanish invaders, and when the prayers designed for the pulpits in 1588 were dusted off and read again in 1599 (Archbishop Whitgift proposed to Cecil that "the same which were used in the year 1588 are also fit for this present occasion and cannot be bettered"[53]). Much had changed in terms of theatrical and political history in the interim; so much, in fact, that the most appropriate form for history was the one that had revealed a decade earlier, in Marlowe's ironic vein, what was at stake in an imperialist world of conquest, honor, and desire.

The political and economic costs to England in the years following the Armada had been enormous. Decisive victory continued to elude the English, and Elizabeth's foreign wars would cost England four and a half million pounds between 1585 and 1603.[54] Historians have gone so far as to characterize the years between *Tamburlaine* and *Henry V* as the "crisis of the 1590s." These years were marked by dearth, bad harvests, inflation, high taxation, threats of invasion almost every year, plague, urban tensions,[55] a crisis of empire, the death of most of Elizabeth's advisors in the Privy Council, and of course the problem of succession.[56] Anxiety about war was prevalent, not just in England, but in much of Europe as well. For I. A. A. Thompson, "[n]ot the least of the crises of the 1590s was a crisis of war itself"; the "wars of the 1590s were wars which nobody really won";[57] the same could be said in retrospect for the triumphant, successive, though finally short-lived victories won by Tamburlaine and Henry V. The "glowing chivalric revival had burnt out" as the decade that began with Sir Philip Sidney would end with Don Quixote.[58]

Although modern histories of the closing years of Elizabeth's reign briefly pass over the Spanish scare of 1599,[59] Londoners that summer lacked the assurance that the Armada was only a threat. Thus, on July 24 Cecil received a letter from William Resould forwarding the disturbing report from the Continent

that the fleet at the Groyne is ready. . . . The whole force will be about 22 galleys and 35 galleons and ships out of Andalusia. . . . They report greater sea forces and 25,000 landing soldiers, and that he goes for England, hoping with this sudden exploit to take the shipping. They go forward in their old vanity of 1588.[60]

In response to this "old vanity" the English would not be caught unprepared. In London the preparations to repulse the invaders were expensive and elaborate. Stow writes in his *Annales* that by royal commandment "the chains were drawn thwart the streets and lanes of the city, and lanthorns with lights of candles hanged out at every man's door, there to burn all night, and so from night to night, upon pain of death, and great watches kept in the streets."[61] London and its suburbs were rapidly filled with troops. A London preacher "in his prayer before his sermon, prayed to be delivered from the mighty forces of the Spaniard, the Scot, and the Danes," reputed to be conspiring in England's overthrow.[62]

By early September, a few weeks before Essex returned unvictorious from Ireland, the scare was over. But what is of interest here is the experience of Londoners who witnessed that spring and summer the inspiring departure of Essex, the public burning of Marlowe's verse, the spectacle of Shakespeare's *Henry V* at the recently erected Globe, the panic attending the threat of the invasion, and especially the arrival of what Stow calls "many thousands of horsemen and footmen . . . well appointed for the wars . . . [who] were brought up to London, where they were lodged in the suburbs, towns and villages near adjoining."[63]

Because the experience of Londoners that spring and summer was double: not only responding patriotically to Elizabeth's call for marshaling troops in defence of the realm, but also, a few months earlier, celebrating Essex's triumphant departure from the city. This patriotic outpouring was balanced, however, by the populace's nervous response to the political implications of the intense military buildup in and around London later that year. There appears to have been considerable confusion over this great stir: On August 1 Chamberlain complained to Carleton that while "the alarm wherof begins to ring in our ears here at home . . . upon what ground or good intelligence I know not, but we are all here in a hurle as though the enemy were at our doors."[64] By August 23 he was better informed, though it seems that his fellow Londoners were not as easily convinced or pacified by the proferred explanations for the mobilization. This time he wrote to Carlton that the

> vulgar sort cannot be persuaded but that there was some great
> mystery in the assembling of these forces, and because they cannot
> find the reason of it, make many wild conjectures, and cast beyond
> the moon; as sometimes that the Queen was dangerously sick,
> otherwhile that it was to show to some that are absent [i.e., Essex],

that others can be followed as well as they, and that if occasion be, military services can be as well and readily ordered and directed as if they were present, with many other as vain and frivolous imaginations as these.[65]

By 1599 the marshaling of so many troops (and the recalling of 2,000 trained soldiers from the Low Countries)[66] could mean any number of things. Was it a show of force by those unsympathetic to the aspiring Essex, say, Cecil's supporters? A signal that Elizabeth was finally dying? Another invasion from Spain? From Scotland? A threatened coup? It was a political climate that clearly invited "wild conjectures" and "cast[ing] beyond the moon." And why not, since within two years just such a coup was attempted? When the "[v]ulgar sort cannot be persuaded but that there was some great mystery in the assembling of these forces" we need to consider the grounds of their insistence on the intended mystification.

Perhaps it is no wonder that critical response to *Henry V* has been divided along similar lines: on the one hand, skepticism, because of Henry's mystification of politics and spectacle; on the other, a simpler, sentimental patriotism.[67] The topical allusion to Essex in *Henry V* touches on what for Elizabethans must have been a series of interconnected political issues: the dangers from Spain (inevitably related to the affairs in Ireland); tension at the English court, where the kind of compromise and indeed factionalism that Elizabeth had actively fostered was breaking down;[68] and the complex set of obligations of London to the Queen[69] and to the expensive foreign wars in the Low Countries where English troops were dying (a concern that finds its way into the background of another 1599 play, Dekker's *Shoemaker's Holiday*[70]). There even appears to have been a brief revival of heroical history, patriotic and topical drama celebrating the recent military exploits of English noblemen against the Spanish. Rowland Whyte's description of the lost *Overthrow of Turnholt* suggests that the kind of jingoism typical of post-Armada drama had returned to the public stage: "This afternoon I saw the *Overthrow of Turnholt* played, and saw Sir Robert Sidney and Sir Francis Vere upon the stage, killing, slaying, and overthrowing the Spaniard."[71]

In such a world Marlowe's *Tamburlaine* must have offered an especially attractive model for the complex political story Shakespeare presents in *Henry V*. Instead of writing against the Marlovian grain, as he had in his earlier histories, Shakespeare in 1599 seems much more comfortable in writing through, or over, Marlovian history. Despite the appearance of ' plays like *The Overthrow of Turnholt,* or the comical histories (like *Oldcastle*) performed at the Rose,[72] it no longer meant the same thing to have, as Thomas Nashe described it in 1592, "Henry the fifth represented on the Stage, leading the French King prisoner, and forcing both him and the Dolphin to sweare fealty."[73] For Shakespeare to retell this story and to do so in the outmoded genre of heroical history in 1599 bespeaks a deeply skeptical political vision. What he writes retrospectively in *As You Like It* holds true for Marlowe's *Tamburlaine* as well: "Dead Shepherd, now I find thy saw of might" (3.5.81).

I am certainly not the first critic to note the resemblance of *Henry V* to *Tamburlaine,* though my interpretation differs sharply from the ahistoric arguments of Irving Ribner (who has described the hero of Agincourt as "Shakespeare's Christian Tamburlaine") and from Robert Egan (who depicts Henry as a humanized version of Marlowe's conqueror).[74] These and other critics have also noted the connections between the protagonists' successive conquests in the face of overwhelming odds; the choruses that orient our response to the ensuing action; the heroes' treatment of followers first as "band[s] of brothers," then as subjects; and moments of unexpected and unwarranted cruelty. Henry's reenactment of Tamburlaine's threats of rape and destruction at the siege of Damascus at his own siege of Harfleur is particularly evocative:

> Therefore, you men of Harfleur,
> Take pity of your town and of your people,
> Whiles yet my soldiers are in my command,
> Whiles yet the cool and temperate wind of grace
> O'erblows the filthy and contagious clouds
> Of heady murder, spoil, and villainy.
> If not, why, in a moment look to see
> The blind and bloody soldier with foul hand
> Defile the locks of your shrill-shrieking daughters,
> Your fathers taken by the silver beards,
> And their most reverend heads dash'd to the walls,
> Your naked infants spitted upon pikes. . . .

> (3.3.27–38)

Henry's savage threats (often cut in performance) evoke Tamburlaine's butchery of the virgins of Damascus, spitted on the "armed spears" of his horsemen (*Tamburlaine, Part One,* 5.1.117).

Even more striking is Shakespeare's appropriation of the endings of both parts of *Tamburlaine* at the conclusion of *Henry V*. We are offered, first, the marriage (to Katherine as to Zenocrate) in which New Comic conventions prevail but with a sardonic twist, for the defeated king must surrender his daughter to his conquering adversary; and then, in the closing Chorus to Shakespeare's play, find this ending undercut as the conclusion of *Tamburlaine, Part Two* is recapitulated, and we discover that the conqueror's son will fail to inherit the qualities that marked his father's success. In Tamburlaine's case this was defined by martial prowess and "working words"; in Henry's, by an understanding of the improvisational basis of politics and rule.

These intertextual connections are complicated by the fact that Pistol, who had so recently passed himself off as the voice of the Tamburlainian conqueror in *2 Henry IV,* competes with Henry as Tamburlaine's heir in *Henry V*.[75] Pistol, as Leslie Hotson has noted, believes himself to be Tamburlaine.[76] And his recollections of Tamburlaine necessarily call into question the similarities that so many critics have noted between Henry and Marlowe's hero. In considering their respective roles in the play we would do well to recall the Chorus's injunction to mind "true things by what their mock'ries be" (4. Chorus. 53). I would like to suggest that in respect to Tamburlaine, Pistol stands as what René Girard would call a "double" to Henry, and it is Henry who must insist on their difference; as far as Pistol is concerned, though he loves the King, he considers himself "as good a gentleman as the Emperor" (4.1.43). The world of *Henry V* cannot safely contain them both. Pistol is only a small-time mystifier, just about able to deceive Fluellen into thinking him heroic; and a small-time thief. We mind true things by what their mockeries be when we turn to Henry, whose powers of mystification are far greater, who can hang petty thieves like Bardolph while overreaching both Commons and Church in financing his wars. Their rivalry comes to a head in Act 4, when Henry in that liminal moment on the eve of the battle of Agincourt wanders disguised among his troops, only to run into that Tamburlainian ghost, Pistol. Not surprisingly, they have little to say to each other. For if Pistol is a Tamburlaine-figure, he is a Tamburlaine who is frozen in time, who cannot escape the cadences, affect, and consciousness of 1588. And yet there is a bit of Pistol that cannot resist parodying the king himself. When Henry gives the command that "every soldier kill his prisoners!" (4.7.37) (a line often cut or transposed in performance), Pistol is given the final word: *"Coup' la gorge."*[77] The offending echo, printed in the Quarto, is removed in the Folio version of the play. Henry's success is defined in part by Pistol's anachronism: while Pistol in the end has no alternative but returning to England as a thief, Henry's understanding of the improvisational basis of the conqueror's role, his impressive appropriation of heroical history, defines and accounts for his success (and, we might add, Shakespeare's).

When Shakespeare was finished with *Henry V,* he would be done with his decade-long exploration of the national history play; not coincidentally, he would also be done with his complex engagement with Marlowe's histories. The solution to the problems raised by both history and Marlowe, in the end, proved simple, because while Marlowe and the Armada could return, the political, historical, and theatrical conditions underlying the heroical history of 1588 were gone forever.

〜

COMEDY

Dead Shepherd now I find thy saw of might,
Whoever loved that loved not at first sight.

(AS YOU LIKE IT, 3.5.81)

AROUND THE SAME TIME that he wrote *Henry V* Shakespeare quoted from Marlowe verbatim in *As You Like It,* explicitly acknowledging and identifying a literary rival for the first and only time in a play or poem. Editors often speak of these lines as an "affectionate remembrance" or an "affectionate farewell" to a poet who had died some years before.[78] For all the resounding assurance of the rhymed couplet, however, neither true love nor Shakespeare's tribute to Marlowe is as straightforward as it would seem to be at first sight. Marlowe may have been dead but the rivalry was not yet over: the poetry of the "dead Shepherd" who is remembered here was being published at an unprecedented pace. "Hero and Leander" was finally available in London's bookstalls, quickly followed by a second edition containing Chapman's "continuation." Petowe's version was also published in 1598. Marlowe's *Lucan* was published a year later (perhaps in response to the recent interest in Marlowe and his works), and the "Passionate Shepherd" shortly thereafter. No doubt adding to his notoriety at this time was the public burning of Marlowe's other extant lyrics, the erotic Ovidian *Elegies*. And fueling reports of Marlowe's disreputable life were the recently published accounts of Thomas Beard and Francis Meres, testifying to the poetic justice of Marlowe's violent end.[79] Arguably, then, as Shakespeare sat down to write *As You Like It*, Marlowe's reputation and his influence as a lyric poet had never been greater.

Shakespeare's recollections of Marlowe in *As You Like It* and in two other comedies written about this time—*The Merchant of Venice* and *The Merry Wives of Windsor*—are thus mediated by a set of complex historical, theatrical and even economic dynamics. Once again, only belatedly do we find intertextual evidence of a rivalry that extended back a decade and, until the closing years of the 1590s, was characterized more by opposition and reaction than by intertextual, parodic interplay. It is not merely avoidance: Shakespeare seems to be very much aware of what Marlowe is up to and chooses to chart a parallel course, virtually stalking his rival. For example, where Marlowe dramatizes the tragedy of Navarre and the Machiavellian French court in *The Massacre at Paris,* Shakespeare takes the same King of Navarre, Dumaine, and others involved in the recent and bitter religious conflict in France, and relocates them in the comic world of *Love's Labor's Lost.* Given the boxoffice success of Marlowe's play on the French court, one can only wonder how audiences must have felt seeing the same protagonists portrayed in a romantic comedy. Where Marlowe had chosen for his long lyric sequence a translation of the three books of Ovid's *Amores,* Shakespeare wrote his sonnet sequence. Where Marlowe had retold in his minor epic Mousaious' famous story of Hero and Leander and rendered it in often comic and deflating rhymed couplets, Shakespeare selected for the "first heir of [his] invention" the Ovidian story of "Venus and Adonis" and constructed it in rhetorically elaborate sestains. In each of these instances (though we do not know for sure that Shakespeare was familiar with "Hero and Leander" when he wrote "Venus and Adonis") Shakespeare appears to stake out a separate territory, an alternative path, especially in challenging Marlowe as rightful heir to Ovid. When Francis Meres recorded in 1598 that "the sweet witty soul of Ovid lives in mellifluous and honey-tongued Shakespeare, witness his *Venus and Adonis,* his *Lucrece,* his sugered *Sonnets* among his private friends" it appears that as far as contemporary literary historians were concerned, Shakespeare had prevailed as the English Ovid.[80]

Only several years after Marlowe's death would this pattern change. Instead of steering around the Marlovian in his comedies, Shakespeare began to experiment with assimilating brief recollections from Marlowe's lyric and dramatic verse. This is especially true for the comedies of the late 1590s. Arguably, part of what is problematic about what critics are increasingly indentifying as "problem" plays like *The Merchant of Venice* (and, to a considerably lesser extent), *The Merry Wives of Windsor,* and *As You Like It* was Shakespeare's difficulty in fully assimilating and thereby neutralizing what he recalls from Marlowe in these plays. I want to focus in this section on how and why Shakespeare returns to Marlowe in these three late Elizabethan comedies, what happens when in the course of displacing and parodying Marlowe he renders his own work vulnerable to the volatile dynamics of Marlowe's dramatic and social vision, and how, by the close of the century, Shakespeare was able to tap his Marlovian source freely in order to interrogate in his plays what he came to see as the increasingly problematic nature of comedy (romantic, festive, or pastoral) itself.

꙳

The Merchant of Venice marks the culmination of an emulative engagement that began in *Titus Andronicus* and *Richard III* in which Shakespeare recalls and appropriates Marlowe's *The Jew of Malta* in tragedy, then history, then comedy. But whereas in the two earlier plays (in which the impact of *The Jew* was relatively limited) Shakespeare had successfully appropriated aspects of Marlowe's play, in *The Merchant of Venice* the result proved more unstable and unsettling. In returning once again to *The Jew* in 1596–97 in a much more direct and therefore riskier encounter, Shakespeare must have recognized that there was something in Marlowe's play that continued to resist the kinds of appropriations to which his drama had already subjected the works of precursors in comedy like Greene, Peele, and Lyly and that had gone far towards rendering their dramatic styles anachronistic. In part, *The Jew*'s resistance to this containment is a measure of its generic slipperiness. While T. S. Eliot perhaps came closest when he described it as savage farce,[81] the work's playful resistance to generic constraints makes any kind of containment precarious.

I want to link the relative failure of these strategies of containment in *The Merchant* to the play's refusal to arrive at satisfying comic closure and to the critical view that *The Merchant* is a "problem play." The idealized vision of Belmont with which Shakespeare's comedy ends ultimately fails to persuade, despite reparative attempts in the fifth Act (following Shylock's humiliation in the Venetian court) to overcome or smooth over tensions by aestheticizing them, because belief in Belmont's distinction of greenworld/everyday world, integral to festive comedy, means ignoring or evading the commercial conditions in the play upon which the green world of Belmont is founded. John Russell Brown warns that "it is undesirable to look too closely for a pattern" in the metaphorical dance of that fifth Act, while C. L. Barber marks a shift in critical evaluation of the play when he acknowledges that upon "reflection" this pattern begins to unravel.[82] Belmont's (and the play's and Brown's) strategy depends upon an unshaken belief in differences: of one suitor from the next, of gold and silver from lead, of one form of venture capital from another, of Shylock from Antonio, of Belmont from Venice. From this perspective there can or should be no hesitation in answering Portia's peculiar question: "Which is the merchant here, and which the Jew?" (4.1.172).

My argument is intended to recall René Girard's claim that characters' insistence in *The Merchant* on their difference from each other (especially Antonio from Shylock) merely accentuates the audience's awareness of the resemblances between them.[83] But I want to extend the way the Girardian lines are drawn: not merely, as Girard would have it, seeing them between one character and another (leaving Shakespeare as author and Girard as critic in privileged positions above the fray), but also seeing then between Shakespeare and his other, Marlowe, and upon the need for the poetic imitator and heir to insist on difference. In short, I want to implicate a "gentle" Shakespeare in the vicious circle of Girardian mimetic desire, and see *The Merchant* as both a product of and a reflection upon that reciprocal exchange and Shakespeare as imitator and as shareholder in a rival company, implicated in a world of competitive appropriation.

Whereas in his earlier emulative encounters with *The Jew* in tragedy and history Shakespeare attempts to overreach Marlowe, his choice in *The Merchant* of romantic comedy reveals an alternative strategy of containment. If, as Northrop Frye has suggested, we view the action of tragedy as incomplete comedy, it then becomes easier to understand why Shakespeare recalls (and thereby moves towards containing) Marlowe's tragical-comical-farcical action within the larger design of his own romantic comedy.[84] The strategy brings with it certain risks: while it succeeds, say, in the comic absorption of the benign "tragic" tale of "Pyramus and Thisbe" in *A Midsummer Night's Dream*, the introduction of the Marlovian into *The Merchant* wrenches the play off its comic course and prevents the comedy's movement towards comfortable closure. The unresolved "problem" of this problem comedy (and perhaps the source of its great popularity, too) stems from Shakespeare's inability to assimilate thoroughly enough what he takes from Marlowe.

Significantly, Shakespeare's echoes of Marlowe in *The Merchant* pervade not only the world of Venice but that of Belmont as well. M. C. Bradbrook has argued compellingly that Shakespeare closely modeled the Prince of Morocco's speech over the caskets on Tamburlaine's famous speech upon the death of Zenocrate (*Tamburlaine, Part Two*, 2.4. 96–142), where Morocco says:

> From the four corners of the earth they come
> To kiss this shrine, this mortal breathing saint.
> The Hyrcanian deserts and the vasty wilds
> Of wide Arabia are as throughfares now
> For princes to come view fair Portia.
>
> (2.7.39–4)[85]

Yet even closer to its Marlovian archetype, I would argue, is Morocco's earlier speech, where he conflates prowess in the field with winning the object of his desire:

> By this scimitar
> That slew the Sophy and a Persian prince,
> That won three fields of Sultan Solyman,
> I would o'erstare the sternest eyes that look,
> Outbrave the heart most daring on the earth,
> Pluck the young sucking cubs from the she-bear,
> Yea, mock the lion when 'a roars for prey,
> To win thee, lady.
>
> (2.1.24–31)

The lines, like Morocco himself, seem oddly out of place in this romantic comedy. Shakespeare easily burlesques Marlowe's aggressive overreachers by relocating them within a comedy where their heroic visions are misplaced and estranged. At the same time, Shakespeare demonstrates his ability to re-present Marlowe's mighty line (while emphasizing the artificiality of Marlowe's style by juxtaposing Morocco's verse paragraphs with

Portia's naturalistic prose). Hazarding has taken on new meaning: the world of Belmont is one in which o'erstaring, outbraving, plucking, and mocking count for little. Although she admits to Nerissa that "it is a sin to be a mocker" (1.2.54), the only mocker is Portia, who later bids a "gentle riddance" to the dark-complexioned Morocco. As Morocco rightly observes, it is a world where "Hercules and Lichas" can "play at dice/ Which is the better man," while "the greater throw/ May turn by fortune from the weaker hand" (2.1.32–34). Herculean or Marlovian heroes have no place, and mythic labors like the search for the "golden fleece" (i.e., Portia) are now achieved by infusions of venture capital and Bassanio's mercantile hazarding.

Portia's other unsuccessful suitor, the Prince of Arragon, offers another example of the disjunctive imposition of the Marlovian figure in the play. Nicholas Brooke was the first to suggest that Arragon is "even more distinctively descended" [86] from the Guise in Marlowe's *The Massacre at Paris* than Morocco from Tamburlaine. Brooke traces Arragon's assertion that

> I will not choose what many men desire,
> Because I will not jump with common spirits,
> And rank me with the barbarous multitudes,
>
> (2.9.31–33)

to the Guise's claim in *The Massacre at Paris:*

> What glory is there in a common good,
> That hangs for every peasant to achieve?
>
> (1.2.40–41)

Indeed, the competition of the lovers in the casket scenes at Belmont is hard to disentangle from Shakespeare's poetic competition with Marlowe in which the unsuitable (and Marlovian) voices of Morocco and Arragon are exposed and dismissed: the Marlovian choices prove to be dead ends.

Through these parodies Shakespeare asserts his command over Marlowe's style, confirming his power to pluck out the heart of its mystery, to subdue it to his own artistic design. By introducing the Marlovian in order to parody it Shakespeare renders his own text vulnerable to Marlowe's, whose work now threatens to expose the limitations of Shakespeare's art: Shakespeare's comedy is revealed as problematic when nobility (as Morocco and Arragon ruefully discover) is contingent upon venture capital and when communal harmony is achieved by the exclusion of the alien (and Marlovian) Morocco, Arragon, and Shylock.

When we turn from the world of Belmont to that of Venice, we encounter once again Shakespeare's attempt to evoke, then reject and exclude what he borrows from Marlowe. This time it is Shylock who is denied a share in succession. Maurice Charney and others have noted correspondences between Shakespeare's and Marlowe's main plots: the usurious, treacherous Jew; the daughter's betrayal of her father; the absent mother; the legal and political expediency whereby the Jew and his money are separated; the sidekick servant; the Christian wooers of his daughter; and even the self-reflexive allusion in *The Merchant* to "the stock of Barrabas" (4.3.292).[87] And Shakespeare echoes Barabas' happy cry, in which daughter and ducats are linked—"O girl, O gold, O beauty, O my bliss!"—in Solanio's account of Shylock's agonized discovery of his daughter's flight:

> My daughter! O my ducats, O my daughter!
> Fled with a Christian! O my Christian ducats!
> Justice! The law! My ducats and my daughter!
>
> (2.8.15–17)

We find in Shakespeare's rendering of Shylock the most realized expression of the repeated pattern in which he tries to recall, outdo, and then reject Marlowe. Perhaps the most decisive revisionary strategy was Shakespeare's repositioning of the trial scene—in which the Jew is required to render up his goods and is threatened with conversion—from the opening Act of Marlowe's play to the climax of his own play. In so doing he takes what in Marlowe's play provided a barely plausible justification for Barabas's desire for revenge and transforms it into a harrowing and nearly tragic confrontation, reversing the movement in Marlowe's play from potential tragedy to comic farce and steering the play towards the verge of tragedy. Indeed, productions that have ended the play at that point, or have Shylock stab himself as he exits, are really only pushing the tragic potential of this scene a small step farther than Shakespeare allows.

In a play that struggles to replace a Marlovian paradigm with a Shakespearean one, the Marlovian Morocco, Arragon, and Shylock are denied successors and are prevented from reproducing themselves. The struggle is not entirely successful, in part because Shakespeare's play would project upon Marlowe's the same kind of raw, aggressive impulses that the world of Belmont needs to hide from itself, since to acknowledge this competitive exchange is to admit to complicity in it. As critics increasingly recognize, Belmont is much more like Venice than it would like to acknowledge; the distinctions between the two worlds, nervously insisted upon by Belmont, begin to collapse (in much the same way that by the end of *The Jew of Malta* Christians, Jews, and Turks are indistinguishable in their Machiavellian scheming). *The Merchant* is thus much more Marlovian than its romantic plot would lead us to believe, especially in its capacity to invite doctrinal readings while subverting the religious, judicial, social, and economic practices and ideologies upon which those doctrines are founded. Put another way, if *The Jew* ends with the dark humor of Barabas cooked alive, *The Merchant* ends with one of the stalest of Renaissance dirty jokes; neat comic closure, to the very end, is undermined.[88]

It is no accident, then, that Marlowe resurfaces a final time in the play in the decisive fifth Act, in which the play scrambles to regain the comic equilibrium that was threatened in the courtroom scene in Act 4. Hitherto, the recollections are drawn from Marlowe's overreachers: Tamburlaine, the Guise, and Barabas. This final recollection is taken instead from Marlowe's erotic *Elegies.* Nicholas Brooke was also the first critic to note the echo of Marlowe's "The Moon sleeps with Endymion every day" (*Poems,* 132), in Shakespeare's "Peace, ho! The moon sleeps with Endymion" (*Merchant,* 5.1.109).[89] The line is taken from Marlowe's version of Book One, "Elegy XIII" of Ovid's *Amores.* "Elegy XIII" is one of the most remarkable in the collection and was among the ten poems that appeared in the first and second editions of the *Elegies,* published in 1594–95, about two years before Shakespeare wrote *The Merchant.*[90]

Portia echoes the line from Marlowe's translation when coming upon the sleeping lovers Lorenzo and Jessica (the stage direction reads "Jessica lying entranced with Lorenzo"). Like the lovers' competitive exchange with which Act 5 begins, as Lorenzo and Jessica try to outdo each other with tales of what ancient (and, ironically, doomed) lovers like Troilus, Thisbe, Dido, and Medea did on such a moonlit night, the Marlovian echo brings us back to the problematic and potentially tragic dynamics of romantic love: the gist of Marlowe's Ovidian aubade is that morning inescapably brings with it the harsh light of day. One last time in the play, then, the Marlovian serves to check the play's drive towards unqualified or idealized romance.

But where the Elegy ends with the arrival of that dawn and the return of the harshness of human social and economic relations (a world, for Marlowe, of exhausted laborers, toiling women, and, closer to the world of *The Merchant,* lawyers, clients, and those "undone" by sureties [*Poems,* 132]), Shakespeare stops just short of reverting once again to tragedy. The fifth Act thus reiterates the pattern of the fourth: comedy veering towards a tragic potential (that in both cases is mediated by a Marlovian recollection) from which Shakespeare, at the last minute, retreats. *The Merchant* thus ends before the return of that depressing dawn: according to Gratiano it "being two hours to day," Nerissa must therefore choose "Whether till the next night she had rather stay,/ Or go to bed now" (302–3). Gratiano's—and the play's—crass final lines hearken back a final time to the spirit of Marlowe's Ovidian speaker:

> But were the day come, I should wish it dark
> Till I were couching with the doctor's clerk.

> (5.1.304–5)

Like Marlowe's poem, Shakespeare's play ends undermining the very aubade tradition Gratiano here invokes. This is no Passionate Shepherd's invitation to love, but the sexual innuendo of an opportunist whose attitude towards love recalls the jaded tone of Marlowe's narrator:

> The Moon sleeps with Endymion every day;
> Thou art as fair as she, then kiss and play.

> (*POEMS,* 132)

What distinguishes Shakespeare from Marlowe here is that Gratiano's remarks are conditional: "were the day come." It is a conditional that allows Shakespeare to have it both ways, remaining within the formal confines of romantic comedy but, through the imposition of a more cynical Marlovian vision of love and community, refusing to ignore the darker possibilites that dawn (or the London world beyond the "Wooden O") will bring.

It is a recognition that extends to Shakespeare's own relationship to his predecessor. If we are to speak of influence and intertextuality in relation to Shakespeare, we need to move beyond merely a literary encounter and confront the larger, economic terms that governed his response to Marlowe. *The Jew of Malta* was one of the most popular plays in the repertoire of Shakespeare's major rivals, the Admiral's Men. It had been staged by them at least thirty-six times in London during the early years of the decade, six times alone in 1595–96.[91] At this time, the Admiral's Men were engaged in serious competition with the Chamberlain's Men, who were in ascendancy and effectively challenging Henslowe's company commercially and at court. Shakespeare's exploration of socioeconomic exchange in *The Merchant* thus needs to be viewed alongside his own involvement in the capitalist hazarding of the London stage in the mid-1590s. And readings that place Shakespeare above or beyond implication in this process underestimate the extent to which the concerns of *The Merchant of Venice* intersect with those of an increasingly prosperous merchant of Stratford.

In recalling Marlowe's play in 1596–97 Shakespeare also signals the extent to which theatrical practice had changed in a remarkably short time. Hazarding had also taken on new meaning in the managing of theater companies. In order to finance the acquisition of new costumes, props, and plays demanded by an expanding and competitive popular theater, entrepeneurs like Philip Henslowe and Francis Langley were needed, and they in turn resorted to extortionate bonding of individual players and, ultimately, of entire companies.[92] Even if Shakespeare's Chamberlain's Men could avoid the kind of arrangements Langley and Henslowe imposed upon their tenant companies, they nevertheless understood that to be a "sharer" meant to invest in the company a sizable sum, a sum that enabled a Shakespeare to avoid the penury that faced dramatists like Dekker who were paid on a per-play basis. And so in the mid-to-late 1590s Shakespeare prospered, applying for a coat of arms, speculating in malt, and acquiring property in Stratford.[93] In doing so, he followed in the footsteps of his father's early business successes, a father who in 1570 was "twice accused of breaking the stringent usury laws by making loans of £80 and £100 . . . and charging £20 interest in both cases." In one of these usury cases he was fined forty shillings; other cases (including charges of illegal wooldealing) "ended inconclusively."[94] This family history was not unearthed from Exchequer records until 1983; perhaps subsequent findings will cast further light on the Shakespeares' implication in bonding, borrowing, and usury.

Critics are fond of saying that the green world of Belmont is not quite the same as that untroubled forest of happy transformations in Shakespeare's earlier festive comedies. No doubt, too, for Shakespeare in 1596–97, that world of escape across the Thames or in the Liberties, at the Theatre or the Swan, was also compromised, also colored by urban constraints and commercial exchange. It is hard to imagine Shakespeare writing of bonding, borrowing, and sharing in *The Merchant* without some awareness of the darker implications of these terms for his art and for his professional world. *The Merchant,* not surprisingly, marks the end of what have been called Shakespeare's "happy comedies." Not coincidentally, it also ushers to a close his intensive, competitive, and emulative response to Marlowe's *The Jew of Malta.*

❧

It is tempting to believe that Shakespeare, having discovered both the risks and rewards of recollecting Marlowe in *The Merchant,* consciously returned to Marlowe in a more controlled fashion, in two subsequent comedies. By 1598–99 Marlowe's voice thus appears to be less of a threat than a trope that allows Shakespeare to call into question some of the comfortable assumptions of romantic comedy. This is especially the case with pastoral, a genre that invokes an idealized vision of a simpler past (the attractiveness of this model to a dramatist recalling his predecessors is easily imagined). A good instance of Shakespeare's recollection of Marlovian lyric in his comedy occurs in *The Merry Wives of Windsor,* where a quotation from Marlowe's poetry helps cast a long shadow over the conservative orientation of the community in this bourgeois comedy.

In Act 3, scene 1 of the play, a most unexpected figure in a most unexpected situation—a terrified Welsh parson anticipating a duel with a French doctor—recites a mangled version of "The Passionate Shepherd." The Folio version (italicized, but not lineated as verse) reads:

To shallow rivers, to whose falls melodious birds sings madrigals;
there will we make our peds of roses, and a thousand fragrant posies.
To shallow—

(3.1.16–20)

After admitting "a great disposition to cry" Parson Evans continues:

Melodious birds sing madrigals—Whenas I sat in Pabylon—
And a thousand vagram posies. To shallow, etc.

(3.1.22–25)

And, once again, as his feared rival is thought to approach, he returns to the words of Marlowe's lyric: "To shallow rivers to whose falls—" (3.1.28).

Evans is scared to death and, as the Arden editor suggests, to "keep up his spirits . . . sings snatches of Marlowe's famous lyric."[95] Considerably more than this, though, is going on at this intertexual moment. Most obvious in the impropriety of Evans, an aging Pastor cast in the role of a duelist, reciting the Passionate Shepherd's lines. And the lines are here addressed, not to a beloved, but to himself, as a kind of mantra, to keep his terror at bay.

By relocating this pastoral vision within the suburban landscape of Windsor, Shakespeare—for the briefest of moments—exposes the transitory qualities of the fragile world Marlowe had created just as powerfully as Raleigh's (and the Nymph's) reply had done. The magical has become the familiar, indeed, so overfamiliar that the words have lost their meaning.

In his terrified state, Evans's imagination drifts towards another fragment lodged in his memory—Psalm 137, "By the rivers of Babylon" —perhaps shifting here, by association of ideas, from the shallow rivers of Marlowe's poem to a parson's recollection of the rivers of Babylon where the Israelite exiles sat and wept (and perhaps having the entire poetic fragment set in motion by his wishful thinking about "Shallow," a word that occurs in each refrain and also alludes to Windsor's Justice of the Peace, Shallow, who could stop the duel and in fact enters a few lines later to do just that).

Marlowe's words are at once demystified, stripped of their fragile context, contaminated by their having been grafted onto their poetical opposite: the harsh realism of a Biblical poem in which exiles lament their captivity and, longing for return to Zion, repudiate song, hanging their "harps upon the willows." Any connection between these powerfully felt emotions and a lover's earnest address to his beloved is severed; stripped of their original connotation, Marlowe's words just kill time.

Shakespeare's recollection here provides not only a critique of Marlowe's pastoral vision but also a challenge to the kind of comic world he has constructed in *The Merry Wives*. For what is missing in *The Merry Wives* is the desire that suffuses the vision of what Marlowe's shepherd proposes. The most serious candidate for romantic wooer in this play is Fenton, who freely admits to his beloved that

> thy father's wealth
> Was the first motive that I woo'd thee, Anne.

(3.4.13–14)

Of course, compared with his aging and ludicrous rivals, Fenton cannot help but fare well. But the impulse to step outside societal bounds, the power to fantasize, and above all, the power to desire, belongs to the libidinous Falstaff, who is summarily warned at the play's end (at least in the Folio text) to "leave [his] desires" (5.5.130–131).

Shakespeare briefly introduces Marlowe's lyric into his comedy in part to show what is absent from his play, yet what we would expect to find intrinsic to romantic comedy. In the world of Windsor, bourgeois desire is not *for* something but rather *against* threats to what it has secured: against infidelity, against the kind of passion that would drive passionate lovers to fight for their love, against the kinds of things that threaten community. If, at the risk of oversimplifying a complex genre, comedy demands the establishment of a new order, as well as movement towards communal harmony, *The Merry Wives* satisfies the latter at the expense of the former. Comic resolution is costly, since in the conservative world of Windsor it demands the scapegoating and rejection of vitality, energy, exuberance, spontaneity, or simply of passion (embodied here in the overreaching Falstaff). This passionate impulse, the irrationality and antisocial qualities of the kind of love embodied in Marlowe's lyric, are too subversive, too romantic, and too unstable for comedy to accept. It is therefore neutralized and domesticated, quite literally domesticated, as Falstaff is contained and cast out in the Fords' laundry basket. What is gained is safety, what is lost is desire. But when you have lost desire you have abandoned the force that drives comedy.

All this suggests that Shakespeare's conception of comedy in *The Merry Wives* may be altogether darker than most critics seem to believe (though some, like Ralph Berry, have already argued that it presents a brutal farce).[96] I would propose instead that, as Shakespeare moves from romantic to problem comedy in the late 1590s, he begins, in David Kastan's formulation, to see comedy itself as a problem;[97] to see the impermanence of the passionate impulse of the Passionate Shepherd irreconcilable with the defensive demands of comic, bourgeois communities, as young Fentons turn into old, jealous Fords; to see the comic uncomfortably situated within comedy itself. To the extent that absence signals presence, the fleeting glance at the absence of passion—made present by the lines quoted from Marlowe's lyric—points to this movement in the development of Shakespeare as comic dramatist. It underscores as well his sense of the limitations of Marlowe's vision, its failure (as Raleigh's Nymph's reply reminds us) to acknowledge the complexities of life within community, and perhaps provides some clues as to why Marlowe never turned his hand toward writing comedies.

❧

Shakespeare's brief and final engagement with Marlovian lyric in *As You Like It* seems to be the most personal of all his recollections and extends beyond the parodic to the biographical. Anne Righter [Barton] is surely on target when she observes that Shakespeare's allusions to Marlowe in this play "are so diffident, so deeply buried in their own dramatic context, that one almost wonders if they were intended to evoke the image of Marlowe for the playgoers at The Globe, or whether they represented some purely private rite of memory."[98] It is difficult, otherwise, to account not only for the invocation to the "dead shepherd," but also for Touchstone's inexplicable statement to Audrey that:

> When a man's verses cannot be understood, nor a man's good wit seconded by the forward child, understanding, it strikes a man more dead than a great reckoning in a little room.

> (3.3.10–13)

O. W. F. Lodge was the first to suggest that in this dense passage Shakespeare alludes to Marlowe's death at the Inn at Deptford over what the court deposition calls "le recknynge," and conflates that with Marlowe's famous line about "infinite riches in a little room" from *The Jew of Malta*.[99] What Shakespeare's meaning is here is harder to construe. Just possibly, Shakespeare may be commenting on the recent misprisions of Marlowe's poems by Chapman and Petowe—implying that a poet is only really killed off by having been misunderstood, like the recently published moralistic and romantic continuations of "Hero and Leander" that struck Marlowe "more dead" than the fatal blow of Ingram Friser or the recent burning of his poems in London. As with the allusion to "dead shepherd," Shakespeare seems particularly interested in the nature of Marlowe's poetic legacy as a dead poet.

It is tempting, though surely an oversimplification, to think of *As You Like It* as Shakespeare's definitive response to both "Hero and Leander" and "The Passionate Shepherd." Certainly, the conflation of the two in Phoebe's allusion to the the dead shepherd's "saw of might" suggests that the pastoral and idealized worlds of love imagined in these poems were in Shakespeare's mind as he sat down to write his own pastoral comedy. It would also be tempting, though an even greater oversimplication, to read Rosalind's witty dismissal of the love of Hero and Leander as Shakespeare's response to Marlowe's poem:

> The poor world is almost six thousand years old, and in all this time there was not any man died in his own person, videlicet, in a love-cause. Troilus had his brains dashed out with a Grecian club, yet he did what he could to die before, and he is one of the patterns of love. Leander, he would have lived many a fair year though Hero had turned nun, if it had not been for a hot midsummer night; for, good youth, he went but forth to wash him in the Hellespont, and being taken with the cramp, was drowned, and the foolish chroniclers of that age found it was Hero of Sestos. But these are all lies: men have died from time to time and worms have eaten them, but not for love.
>
> (4.1.89–102)

The skepticism of Rosalind's account resembles that other prose version of Marlowe's story, Nashe's *Lenten Stuff,* which may have influenced this speech. Like Nashe's response, it is as much tribute to Marlowe's poem as one of the "patterns of love" as it is a parody of its romantic aspirations.

But in Shakespeare's version the context of Rosalind's remarks—along with those of Pheobe's when she recalls Marlowe's lines—subtly undermines the foundations of their claims. Rosalind, after all, had been lovestruck at the first sight of Orlando, to whom she addresses these lines. And ironically, Phoebe, who speaks of being struck in love in this way, is deceived in the object of her love, Rosalind disguised as a young man. The ironies run deeper, as Phoebe, a "shepherdess," resembles Marlowe's lovers in her urbanity, sophisticated enough to be familiar with fashionable love lyrics. Shakespeare, then, makes explicit that which is suppressed or only hinted at in Marlowe's pastoral worlds: the dynamic tension between the pastoral and the harsher urban realities that are only temporarily left behind, as well as the superfluousness of language when human beings fall in love with each other (Rosalind, like Hero, were each won before Orlando or Leander wooed).

There is a playfulness in Shakespeare's recollections of Marlowe here, a playfulness in tune with the spirit of Marlowe's own handling of love.

Here, at the end of the century, it seems as if a literary age has passed. From the perspective of the late 1590s, when the genre of satire (neatly captured in his depiction of Jacques) was in vogue, Shakespeare appears to be glancing back nostalgically to what was emerging as a previous literary epoch, one that had existed just six years before, when Lodge in his *Rosalynde* (the primary source of *As You Like It*) could happily evoke a more or less idealized pastoral vision. Marlowe seems to straddle both worlds, though Shakespeare gently nudges him back into anachronism. Though his poems may well provide the hint of the kind of social and economic tensions that lurk within the pastoral world, Marlowe's works are nonetheless represented here as those of a simpler, anachronistic past. Marlowe may well have been on Shakespeare's mind in subsequent comedies and romances; but the pressure of his lyric and comic worlds was past by 1600, and his words would never break the surface of Shakespeare's comedies again. Indeed, even with *The Merry Wives* and *As You Like It*, we have seen that the pressure exerted by Marlowe had slackened considerably, as Shakespeare's digestion and appropriation of Marlowe's lyric poetry was virtually complete. By 1599, with Ben Jonson's recent successes in satirical comedies like *Every Man in* and *Every Man out of His Humour*, the voice that challenged Shakespeare's predominance in comedy belonged to a new rival.

TRAGEDY

CRITICS GENERALLY AGREE that Shakespeare's earliest tragedy, *Titus Andronicus*, is very much concerned with emulation: filial, fraternal, and, most of all, literary. Titus' desire to find "a pattern, precedent, and lively warrant" (5.3.44) for an act of revenge that (like Shakespeare's art) is both mimetic and belated underscores how obsessively the play explores (as it enacts) the problems of imitation. But the same critics have disagreed sharply in identifying the source of Shakespeare's own poetic pattern and precedent. Some, like Eugene Waith, have championed Ovid,[100] others Seneca, even Virgil. The claims for the unmediated influence of Roman poets has been greatly overstated, however, and a good deal of the blame can be placed on Shakespeare himself, who litters his play with handfuls of classical quotations. There are famous bits from Seneca (e.g., "*Magni dominatur poli, Tam lentus audis scelera, tam lentus vides?*" [4.1.80–81]);

from Horace's *Odes* (e.g., *"Integer vitae, sceleris purus, Non eget Mauri iaculis, nec arcu?"* [4.2.20–21]); allusions to Virgil's "story of that baleful burning night/ When subtle Greeks surprised King Priam's Troy" (5.3.82–83); and plot material from "Ovid's *Metamorphoses*" (4.1.42), a text that literally appears onstage in Act 3. Yet for the most part these are not particularly complex evocations, and call to mind Thomas Nashe's criticism of those derivative fellow dramatists who "could scarely Latinize their neck-verse if they should have need; yet [for whom] English Seneca read by candlelight yields many good sentences."[101] We might simply compare Marlowe's roughly contemporaneous quotation from Ovid's *Amores* in Doctor Faustus's cry — *"O lente, lente, currite noctis equi"* (line 5.2.152) — a deeply ironic recontextualization in which a lover's desire that 'the horses of the night run more slowly' is transposed onto the agony of a man who has sold his soul, frantically hoping to forestall the endless damnation that awaits him.

Not only their relatively uncontestatory nature but also the very profusion of the classical quotations in *Titus* should render them suspect. My own sense is that they are a feint, a deceptive strategy on Shakespeare's part, whereby the classical allusions are foregrounded in order to deflect our attention from the far more disturbing pressure of contemporary rivals, notably Kyd and Marlowe, neither of whom is quoted or acknowledged directly. To the extent that these explicit allusions to Ovid and Virgil are moments of substantial emulative engagement on Shakespeare's part, they serve a complex mediating function, through which Shakespeare, as rival heir to these Roman poets, indirectly confronts Marlowe's achievements in rendering Virgil (in *Dido*) and Ovid (in the *Elegies*) in his own imitations of these classical antecedents.

To those who would still insist that *Titus* is more indebted to classical than native sources, perhaps the most compelling rejoinder is provided by the recent and highly praised staging of the play, under the direction of Deborah Warner, at the New Swan Theatre at Stratford-upon-Avon in 1987, a production that revealed how this play's "classicism" is a creation of the study more than the stage.[102] The production began high Marlovian fashion, as Titus enters riding in triumph, borne by his chained captives. Brian Cox, who plays the title role, has acknowledged the Marlovian origins of this entrance and traces its roots back to his own role as Tamburlaine's lieutenant, Techelles, in the 1976 production of *Tamburlaine* at the National Theatre.[103] Titus' reference to his "chariot," which, along with his sword and prisoners, he will "consecrate" to Saturninus (1.1.252–3), further raises the possibility that in Elizabethan stagings the scene would have visually recalled Tamburlaine's triumphant entrance in his chariot (perhaps, when *Titus* was staged at Henslowe's Rose in 1594, the very same prop), drawn by captive kings.[104]

Titus includes a number of other visual recollections of Marlowe's work. Take, for example, Tamburlaine's reflexive slaughter of his disobedient son, which is imitated in Titus' killing of his son Mutius, or Tamburlaine's self-wounding, repeated in Titus'. Aaron's delight in the self-destruction of his adversaries (he "laughed so heartily That both [his] eyes were rainy like to [Titus']" [5.1.116–17]) recalls Barabas's joy in watching his foes destroy themselves as a result of his stratagems. The confluence of violence, pain, physical humiliation, and laughter in such scenes in *Titus* is something we would more readily identify with Marlowe's dramaturgy. More generally, the static, emblematic nature of many scenes in *Titus* also bears a closer resemblance to Marlowe's practice than to Shakespeare's other early plays.

It is Marlowe's language, however, that appears to have commanded Shakespeare's greatest interest. The "high astounding terms" of Aaron's first soliloquy is the most obvious example of Shakespeare's debt to the soaring vein of the Marlovian overreacher:

> Now climbeth Tamora Olympus' top,
> Safe out of fortune's shot, and sits aloft,
> Secure of thunder's crack or lightning flash,
> Advanced above pale envy's threatening reach.
>
> .   .   .
>
> Then, Aaron, arm thy heart, and fit thy thoughts,
> To mount aloft with thy imperial mistress,
> And mount her pitch, whom thou in triumph long
> Hast prisoner held, fettered in amorous chains
> And faster bound to Aaron's charming eyes
> Than is Prometheus tied to Caucasus.
>
> (2.1.1–4; 12–17)

The speech reads like a compendium of Marlovian rhetorical and metrical devices: long verse sentences, stitched together out of conjuctive clauses and end-stopped lines; reiterated images of climbing, advancing, and mounting aloft; the familiar icon of prisoners bound fast; even the repeated polysyllabic classical and geographical allusions. These are the building blocks of "Marlowe's mighty line," and Shakespeare renders this style quite capably, though he stops far short of an evaluative or parodic treatment of this style.

Shakespeare does go further than simply replicating its features, though, when in Act 5 Aaron overreaches the hyperbolic claims of the Marlovian protagonist when he outdoes Barabas's catalogue of villainies. Where Barabas brags:

> As for myself, I walk abroad a-nights,
> And kill sick people groaning under walls.
> Sometimes I go about and poison wells;
> And now and then, to cherish Christian thieves,
> I am content to lose some of my crowns,
> That I may, walking in my gallery,
> See 'em go pinioned along by my door.
>
> . . .
>
> I filled the gaols with bankrupts in a year,
> And with young orphans planted hospitals,
> And every moon made some or other mad.
>
> (2.3.179–90; 198–200)

Aaron's evil is even more destructive: "Even now I curse the day,"

> Wherein I did not some notorious ill;
> As kill a man, or else devise his death;
> Ravish a maid or plot a way to do it;
> Accuse some innocence, and forswear myself;
> Set deadly emnity betweeen two friends;
> Make poor men's cattle break their necks;
> Set fire on barns and haystacks in the night,
> And bid the owners quench them with their tears.
>
> (5.1.124–34)

And where Barabas had "now and then [made] one hang himself for grief,

> Pinning upon his breast a long great scroll
> How I with interest tormented him.
>
> (2.3.201–203)

Aaron goes one step farther, claiming that:

> Oft have I digged up dead men from their graves,
> And set them upright at their dear friends' door,
> Even when their sorrow almost was forgot,
> And on their skins, as on the bark of trees,
> Have with my knife carved in Roman letters,
> "Let not your sorrow die, though I am dead."

> (5.1.135–140)

Barabas's speech seems to invite outdoing: just as his sidekick Ithamore responds to Barabas's boasts with his own even more heinous catalogue of evildoings, so too does Shakespeare take up the implicit challenge and outdo Marlovian excess. To overreach Marlowe in this fashion may be easy, but not easy to sustain, because Marlovian rant constantly threatens to topple into absurdity and self-parody, and parodists run an even greater risk, since their exaggeration of stylistic features draws the imitation even closer to the verge of absurdity. Nonetheless, Shakespeare's imitative effort here stops short of a complex evaluative engagement with Marlowe's passage (though, as M. C. Bradbrook observes, its repositioning as a man's dying confession may give Shakespeare's version "more force").[105] The passage reads like a setpiece, not fully integrated into the world of the play, an exercise, albeit a successful one.

Bradbrook has also suggested that Shakespeare may not himself have known exactly what he was up to in *Titus Andronicus*. This claim, often taken to an extreme by the play's many detractors, underestimates just how compelling and coherent a play it is. It is also remarkably disturbing theater, not only in its handling of violence that approaches Marlowe's savage farce, but also in its forced and unsatisfying resolution, a point in the play where Shakespeare comes closest to the kind of ironic playfulness characteristic of the endings to Marlowe's *Jew of Malta* and *Tamburlaine* plays (and the open-endedness found in the conclusions to his early and roughly contemporaneous histories *2 and 3 Henry VI*).

This Marlovian cast has been obscured by editors who, in trying to make the play fit a model of what we consider normative "Shakespearean tragedy," have altered a number of key features of the play's ambiguous ending. The reassuring closing speech that first appeared in the second Quarto—"order well the state/ That like events may ne're it ruinate"

(5.3.200.3–4)—is perhaps the first example of this recuperative strategy. Twentieth century editors have built on this precedent, for example, assigning to Rome's populace (rather than to a Marcus trying to gather support for the Andronici coup d'etat) the repeated refrain "Lucius, all hail, Rome's royal Emperer!" (5.3.141), a scene that in the original Quarto version calls to mind Buckingham's political gambit in *Richard III* when he tries to sway the crowd in Gloucester's favor. Other editorial revisions that smooth over the political ambiguities of the denouement of *Titus* include the reassignment (again, to Marcus!) of a Roman Lord's skeptical reception of the Adronici's call for Lucius to rule and, in Waith's recent Oxford edition, the unwarranted switch in this speech from "Let Rome herself be bane unto herself" (5.3.73) to "Lest Rome. . . . " Despite Lucius' canonical invocation of Troy, we know that the end of Rome and the triumph of the Goths is imminent. When viewed within the context of the political drama that Shakespeare was writing around 1590 or so, the ending to *Titus* emerges as considerably bleaker than the doctored contemporary editions we now study might suggest.

Insofar as Shakespeare drew upon the dynamics of Marlovian tragedy in *Titus,* it apparently proved to be a deadend for him. Having partially opened his tragedy to the influence of Marlowe's sensibility, Shakespeare did not (and perhaps could not) quite wrestle Marlowe's universe into submission and contain it within the confines of his own inchoate tragic vision.

I suspect that this unresolved early encounter with Marlowe in tragedy may help explain why (with the exception of *Romeo and Juliet*) Shakespeare would subsequently avoid writing tragedy for almost a decade. And when Shakespeare did return briefly to tragedy in *Romeo and Juliet* it would be through a diferent path, via romantic comedy. Shakespeare's tragic practice thus resembles the pattern we found characteristic of his histories plays: an early, though relatively unacknowledged engagement that would only culminate a decade later in parodic recollections that pay tribute to Marlowe's achievement at the same time that they reveal its limitations. Studies of literary influence depend upon the evidence of borrowings and echoes; in the case of Shakespearean tragedy in the 1590s, however, the absence (and perhaps avoidance) of an emulative engagement with the kind of tragedy that Marlowe was writing signals the greatest tribute to the influence of a poet Robert Greene grudgingly called the "famous gracer of tragedians."

When Shakespeare returned to Roman and revenge tragedy in *Julius*

Caesar in 1599 he would also return briefly to Marlowe. Marlowe's voice does not figure significantly in the play (despite the claims of turn-of-the-century critics who insisted that Shakespeare was simply touching up a Marlovian original[106]). But when Marlowe's style does surface in *Julius Caesar* its recontextualization reveals the mastery Shakespeare now had over his rival's style: he could draw on it to underscore a point, delineate a character trait, or recall a heroic and absolutist world, simply by quoting a line or two. Marlowe's style, at long last, had been reduced to a trope.

This is exemplified in Shakespeare's depiction of Caesar in Act 2 scene 2, when he ignores Calpurnia's warnings and prepares to goes forth on the Ides of March to the Senate:

> *Caesar shall forth.* The things that threatened me
> Ne'er looked but on my back. When they shall see
> The face of Caesar, they are vanished.
>
> [2.2.10–12 (italics mine)]

Some twenty lines later he reiterates:

> *Yet Caesar shall go forth;* for these predictions
> Are as the world in general as to Caesar.
>
> [2.2.29–30 (italics mine)]

And again, a dozen lines later, Caesar proclaims that:

>   danger knows full well
> That Caesar is more dangerous than he.
> We are two lions littered in one day,
> And I the elder and more terrible;
> *And Caesar shall go forth.*
>
> [2.2.43–47 (italics mine)]

His repeated insistence that "Caesar shall go forth" echoes the identical words spoken at the climax of Marlowe's *The Massacre at Paris* (which Shakespeare possibly acted in during his association with Pembroke's Men). When similarly warned of his impending assassination (a murderer tells him that "the rest have ta'en their standings in the next room, therefore good my Lord go not forth" [5.2.68–70]) Marlowe's Guise haughtily responds:

> *Yet Caesar shall go forth.*
> Let mean conceits and baser men fear death:
> Tut, they are peasants. I am Duke of Guise;
> And princes with their looks engender fear.
>
> [5.2.71–74 (italics mine)]

The Guise goes forth, is immediately attacked and stabbed, and dies echoing the refrain:

> *Thus Caesar did go forth,* and thus he died.
> [5.2.94 (italics mine)][107]

Shakespeare is capitalizing here on his audience's familiarity with the climactic moment of his rival's boxoffice hit. Remembering the Guise's identification with Caesar in his death scene, Shakespeare reassigns those lines to Caesar himself when he chose to dramatize Caesar's assassination. In doing so, he renders even more complex the way in which theatrical representation and imitation are appropriated in order to rewrite political history. The issue of dramatic imitation is central in *Julius Caesar,* in part because the protagonists understand that their "original" action takes on meaning through its re-presentation onstage. Cassius exclaims how "ages hence,"

> Shall this our lofty scene be acted over
> In states unborn and accents yet unknown.
>
>   .   .   .
>
> So oft as that shall be
> So oft shall the knot of us be called
> The men that gave their country liberty.
>
> [3.1.112–13; 117–19]

But the causal link between theatrical representation and how one is remembered historically is not as simple as Cassius imagines. What does one do with a misappropriation of theatrical antecedents, such as the Guise's identification with Caesar? In a play in which the protagonists project into the future in imagining their words and actions imitated onstage, Shakespeare returns to a past moment when, before his own characters (though not their originals) were created, their very words had been spoken—and willfully appropriated in the service of rewriting history. By deliberately recollecting Marlowe and "acting over" the lines from his play in its "original" context, only to have his "originals" misconstrue how their lines will be repeated in future times and lands (like Paris, during the Massacre of St. Bartholomew), Shakespeare reveals the slipperiness with which history is reconstructed through theatrical representation.

This intertextual recollection serves yet another purpose. By identifying Caesar with Marlowe's protagonist at this decisive moment Shakespeare also draws attention to the more disturbing aspects of Caesar's character. To the extent that Caesar here resembles a Marlovian overreacher like the Guise, we admire Caesar's heroic self-assurance. Yet this very quality renders him increasingly suspect, politically. What place can a man who distinguishes himself from his fellow citizens have in a world of political (near) equals? The debate over whether the conspirators were justified in killing Caesar (which still rages in contemporary criticism of the play) recalls a similar critical dispute over how we should respond to Marlowe's personally compelling but politically unsavory heroes. Shakespeare here exploits the ringing and unmistakable self-assertiveness of Marlowe's heroes, individuals who are oblivious to the dangers that confront them and unwilling to subordinate their herculean greatness to the pettiness of the world around them.

By evoking and then relocating this bombastic self-assertion within a political world that no longer has room for these kind of heroic claims, Shakespeare shows how difficult it is to judge such individuals without acknowledging at the same time that the possibility of political heroism in a shrinking world is severely circumscribed. From this tension would subsequently emerge Shakespeare's tragedies of nostalgia, heroic tragedies like *Antony and Cleopatra* and *Coriolanus* in which characters who inherit the heroic aspirations and self-assertion typical of Marlowe's Elizabethan overreachers find themselves helplessly trapped in worlds of petty Jacobean intrigue. Neither Jonson (who found these kinds of lines in *Julius Caesar* "ridiculous") nor Dryden (who condemned Shakespeare's propensity for bombast) quite grasped why Shakespeare would invoke this Marlovian style in rendering more complex the political and ethical texture of his drama. Marlowe's style, once reduced and reproducible in this way, became a shorthand for evoking, not only a type of character, but also a fairly narrow range of moral and political conditions within which that character operated. What made this kind of appropriation possible was the anachronism of Marlowe's bombastic style and the anachronism of the absolutist political world in which it had operated. Cultural values change and theatrical and metrical styles go out of fashion; both processes, though, were accelerated by Shakespeare, who, having helped render them obsolete, returned and recalled both Marlowe's style and the Marlovian dramatic universe, one last time, in the Player's speech in *Hamlet*.

ॳ

With the Player's speech we move beyond parody, or at least to its outermost verge. It is Shakespeare's last and greatest recollection of Marlowe and it occurs in a play that, ushering in the new century, glances back a final time at the dramatic world that had passed and that it had helped efface and render obsolete—not simply the "Ur-Hamlet," which *Hamlet* writes over, but the assumptions and direction of Kyd's *Spanish Tragedy*, as well as the dramatic conditions of Marlovian tragedy. *Hamlet* is a recollective play and a nostalgic one, in which the protagonist must come to grips with a past that continues to haunt, with a progenitor who offers a model of heroism that is impossible to emulate. Shakespeare can recall his dramatic antecedents as he does here precisely because a historical break and an awareness of anachronism has occurred. The struggle with these rivals was a thing of the distant past. Marlowe, Kyd, Greene, Peele, Lodge, and Nashe were dead. The Curtain was empty, the Rose abandoned by the Admiral's Men, the Theatre knocked down to provide the timber for the newly erected Globe. As Rozencranz make clear in the scene leading up to the Player's speech, it was the present, not the past, that was the source of the playwright's current anxiety: there is "an aery of children, little eyases, that cry out on the top of the question, and are now most tyrannically clapped for 't. These now are the fashion" (2.2.339–41). The children's companies that had begun to perform in London in 1599 "carry it away. . . . Hercules and his load, too" (2.2.360–01), threatening the preeminence of the adult companies, including Shakespeare's Chamberlain's Men.

Shakespeare also composed *Hamlet* at a time of revivals, including revivals of children's plays, including, quite possibly, *Dido, Queen of Carthage*. Henslowe records in his *Diary* payments on January 3, 1598 for costuming a boy actor in the play, and his inventory of stage properties includes a tomb of Dido, Cupid's bow and quiver, and Dido's robe.[108] The evidence does not rule out the existence of another *Dido* play, though Henslowe records no payments for the writing of such a play. In addition, there was a recorded revival of the play for a private evening performance.

These facts have invited speculation that the speech that Hamlet says he "chiefly loved," "Aeneas' tale to Dido," was patterned, however indirectly, upon one from Marlowe's play:

> I heard thee speak me a speech once, but it was never acted, or, if it was, not above once, for the play, I remember, pleased not the million; 'twas caviary to the general. But it was—as I received it, and others, whose judgements in such matters cried in the top of mine—an excellent play. . . . One speech in't I chiefly loved: 'twas Aeneas' tale to Dido, and thereabout of it especially when he speaks of Priam's slaughter.
>
> {2.2.434–39; 445–48}

H. J. Oliver, who edited the Revels edition of *Dido,* writes that "[c]onceivably, then, it was when Henslowe tried to revive *Dido* that Shakespeare saw it, and that it 'please not the million,' and was 'caviary to the general.'.. and this would at least explain how a play not originally written for the 'general' public could nevertheless have come to their notice."[109] Whether or not a revival of *Dido* (that Shakespeare may or may not have seen, in a public or private production) is behind Hamlet's account, the Player's speech that follows unmistakably recalls Aeneas' speech to Dido in Marlowe's play.

The Player's speech is written in a remarkably anachronistic style; so much so, that early critics thought that Shakespeare was inserting an unused bit from his early work as a dramatist. Others sought to deny Shakespeare's hand in the speech entirely, assigning it to various playwrights, including Marlowe. Dryden's remarks are typical. He writes in his *Preface to "Troilus and Cressida"* (1679):

> What a pudder is here kept in raising the expression of trifling thoughts. Would not a man have thought that the poet had been bound prentice to a wheel-wright for his first rant? and had followed a ragman, for the clout and blanket, in the second? Fortune is painted on a wheel; and therefore the writer in a rage, will have poetical justice done upon every member of that engine.[110]

Dryden apparently refused to believe that Shakespeare wrote these lines; at the same time he uses them as a basis of his attack upon Shakespeare's propensity for bombastic excess, his tendency at times to "say nothing without a metaphor, a simile, an image, or description." [111]

Theories of attribution abound. Fleay, in his *On the Extract from an Old Play in Hamlet* (1874), asserts that the "scene was written by Shakespeare in 1594, as a supplement to Marlowe's unfinished play, in competition with Nashe, and that it was introduced by him into the first draught of *Hamlet* in 1601." [112] Not to be outdone, C. W. Wallace, writing in 1910, argued that Jonson was behind the Dido speech. [113] While these claims may seem ludicrous today, as reputable a scholar and editor as G. L. Kittridge considered the debate over quotation or original composition "insoluble." [114]

Pope may have been the first to suggest that the speech was written for parodic purposes, though even he is unsure of its authorship: "This whole speech of Hamlet is purely ironical; he seems to commend this play to expose the bombast of it. Who was its author is not come to my knowledge." [115] And Malone first suggested the affinity with Marlowe's style, though he does not make the specific connection with *Dido:*

> I formerly thought that these lines were extracted from some old play, of which it appeared to me probable that Marlowe was the author; but whatever Shakespeare's view in producing them may have been, I am now decidedly of opinion that they were written by himself, not in any former unsuccessful piece, but expressly for the play of *Hamlet.* [116]

When we turn to the corresponding passage in *Dido,* however, the number of unmistakable correspondences are quite few. The strongest (and one that has led Geoffrey Bullough to claim that Shakespeare's definitely used Marlowe as a source) occurs in the comparable descriptions of Pyrrhus' blow, not found in the Virgilian source. [117] Shakespeare writes how:

> Unequal matched,
> Pyrrhus at Priam drives, in rage strikes wide,
> But with the whiff and wind of his fell sword
> Th'unnerved father falls.

> (2.2.471–74)

In Marlowe's version, Priam

> would have grappled with Achilles' son,
> Forgetting both his want of strength and hands,
> Which he disdaining whiskt his sword about,
> And with the wind thereof the King fell down.
>
> (2.1.251–54)

Bowers and virtually all editors of Marlowe (except Oliver) have accepted Collier's emendation of "wind" for "wound" (which appears in the Quarto version of *Dido*) in the last line of Marlowe's speech. The problem here is that the speech has been read back through Shakespeare's, so that the emendation is premised on the assumption that Shakespeare's borrowing gets right what the compositors got wrong. Influence, again, can work in reverse.

I am less interested, however, in word-for-word correspondences in the passage (which I think Shakespeare pretty deliberately avoids here) than in the ways in which Shakespeare creates the "feel" of a Marlovian speech. In this respect I follow Stratchey, who suggestively argues that though

> there is not a line, hardly a thought of them, the same as the passage
> which the Player recites, and which is of course Shakespeare's own,
> still the style is so like, that the audience would probably have been
> reminded of Marlowe's play, and so have experienced the sensation
> of hearing real men quoting a real play; nay, if they retained only a
> general recollection of the original, might have supposed that the
> quotation was actually from Marlowe's tragedy. [118]

Before examining more closely how this effect is achieved and why Shakespeare does so at this point in his play it is worth quoting briefly from each of the two passages. First, Marlowe's:

> At last came Pyrrhus, fell and full of ire,
> His harness dropping blood, and on his spear
> The mangled head of Priam's youngest son,
> And after him his band of Myrmidons,
> With balls of wild-fire in their murdering paws,
> Which made the funeral flame that burnt fair Troy:

. . .

And at Jove's altar finding Priamus,
About whose withered neck hung Hecuba,
Folding his hand in hers, and jointly both
Beating their breasts and falling on the ground,
He, with his falchion's point raised up at once,
And with Megaera's eyes stared in their face,
Threatening a thousand deaths at every glance. . . .

                    (2.1.213–218; 225–31)

And Shakespeare's:

The rugged Pyrrhus, he whose sable arms,
Black as his purpose, did the night resemble
When he lay couched in the ominous horse,
Hath now this dread and black complexion smeared
With heraldry more dismal. Head to foot
Now is he total gules, horridly tricked
With blood of fathers, mothers, daughters, sons,
Baked and impasted with the parching streets
That lend a tyrannous and a damned light
To their lord's murder. Roasted in wrath and fire,
And thus o'er-sized with coagulate gore,
With eyes like carbuncles, the hellish Pyrrhus
Old grandsire Priam seeks. . . .

                    (2.2.452–64)

It is not hard to see why this is a speech Hamlet "chiefly loved." It
recalls a lost world, one in which remorseless killers like Pyrrhus could
revenge the death of a father and murder a king without a moment's
hesitation, notwithstanding that instant in which Phyrrus is distracted
from his revenge by the toppling of Troy's towers, the briefest of delays
that stands in such sharp contrast to Hamlet's immobility; in this Shakespeare recalls Marlowe's version, where the only thing that stops Phyrrus
is the gridlock of "slaughtered men" in the streets of Troy. Pyrrhus,
coated in red and black, visually calls to mind Marlowe's bloody Tamburlaine, who unhesitatingly slaughters the virgins of Damascus and unflinchingly avenges himself upon his other foes. Hamlet's problem is that
this kind of hero is no longer an adequate "pattern, precedent, and lively
warrant" (*Titus*, 5.3.44). As such, the speech is a nostalgic one, a longing

for a simpler, clearer past that is no longer recoverable. Phyrrus is an anachronism, a throwback to the revengers of the drama of a previous decade, to Marlowe's heroes and to Shakespeare's own Titus Andronicus, predecessors who were not overwhelmed, like Hamlet, by a mountain of ethical constraints (Could he trust that his father's ghost was not a devil? Could Claudius be killed at prayer? What about the canon 'gainst self-slaughter? To be or not to be?).

Hamlet calls it a "passionate" speech, a term that conveys both rhetorical and erotic connotations: powerful enough to move the Player to tears over Hecuba's grief and sufficiently compelling to provoke Dido's fatal passion for Aeneas (in this sense it recalls Marlowe's seduction poem, "The Passionate Shepherd"). For a Hamlet who has repudiated his passion for Ophelia and who is obsessed with his mother's adulterous passion for Claudius, the vision of an aged queen Hecuba (her "loins" now "lank and all o'er-teemed") loyal to her dying husband also offers a nostalgic alternative to the sexual confusions of Elsinore.

Perhaps Shakespeare, too, chiefly loved this speech and found in it his own moment for nostalgic recollection. The revenge play had changed, and Shakespeare himself had helped render simple revenge tragedy impossible. Not only the actions but also the language of the Marlovian hero were outdated, irrecoverable, anachronistic. The gradual shift in the 1590s to a more naturalistic dramatic language onstage had rendered Marlowe's style stiff and unnatural. It is no accident that Shakespeare embeds the Player's speech with the framework of Hamlet's colloquial prose, thereby drawing further attention to its artificiality and, indirectly, to its (relative) failure to render "reality" adequately. Moreover, because the speech is so bombastic we are also distracted from Hamlet's own propensity for this style throughout the play. A good example occurs in Act 5, when he confronts the mourning Laertes at Ophelia's grave and exclaims, "Nay and thou'll mouth, I'll rant as well as thou":

> And, if thou prate of mountains, let them throw
> Millions of acres on us, till our ground,
> Singeing his pate against the burning zone,
> Make Ossa like a wart!

> (5.1.280–83)

Gertrude describes the speech as "mere madness" (5.1.284); normal people just do not speak like this. Once again, Shakespeare is having it both ways: appropriating Marlovian excess, while distancing himself from it.

Rather than parody Marlowe's style on a word-by-word basis, as he had earlier in previous recollections, Shakespeare in the Player's speech exaggerates the defining features of that style, in order to recreate its effects. Part of Shakespeare's task here is to recapture the sense of the newness, the strangeness that Marlowe's style must have had for its initial audiences. One of the ways he achieves this effect is by introducing a number of new words into the language (the speech must hold a record for first recorded entries in the *OED*). In addition, rather than end-stop all the lines (as is typical of Marlowe's practice) Shakespeare recreates a sense of Marlowe's verse paragraph by breaking up the long sections in midline, a feature that makes those pauses between the sections of the speech even more pronounced. The extended similes and metaphors, alliteration, repeated exclamations, and digressive flights all compound this effect. Strachey is undoubtedly on target when he concludes that the "audience would probably have been reminded of Marlowe's play, and so have experienced the sensation of hearing real men quoting a real play."

For Hamlet, Pyrrhus is a tiger, a Hyrcanian beast (the identification is so strong he gets the first line of the speech wrong because of this):

> "The rugged Pyrrhus, like th'Hyrcanian beast" —
> 'Tis not so. It begins with Pyrrhus:
> "The rugged Pyrrhus, he whose sable arms. . . .

> (2.2.450–2)

It is perhaps only accidental that the image recalls the earliest identification of Shakespeare as Marlowe's derivative imitator, when Robert Greene, parodically transposing a line from *3 Henry VI*, described Shakespeare as possessed of a "'tiger's hart wrapt in a player's hyde,' [and] supposes he is as well able to bombast out a blank verse as the best of you." In the course of the decade separating Greene's remarks from *Hamlet*, Shakespeare has gone from rapacious to gentle, from derivative imitator to generous recollector of his rival's gifts. There is a long-standing tradition that Shakespeare performed the part of the Ghost in *Hamlet*. What is often forgotten is that this role is usually doubled with that of the First Player.[119] If this was the case, Shakespeare himself acted this final bit of 'scenical strutting and furious vociferaction.' The rivalry, at long last, was over.

IV

JONSON AND SHAKESPEARE

N ANECDOTE CIRCULATING in the early seventeenth century relates how "Mr. Ben Jonson and Mr. William Shakespeare being merry at a tavern, Mr. Jonson having begun this for his epitaph:

> *Here lies Ben Jonson that was once . . .*

He gives it to Mr. Shakespeare to make up, who presently writes:

> *Who while he lived was a slow thing,*
> *And now being dead, is nothing.*[1]

The story, which survives in a number of contemporary manuscripts, portrays a Jonson struggling to get his own epitaph right, surrendering it to a not-so-gentle Shakespeare, who wittily obliterates the memory of his rival.[2] This is a Jonson obsessed with rendering how he should be remembered, though at the same time unsure of exactly what he is to be celebrated for: he starts by writing "Ben Jonson that was once . . ." only to trail off. If Jonson struggles at self-definition, Shakespeare, instead of helping out his friend and rival, strips him of his poetic identity. In another version of the story Shakespeare even takes away Jonson's pen. For Shakespeare, who plays on his rival's reputation as a painstakingly slow writer (hence the allusion to "slow thing"), Jonson—"now being dead" —is now no writer, and therefore no thing, at all. Scratch the surface of this tavern jest and one of the darker sides of how influence works is uncovered. This is a different kind of influence than we have encountered so far: not the struggle of young playwrights seeking mastery over precursors they found difficult to surpass, but the weightier influence that an established dramatist can wield over a rival's place in literary history. It is this kind of influence, and the intertextual strategies that it gives rise to, that is the main interest of this chapter.

One of the reasons that this story may have proved so popular is that it assigns to Shakespeare a role that he so studiously avoided and that Jonson so doggedly pursued. It was Jonson, after all, not Shakespeare, who would introduce his rival in poetic epitaphs that to this day shape our sense of who Shakespeare was: that soul of an age and sweet swan of Avon who knew little Latin and less Greek. Unlike the overwhelming majority of his fellow playwrights and poets, though, the "real" Shakespeare (to the best of our knowledge) never wrote a dedication, elegy, or epitaph for another writer. The anecdote thus invites us to imagine how Shakespeare might have acted in such a situation. Of course, to participate in the business of writing prefatory poems is necessarily to define oneself in relation to others within a literary hierarchy and a system of poetic relations. This is not to say that Shakespeare was totally free from being implicated in such systems: he wore the King's livery, paid (along with his fellow shareholders) for plays, and contributed poems (like "The Phoenix and the Turtle") for collaborative collections. He demurred, though, from defining himself, specifically, in relationship to his rivals. It would be left for them to define him.

Jonson did not have that luxury, nor for that matter the kind of personality that could long stay silent on the subject of literary rivalry.[3] At some point around the time that a prosperous Shakespeare retired from the stage, Jonson seems to have grasped to what extent his own reputation as a dramatist was contingent upon Shakespeare's. The anecdote describing their tavern encounter hints at how frustrating it must have been for Jonson to accept this and to accept Shakespeare's silence about him. Almost everything we know about Jonson's career suggests that he understood how vital it was to be placed correctly in relation to canonized predecessors and rivals. This positioning had become quite literal by the 1630s, when being assigned a plot in Poets' Corner at Westminster Abbey helped guarantee one's place among the greatest of English writers.

Jonson seems to have been so anxious that a place be secured for him among those monuments that he was teased about it by contemporaries. According to a seventeenth-century account,

> one day being rallied by the Dean of Westminster about being buried in the Poets' Corner, the poet is said to have replied. . . . "I am too poor for that, and no one will lay out funeral charges upon me. No sir, 6 feet long by 2 feet wide is too much for me: 2 feet by 2 feet will do for all I want." "You shall have it," said the Dean, and thus the conversation ended.[4]

The story (and another version, in which a similar request is made of King Charles) may well have some basis in fact, for when Jonson's bones were uncovered by gravediggers making room for Lady Wilson's remains in 1823, a witness who happened to be visiting Westminster at this hour, one "J. C. B.," wrote to a friend about the disturbance of Jonson's grave, including the information that it "is remarkable that the back is turned towards the East, and more remarkable that the corpse was buried with his head downwards, the feet being only a few inches below the pavement of the Church."[5] Subsequent gravedigging in 1849 (this time for Sir Robert, Lady Wilson's husband) confirmed the account that Jonson was buried not only vertically but upside down. Francis Buckland, who reported this incident, sought to preclude looting by souvenir hunters and removed Jonson's skull from the rest of his skeleton, hiding it on the "velvet covered top of the leaden coffin of the famous surgeon, John Hunter," where in all likelihood it remains to this day.[6] For all of Jonson's care in seeing that he received his rightful place in Poets' Corner, where his remains—skeletal and literary—might lie undisturbed, his plans for an eternal resting place (if we are to place any credence in the correspondence of anecdote and the subsequent reports of his burial) were overturned.

And what of Shakespeare's concern with "what he hath left us"? Shakespeare, if less interested in occupying a place in Westminster, proved more prescient than Jonson about how his remains would be treated. Shakespeare appears to have placed little value on being monumentalized; the famous epitaph on his gravestone (the one situated between those of Anne Shakespeare and Susanna Hall in the chancel of Stratford Church) bears no name. It reads simply:

Good friend, for Jesus' sake forbear
To dig the dust enclosed here.
Blessed be the man that spares these stones,
And cursed be he that moves my bones.[7]

The tradition that Shakespeare himself wrote these lines dates back to Dowdall in 1693, who got the information from an aged clerk who showed him around the church.[8] If this indeed is Shakespeare's tomb, and if the lines are his own, they are remarkable in their anonymity: Shakespeare demonstrates no concern here, as Jonson had, with naming himself or with recalling his achievements. Only a desire at this point to be left alone. His main concern seems to be over the possibility of "a transfer of his bones to the charnel-house," a legitimate fear, given the frequency of this practice in the overcrowded Stratford Church.[9]

After Shakespeare died William Bass wrote:

Reknowned Spenser, lie a thought more nigh
To learned Chaucer, and, rare Beaumont, lie
A little nearer Spenser, to make room
For Shakespeare.[10]

Bass was wittily conflating the place of literary and skeletal remains at Westminster. What had begun with Chaucer's burial there in 1400 took on increasing canonical significance with the burial of Spenser in 1599, an event that both Shakespeare and Jonson, along with other leading writers, may well have attended. At a time when literary reputation was increasingly institutionalized, burial at Westminster, along with the emergence of the laureateship, served to confirm one's place in the canon of English poets and—surprisingly—dramatists as well. The ranking in Westminster was based on a careful hierarchy: the inscription on Chaucer's tomb compared him with Homer, and Spenser, in turn, was likened to Chaucer. The pace would accelerate as Beaumont assumed a place in 1616, Camden in 1623, and Drayton in 1631.

In his poem prefacing the 1623 Folio of Shakespeare's plays, Jonson would amend Bass's lines to read:

My Shakespeare, rise; I will not lodge thee by
Chaucer, or Spenser, or bid Beaumont lie

A little further, to make thee a room:
Thou art a monument, without a tomb.

(H&S 8:391)

Jonson steers clear of Bass's clumsy exhumation and instead assumes the
authority to "lodge" Shakespeare outside of the institution of Poets'
Corner. While he confirms that Shakespeare is a monument without a
tomb, he takes for himself the role of monumentalizer, making Shakespeare stand in need of one who can place his remains properly. Pointedly,
he refuses to link Shakespeare (as Chaucer and Spenser had been linked)
with a notable predecessor. The obvious but unspoken comparison was to
Jonson himself. The irony is that history would be doubly cruel to Jonson.
He would outlive Shakespeare, but he would not eclipse him as a writer.
And though Shakespeare never completed Jonson's epitaph, and Jonson
would pen that of his rival's, it is Shakespeare's remains, his literary
reputation and his bones, that have remained undisturbed.[11]

If previous chapters have focused on the role influence plays in the
formative years of a dramatist's development, the interest in this chapter
shifts to the effect of influence upon poetic legacy and upon the ways in
which writers are canonized and remembered. The anecdote with which
this chapter began hints at the close literary engagement between Shakespeare and Jonson from the closing years of Elizabeth's reign until (and
even after) the posthumous appearance of Shakespeare's works in Folio in
1623. Yet little hard evidence of their rivalry survives, especially in regard
to the formative years of their relationship. What, one wonders, was
Jonson's response to Shakespeare's comedies and histories in the mid-to-
late 1590s? Did he act in Shakespeare's plays during the period when he
is reputed to have been performing in the provinces, perhaps with Pembroke's Men as early as 1592?[12] Did Shakespeare really rescue Jonson's
rejected manuscript of *Every Man in His Humour* in 1598?[13] And how did
Shakespeare feel about acting under Jonson's direction in rehearsals of
Every Man in and *Sejanus?* Why (if we follow Jonson's Folio) did Shakespeare not act in *Every Man out, Volpone,* and *Cataline?* Was Shakespeare
Jonson's unacknowledged collaborator in *Sejanus,* and if so, why did
Jonson erase any record of his rival's share? (And why, if this was the case,
did Shakespeare never complain about being edited out of the published
text?) What "purge," if we are to believe the authors of *Return from Par-*

nassus, Part 2, did Shakespeare administer to Jonson as part of the Poets' War? What was the extent of their mutual involvement at roughly the same time in supplying poems for Chester's *Love's Martyr* (1601)? The list of virtually unanswerable questions could easily be extended. The problem remains. It is indisputable that the two had a long, extensive, and diverse professional relationship, but where, exactly, is the presence of Shakespeare and Jonson in each other's work and how is its pressure signaled?

Recent critics searching for signs of this presence have seen it manifested in two ways.[14] The first is in intertextual allusions, the kind that form the basis of analysis in earlier chapters in this book. Following the lead of Anne Barton and E. A. J. Honigmann, critics have argued that the plays of Shakespeare and Jonson reveal an ongoing and at times obsessive struggle that can be identified on a textual level in verbal parody. Surprisingly, however, given the playwrights' extensive interaction over several decades, we do not find nearly as much evidence as we might expect in their plays and poems of the kind of intertextual struggle embodied in parodic recollections that was so characteristic of each of their responses to other dramatists, including Marlowe. And we find far less in Shakespeare than in Jonson. An important distinction needs to be drawn, then, between being responsive to and being influenced by another writer. Neither Jonson nor Shakespeare was a formative influence upon each other, and apparently, as a result, there was considerably less need for verbal or visual parody. Moreover, after 1600 Shakespeare does not really echo contemporary dramatists at all, other than the early Shakespeare. And when Jonson deliberately recalls and parodies rivals in his plays—as he does with Marston and Dekker—he does so to hold up fellow playwrights to ridicule. Shakespeare was not so easily ridiculed; and he proved remarkably immune from successful parody, even by a talented versifier like Jonson.

If some critics have searched Shakespeare's and Jonson's plays and poems for echoes or scattered bits of parody, others have looked instead at entire plays as engaged in a sustained dialogue. This second approach, most recently and forcefully advocated by Russ McDonald in his *Shakespeare & Jonson/Jonson & Shakespeare,* operates by pairing roughly contemporaneous plays, like *Every Man in* and *The Merry Wives,* or *Bartholomew Fair* and *The Tempest.* There is, after all, contemporary evidence even before the Poets' War (e.g., the Admiral's Men's *Oldcastle* play of 1599) that plays could be written with such an objective in mind. One of the problems with this approach though is that in the absence of extended and unmistakable topical allusion, it is difficult to prove that multifaceted plays were conceived primarily as sustained attacks upon each other's art or as defenses of their own. Moreover, this approach to literary influence tends to bring to the plays hardened preconceptions of the literary styles and values we call "Shakespearean" and "Jonsonian" and to run the risk of merely confirming these stereotypes.

To these two approaches, which I review and try to build upon in the following pages, I offer a third, and I believe predominant and largely undervalued approach, one that locates the primary site of their literary struggle, not in the plays or poems themselves, but in the retrospective prefaces, prologues, inductions, and critical prose that Jonson composed only after Shakespeare had stopped writing plays. Jonson, who had introduced a series of poetasters in coming to terms with Marlowe's influence, hit upon another device in responding to Shakespeare. Print, and the increasing control a dramatist could have over the publication of his plays, allowed Jonson to move the site of intertextual struggle from the plots and language of the plays to their margins, such as the prefatory material we find in the Induction of *Bartholomew Fair* (1614), the revised Prologue to *Every Man in* (1616), the *Conversations with Drummond* that date from 1619 or so, and his posthumously published *Discoveries* (c. 1623–25, pub. 1640 (H&S 11:213)). The climax of this strategy whereby a reader's path to Jonson was mediated by the presence of Shakespeare, and access to Shakespeare likewise mediated by Jonson, occurs in the prefatory poems and inductions to the two great collections of plays in these years: the Folio editions of Jonson's (1616) and Shakespeare's (1623) *Works*. In each case we approach the work of one dramatist with the accomplishments of the other firmly in mind. Against this stands Shakespeare's stony, deliberate, and, no doubt for Jonson, infuriating silence.

The force of that silence should not be underestimated. That Shakespeare took from Jonson, that Jonson powerfully shaped Shakespeare's dramatic output, neither man could have doubted. As David Bevington, R. A. Foakes, and others have noted, Shakespeare's strong interest in satire and in the satirist in plays like *As You Like It, Troilus and Cressida,* and *Measure for Measure* betrays a considerable debt to Jonson's recent comical satires. And surely, the various masques in Shakespeare's late plays are influenced by Jonson's masterful experiments in that genre at Court. Shakespeare may even have been among the members of the King's Men who acted in Jonson's masques before King James.[15] Yet in both instances Shakespeare's debt to Jonson is never signaled, and what is

Jonsonian is quietly, seamlessly absorbed into a Shakespearean framework. Only on the rarest of occasions—as when the "armed Prologue" to *Troilus and Cressida* tilts at the Prologue of Jonson's *Poetaster*—does this rivalry break the placid surface of his drama.[16] Whatever Shakespeare felt, and he surely felt something, he kept to himself. In retrospect, this must have taken considerable self-restraint. Having worked in the same professional circles as Jonson for close to two decades, having witnessed his plays and masques, and having seen some of Jonson's early quartos published with sly digs at his own drama, what is extraordinary is that Shakespeare never responded, and above all scrupulously avoided letting Jonson's language permeate his own, as Marlowe's, Kyd's, and Lyly's once had. This is all the more remarkable, since Shakespeare, who acted in several of Jonson's plays, knew stretches of Jonson's drama by heart. Yet his plays yield no Jonsonian equivalent to Pistol's Marlovian rant or to the parody of Lyly's Euphuism in Don Armado's speeches in *Love's Labor's Lost*. Silence and gentleness are also carefully constructed strategies and ones that can effectively silence critics too.[17]

Their respective strategies would have a profound effect on the ways in which both Shakespeare and Jonson have been read and canonically positioned for the past four centuries. The binary oppositions to which their poetic practices were reduced through Jonson's retrospective labeling of "Shakespeare" and "Jonson" (e.g., easyflowing vs. labored, native vs. classical, natural vs. artificial) would be appropriated (for very different ends) by such canonical figures as Milton, Dryden, Pope, Johnson, Wordsworth, and Coleridge. And in three of the most significant and influential works of literary theory from the Restoration to the Romantic periods—Dryden's *An Essay of Dramatic Poesie*, Johnson's *Preface to Shakespeare*, and Wordsworth's *Preface to Lyrical Ballads*—these terms, and the constructed and still prevalent opposition of "Shakespeare" and "Jonson," would be appropriated in order to advocate literary values markedly different from those Jonson originally had in mind.

The reductiveness that we have seen to be so crucial to effective parody would be translated into a reductiveness central to the making of the English literary canon. Viewed in this light, canonization emerges as an extension and formalization of parody. Where parody succeeds in reducing the complex social, linguistic, political, and formal properties of an artist's work to a catchphrase, the act of locating a writer within literary history often comes to depend upon a similar act of reductiveness, through which a writer's work often becomes identified with one of a set of binary categories. The chapter thus concludes with some speculation on the effect of the personal rivalry of Jonson and Shakespeare on the system of canonical valuation we have inherited from the seventeenth, eighteenth, and early nineteenth centuries.

❧

It is one thing to insist, as Anne Barton and E. A. J. Honigmann recently have, that Jonson is "obsessed" with Shakespeare in the early years of the seventeenth century (for Honigmann, Jonson is even the rival poet of the sonnets).[18] It is another to identify the ways in which that obsession was displayed in the plays that Jonson wrote in those years. Where are the textual traces, or shards, of this literary encounter to be found? The cumulative claims of scholars who have identified connections in the plots, characters, and language of Jonson's (and to a lesser extent Shakespeare's) plays during these years are a little staggering. And the force of all these allusions, taken together, would seem to make a formidable case for a sustained interpenetration of their work. Given the considerable emphasis placed on these kinds of recollections in earlier chapters of this book, it seems the obvious point of departure in examining the rivalry of Shakespeare and Jonson. It is important to acknowledge from the outset, then, that the evidence is not as compelling as it has been made out to be and that the claims need to be reviewed on a case-by-case basis.

While there is considerable evidence that Jonson was active in the theater as early as 1595, the first documented information concerning his relationship to Shakespeare does not occur until 1598 when the Chamberlain's Men performed *Every Man in.* Shakespeare's name heads the list of actors included in the Folio edition of the play. Although critics have not identified any echoes of Shakespeare in the play, some connections to Shakespearean practice have been noticed. Barton has suggested that "Bobadilla anticipates, and indeed may have influenced Shakespeare's Ancient Pistol" (though both characters may be said to draw upon a common ancestor, the braggart soldier of Roman comedy).[19] Barton also raises the possibility that we can trace a Jonsonian recollection of Shakespeare's drama back to 1597; she suggests that there "are moments in *The Case Is Altered* when Jonson seems to be appealing to his audience's recollections of Shakespeare's *Two Gentlemen of Verona*" in the triangulation of the lovers. Again, there is a danger of seeing influence in what may simply be analogous and timeworn comic situations. Barton qualifies her suggestion, adding that what "in Shakespeare had been crucial becomes, in Jonson, only one thread in a complex network."[20]

Of all Jonson's early plays, *Every Man out* (1599) has struck critics as the richest in intertextual allusions to Shakespeare. Yet even here the casual references to Shakespeare do not add up to much. Nevertheless, Honigmann has urged that the play "bristles with allusions to Shakespeare . . . right to the play's very last words."[21] This last claim is somewhat deceptive. In the third ending written for the play and published in a 1601 Quarto, Macilente invites our applause, which "may (in time) make lean MACILENTE as fat, as SIR JOHN FALSTAFF" (H&S 3:598). It is unclear whether this is a plug for another Chamberlain's Men play in repertory at the Globe or a jealous swipe at a rival's success. The same holds true for an allusion to *2 Henry IV* in Brisk's description of Fungoso as "a kinsman to justice Silence" (H&S 3:567). More frustratingly, we do not know whether the allusion to Falstaff (or to Silence) was ever heard by audiences at the Globe or, like so many other changes in the Quarto versions that were greatly revised and padded for publication, whether Jonson added this a couple of years later when he was no longer writing for the Chamberlain's Men and when his relationship to Shakespeare's dramatic practice may have changed in some fundamental way. The same holds true for other allusions: it is hard to imagine Shakespeare the shareholder pleased with a remark that ridicules his aspirations to gentility (if this in fact is what Jonson intended in the line that appears to parody the motto of the Shakespeare family's recently acquired coat of arms—"Non san droit": "not without mustard" (3.4.86), an allusion that would undoubtedly be lost upon all but a tiny handful of theatergoers). Certainly, the allusions to *Julius Caesar*—the recontextualized echo of "Et tu Brute" (5.6.79), and the parodic twist on Shakespeare's "reason is fled to brutish beasts" in Jonson's "Reason long since is fled to animals, you know" (3.4.33)—are unmistakable recollections, and fit a pattern of Jonson's lifelong delight at parodying lines from *Julius Caesar*. But it is overhasty to conclude from this that "Jonson jeers at Shakespeare and his plays" throughout *Every Man out.*[22]

When we turn to Jonson's other plays from this period the kind of explicit attacks leveled at Dekker, Marston, and others are not directed at Shakespeare, either because they are so veiled as to be unrecoverable or simply because they are not there.[23] In Jonson's *Poetaster,* a play that at many points alludes deliberately to contemporary dramatists, about the only intertextual recollection of Shakespeare that has been claimed is the similarity of Julia's entrances and exits in her "balcony scene" to her namesake Juliet's in *Romeo and Juliet*. And as Barton hastens to add, such to-and-fro is frequently used by Jonson for comic effect; moreover, "Jonson does not seem to have been able to make up his mind, in this scene, as to just how he felt . . . about his Shakespearean model."[24]

Even when we add the collaborative *Eastward Ho* to the list of plays from these years, with its obvious recollections of *Hamlet* in the appearance of the footman named Hamlet who rushes about and is asked "S'foot, Hamlet, are you mad?" (H&S 4:557), the echoes and allusions do not reveal a sustained and coherent act of parody, one that identifies those features of Shakespeare's art as sufficiently threatening to be worthy of displacement or stylistic flaws as sufficiently egregious to be worthy of ridicule. Like the possible recollection of *Twelfth Night* in *Epicoene*,[25] they seem casual, especially when they take their place alongside more sustained (and brashly paraded) parodies of Kyd, Marlowe, Chapman, Dekker, and Marston. While Barton makes about as strong a case as one can in her essay on "Shakespeare and Jonson" (going so far as to see Jonson's description of "cross wooing" in romantic comedy as proleptically parodic of Shakespeare's as yet unwritten *Twelfth Night*!), even she ends up falling back on the stereotypic view of "Jonsonian" and "Shakespearean" practice in trying to support her conviction that "Jonson's ten surviving Elizabethan and Jacobean comedies often seem to invoke conventions, themes, or situations associated with specific Shakespearean plays in a deliberately distorted form."[26] Although many would agree that these plays testify to Jonson's obsession with Shakespeare, it remains the case that his plays of this period fail to reveal more than a handful of instances that reveal this obsession being played out in the kind of parodic practices characteristic of Jonson's art in these years. Shakespeare is always in view; but for the most part he remains on the horizon, just out of range.

We also need to be careful about stereotyping either Jonson's or Shakespeare's dramatic output in these years, applying, retrospectively, a coherence hard to discern at the time. In the closing years of Elizabeth's reign Jonson had a hand in at least fourteen plays and probably more: *The Ile of Dogs, The Case Is Altered, Hot Anger Soon Cold, Every Man in, Every Man out, Page of Plymouth, Robert II, King of Scots, Mortimer His Fall, Cynthia's Revels, Poetaster*, the additions to *The Spanish Tragedy, Richard Crookback*, and *Sejanus*. To this we may add the lost play from which Allott reprinted the speech "Gold is a Suitor" and the early version of *A Tale of a Tub*. He wrote for virtually every company that produced plays, including the Admiral's, Chamberlain's, Pembroke's, and the Children of the Chapel, and he collaborated with most of the major dramatists of the period, including Dekker, Chapman, Nashe, Porter, Chettle, and probably Marston as well. He experimented with a great many dramatic forms. The range of genres includes revenge tragedy, comedy of humours, comical satires, citizen comedy, English history, Scottish tragedy, domestic tragedy, and Roman tragedy. If we add his experiences acting Zulziman at the Paris Garden at one end of the spectrum and his collaborative role in King James's coronation pageantry at the other, there seems little in terms of theatrical representation that Jonson did not attempt.

In light of this remarkable range, we have to be especially cautious when Jonson himself offers a revisionary account of his artistic development, such as the one that appears in the Chorus to *The Magnetic Lady*, that tries to persuade us of the linearity of his career as playwright:

> The author, beginning his studies of this kind, with *Every Man in His Humour;* and after, *Every Man out of His Humour:* and since, continuing in all his plays, especially those of the comic thread, whereof the *New Inn* was the last, some recent humours still, or manners of men, that went along with the times, finding himself now near the close, or shutting up of his circle, hath phant'sied to himself, in idea, this *Magnetic Mistress*. . . . And this he hath called *Humours Reconciled.* (H&S 6:511)

It is an attractive narrative—in Jonson's terms, "how summed a circle" —in that it offers a sense of coherence to Jonson's dramatic production from what he earlier called his first fruits, up until his final Caroline plays. Yet it achieves this coherence only by selectively representing Jonson's wide-ranging dramatic practices. Jonson's own highly selective reconstruction (one he may perhaps have come to believe in) has had such a powerful hold upon his critics that only quite recently have Jonson scholars seriously questioned this received view of the trajectory of his career. In brief, much work remains to be done distinguishing the history of Jonson's career from that of "Jonson's."

Shakespeare's range was also quite extensive at this time, and it is difficult in this case as well to define a "Shakespearean" norm that embraces such disparate works as the late histories: *Henry IV, Parts 1 and 2* and *Henry V;* the romantic, problem, and citizen comedies: *The Merry Wives of Windsor, Much Ado About Nothing, As You Like It, Twelfth Night,* and *All's Well that Ends Well;* the classical and revenge tragedies *Julius Caesar* and *Hamlet;* and the generically elusive *Troilus and Cressida.* Since Shakespeare wrote exclusively for the increasingly dominant Chamberlain's Men (and had a personal investment in the Globe), another dimension that enters into an account of their rivalry in these years is the complex economic competition between companies and playhouses. Thus, we do not know whether Jonson, because of his work for the Children of the Chapel, is implicated in Shakespeare's attack in *Hamlet* on the popularity of the children's companies (which might, in turn, have generated the ripostes in *Eastward Ho* against *Hamlet,* and so on).

So much for the Elizabethan years. A curious methodologic shift occurs when critics direct their attention towards the relationship of Jonson and Shakespeare in their major Jacobean plays. This shift brings us to the second dominant critical approach, in which allusion hunting is largely replaced by allegorical readings of entire plays against other plays. No doubt one reason for this is that intertextual stylistic evidence is even scarcer after 1604 or so. Thus, Harry Levin has argued suggestively that *The Tempest* be read as a magnificent reply to *The Alchemist,* and Thomas Cartelli's elegant *"Bartholomew Fair* as Urban Arcadia" shows how Jonson replies in turn to Shakespeare's pastoral vision.[27] Russ McDonald has taken this approach the furthest. Rather than merely link one festive comedy or Roman tragedy with another, McDonald urges that we juxtapose instead what each author was primarily writing in the early years of James's reign: for Shakespeare, tragedy, for Jonson, a comedy that shared with Shakespearean tragedy an antiromantic impulse in its exploration of powerful collisions "between the world as it is and the world as it should be" in plays populated by characters whose great imaginative visions are ultimately crushed.[28] To this end McDonald explores thematic and ethical links between plays like *Merry Wives* and *Every Man in,* or *Troilus* and *Sejanus.* As suggestive and informative as McDonald's book is, its thesis ultimately tends to compare and contrast styles, rather than pinpoint precisely where Jonson and Shakespeare are provoked into reacting against each other's dramatic practices.[29]

In Honigmann, as in McDonald, the terms of the debate between plays are ultimately too general. Thus, for example, Honigmann argues that *"The Winter's Tale* . . . contains a comprehensive reply to Jonson's charge that Shakespeare's plays run away from Nature, Life and Truth," and "Shakespeare's next two plays appear to refer back to the same debate."[30] To suggest, however, as Honigmann does, that the subtitle of

Henry VIII, "All is True," obliquely mocks Jonson's claims is to fall into the trap of representing Shakespeare responding to claims that Jonson had not yet fully articulated. It is a tendency not limited to Honigmann but at times characteristic of some of the other fine critics of the plays of these years, in part because the plays themselves do not offer much evidence—on the level of intertextual recollections—of the struggle between the great playwrights. Again, this is not to underestimate the extent of their interaction in the early years of the seventeenth century, at a time of what appears to have been extensive collaboration and rivalry between these two leading dramatists. It is to claim that evidence of the ways in which they responded to the pressure of each other's output must be found elsewhere.

More recently, Jonson's Caroline plays have been viewed as sympathetic to and shaped by Shakespearean models. Barton's revaluation of Jonson's late plays, particularly *The New Inn,* in which she is seconded by both Robert Watson and Michael Hattaway, has been especially influential in urging us to see Jonson turning away from the "popular morality tradition to which he had recourse in both *Devil Is an Ass* and *The Staple of News* to re-think the premises of Shakespearean comedy, to explore its attitudes and, up to a point, make them his own."[31] For Barton, "the shaping influence [in *The New Inn*] is Shakespearean,"[32] and Hattaway agrees: "In *The New Inn* Jonson was celebrating another debt to the past, to Shakespeare" in the play's "resurrection of a Shakespearean mode."[33] The argument is attractive, especially when we take into account not only Jonson's exposure to Shakespeare's work when he helped produce the Folio edition of 1623, but also the tendency in the 1620s and 1630s to look back nostalgically at Elizabeth's reign. Once again, however, what is recollected from Shakespeare is basically the kind of plot Jonson employs, here, romantic comedy. And while Shakespeare is undoubtedly an enormously important force for this kind of drama, too little is known of Jonson's early plays—like the collaboration with Chettle on the lost *Hot Anger Soon Cold*—to determine whether Jonson is turning back to his own, earlier dramatic styles (as he seems to have done with *A Tale of a Tub*), or whether he is striking out into "Shakespearean" terrain for the first time. If he is writing in a Shakespearean vein it remains in terms of plot rather than poetic style, for the play yields no verbal echoes or parodic recollections, no sense that the poetic voice is anyone's but Jonson's.

I suspect that Jonson did not take up his proven practice of stylistic parody when it came to Shakespeare's plays because Shakespeare was not a formative influence in the way that "sporting Kyd," or "Marlowe's mighty line" had been for him. Nor did he feel the need, compulsively pursued in his relationship to other contemporaries, to display mastery over the rival's style through parodic recollection and displacement. The exception that would seem to prove the rule here is his response to *Julius Caesar*, touched upon above in the discussion of *Every Man out*. Jonson would write of Shakespeare in his *Discoveries* that "Many times he fell into those things, could not scape laughter; as when he said in the person of Caesar, one speaking to him; *Caesar, thou didst me wrong*. He replied: *Caesar never did wrong but with just cause*, and such like, which were ridiculous" (H&S 584). In the surviving Folio text of Shakespeare's play, perhaps in response to Jonson's jibe, the offending line was altered to the less paradoxical: "Caesar doth not wrong, nor without cause/ Will he be satisfied" (3.1.47–48). Jonson, in one of the rare moments that he had Shakespeare by the hip, would not let go. So that even after his rival's death, in the Induction to *The Staple of News*, Caesar's "ridiculous" words are recalled; when "Expectation," challenged by the "Prologue" that she teaches others to expect "too much," responds: "I can do that too, if I have cause," only to be met with the "Prologue's" rejoinder: "Cry you mercy, you never did wrong, but with just cause" (H&S 6:280). Jonson is still parodying the lines almost a quarter century after Shakespeare's character first misspoke. At this point, one wonders, who would have gotten the joke? Despite its relative ineffectiveness as parody (since parody depends upon a recognition on the part of the audience that must be highly suspect here, and the allusion remains more of a private joke than an intertextual recollection that serves parodic ends) the example nevertheless shows that Jonson could parody Shakespeare onstage if he wished to do so.

The example of *Julius Caesar* indicates that Jonson could and, on rare occasions, did recall and parody Shakespeare's words, despite the difficulty of parodying an author whose works proved so resistant to this kind of treatment. But for the most part Jonson's response to Shakespeare early in his career was primarily selective and reactive. Jonson became obsessed with Shakespeare's formidable dramatic output for different reasons than anxiety over his rival's influence. That reason, I suspect, was literary reputation and legacy, which seems to have become increasingly important to Jonson in the early years of the seventeenth century. Concomitantly, the intertextual strategies Jonson employed changed accordingly.

For Jonson, the ends of parody—displaying for all to see one's mastery over a rival's art—could be achieved through a different kind of intertextuality, one made available by the printing of plays. Print, Jonson realized, offered a kind of intertextual space that the staged play could not: the revised preface, the induction, the dedicatory epistle. Moreover, as he began to see, this space gave the playwright a chance to address his readership directly and a chance to clarify, retroactively, to what extent his aims had been realized in production. The publication of his plays as *Works* was thus far more than a piece of vanity, as some contemporaries saw it, but an opportunity for accomplishing the ends of parody (and canonization) through retrospective critiques of his rivals' art and of Shakespeare's art in particular. I would like to press this point even further: Jonson plays out, in the two most important collections of English drama in his lifetime (the Folios of 1616 and 1623) his struggle with Shakespeare. Before we read a line of either *Every Man in* or *The Tempest* (the first plays in these respective collections) we are confronted with Jonson's revisionary and mediating arguments about the relationship of his art to Shakespeare's. We are back, then, to the premise of the tavern anecdote: Jonson's *Works* (1616), no less than Shakespeare's *Comedies, Histories, and Tragedies* (1623), could not stand as far as Jonson was concerned, without being located in relation to a rival poetic practice. To present "Jonson" was not possible without presenting "Shakespeare," and vice versa. What Jonson could not accomplish on stage he would attempt in print.

The key to Jonson's response to Shakespeare is the presumption of symmetrical contestation, of charges and counter-charges, thrust and parry, a strategy that Shakespeare refused to engage in and that literary historians and critics have nonetheless ascribed to, no doubt because it is hard imagining a contest between two authors that is sustained by only one of them. Honigmann's unpersuasive claim that *The Winter's Tale* constitutes Shakespeare's punishing refutation of Jonson's attack in *The Alchemist* offers the very response that Jonson tried to provoke and Shakespeare refused to supply.[34] Seventeenth-century antecedents that describe their contestation in symmetrical terms abound not only in the anecdotes about witty exchanges at the Mermaid tavern or at christenings but also in the two substantial claims upon which twentieth-century views of a combative rivalry ultimately depend.

The first is Thomas Fuller's famous account of the Wit Combats between Shakespeare and Jonson:

which two I behold like a Spanish great Galleon, and an English Man of War; Master Jonson, (like the former) was built far higher in learning; solid, but slow in his performances. Shakespeare, with the English Man of War, lesser in bulk, but lighter in sailing, could turn with all tides, tack about and take advantage of all winds, by the quickness of his wit and invention. [H&S 11:510]

Herford and the Simpsons are sufficiently drawn to the account to place some credence in it (Fuller, who was born in 1605, could have heard the story from contemporaries); Schoenbaum and others have discredited Fuller's description as mere fantasy. Its attractiveness resides, however, in how it balances the rivalry, making it into a fair (albeit a lopsided) fight, recalling the English defeat of the Armada (though Shakespeare's triumph, like the English one, is providentially assured).

Much the same impulse towards finding symmetry in Jonson and Shakespeare's relationship appears in that other influential document, the pro-Jonson Cambridge play, *Return from Parnassus, Part 2*:

Why here's our fellow Shakespeare puts them all down, aye and Ben Jonson, too. Oh, that Ben Jonson is a pestilent fellow: he brought up Horace [in *Poetaster*] giving the poets a pill, but our fellow Shakespeare hath given him a purge that made him bewray his credit.[35]

This purge may well be *Troilus and Cressida,* or it may be Dekker's *Satiromastix,* performed by the Chamberlain's Men and perhaps mistakenly attributed to Shakespeare. Perhaps there was no purge at all, merely, again, a desire to define their emulative engagement as symmetrical, in much the same way that the confrontations between Harvey and Nashe, Daniel and Campion, and Jonson and Marston were constructed. In this respect, Fuller and the *Parnassus* play's accounts should be read warily, insofar as they fail to correspond with Shakespeare's reluctance to play by Jonson's rules.

What appears to have most frustrated Jonson was not only Shakespeare's refusal to spar with him in his staged plays but also his reluctance in printed texts to blot out lines, to revise for polemical purposes. It was not as if Shakespeare were unaware of how this was done: Hamlet, after all, asks the First Player to add "some dozen or sixteen lines" to *The Murder of Gonzago* (2.2.541–42) that he had written to make its topical application unmistakable. It is just this issue that Jonson addresses in his frustrated remarks in his *Discoveries:*

> I remember, the players have often mentioned it as an honor to Shakespeare, that in his writing (whatsoever he penned) he never blotted out a line. My answer hath been, would he have blotted a thousand. Which they thought a malevolent speech. I had not told posterity this, but for their ignorance, who choose that circumstance to commend their friends by, wherein he most faulted. And to justify my own candor (for I loved the man, and do honor his memory [on this side idolatry] as much as any).

(H&S 8:583–84)

Jonson is clearly frustrated that Shakespeare thought he never needed to revise and rework his verse. Yet "blot" in the late sixteenth century had other connnotations: it also meant to obliterate by way of correction, stigmatize, efface, disfigure, and eclipse. As recent textual scholarship has made clear—and as editors from Pope onward knew, as well as Heminges, Condell, and Jonson—Shakespeare was a tireless reviser of his own plays, as the complex textual histories of works like *Titus Andronicus,* the *Henry VI* plays, *Hamlet,* and, of course, *Lear* demonstrate. But the ends of his revision were markedly different from Jonson's blotting. More, then, is at stake here than simply a sour Jonson criticizing Shakespeare's effortless production. Part of what bothers Jonson here is the kind of revision that Shakespeare avoided, revision with one eye towards rivals, the other towards posterity, the kind that Jonson himself practiced so assiduously.

The intertextual struggle that is absent, suppressed, or subterranean in Shakespeare and in much of Jonson's plays for the stage appears primarily in the interstices or margins of Jonson's published texts. Jonson's surviving marginalia, such as his running battle with Chapman in his copy of the latter's translations from Homer, his recently rediscovered copy of Spenser, and his copy of Chaucer, indicate that he viewed the margins of the printed text as a place where poetic wrongs should be righted. Jonson also appears to have understood, long before others, the power of the marginalized space in printed editions of his works, where he could mediate between his words and his reader's experience of them.

Jonson's consciousness of what is contested in this space is apparent in the address "To the Reader in Ordinary" prefacing *Cataline:*

> The Muses forbid, that I should restrain your meddling, whom I see already busy with the title, and tricking over the leaves: It is your own. I departed with my right, when I let it first abroad.
>
> (H&S 5:432)

Sidestepping the very reservations he raises, Jonson breezily goes on to suggest what should be excused or taken into account in the reader's experience of his play. The meddling is his as much as the reader's, as Jonson, through the various addresses to his plays, shapes his reader's response not just to what he has written but also to how that stands in relation to what his rivals, especially Shakespeare, have accomplished.

The most striking example of this practice in Jonson's work occurs in *Every Man in,* which, as the title page of the 1616 edition indicates, was first acted in 1598, with Shakespeare's name (again, according to the Folio) leading the cast of players. The text of the play thus has it both ways: revised for the Folio, it nonetheless passes itself off as having been written in 1598 (a maneuver that fooled Gifford, one of Jonson's early editors). The ambiguity surrounding the play's date allows Jonson to publish a Prologue in 1616 that would juxtapose the play with the kind of dramatic practices characteristic of the drama of the 1590s, making the play seem as though it was written against this kind of drama. And the Dedication to Camden offering up the play as Jonson's first fruits further underscores the kind of revisionary drama Jonson would seem to have practiced from the start.

The Prologue, written after 1612, and probably around 1614 after Shakespeare had retired to Stratford and while Jonson's Folio was going to press,[36] recalls and challenges a quarter-century of Shakespeare's work, from the early histories to the late romances. Before Jonson introduces us to his own plays he has us review Shakespeare's. All genres are covered: sandwiched between Jonson's critique of Shakespeare's late romances—specifically *Pericles* and *The Tempest*—are challenges to the dramaturgic principles that inform the histories and tragedies. Jonson's allusion to the

> three rusty swords,
> And help of some few foot-and-half-foot words

Fight over York, and Lancaster's long jars:
And in the tiring house bring wounds, to scars,

(H&S 3:303)

returns us to the beginnings of Shakespeare's drama and indicts his rival's mimetic practice from its inception: having a handful of old props and some high astounding terms cannot, Jonson suggests, adequately represent the complex political struggle of the War of the Roses. Shakespeare's most recent Lancastrian history, *Henry V,* comes in for censure as well for its "Chorus [that] wafts you o'er the seas" (H&S 3:303). Where Jonson had faulted the early histories for actually trying to stage battles, he criticizes *Henry V* for merely inviting us to imagine similar actions. Shakespeare abandons his earlier dramaturgic practice in *Henry V* and replaces the staged combat of his earlier histories with a Chorus that challenges the spectators to envision imaginatively what the playwright cannot depict: the vast sweep of time, widely separated locales, and tumultuous battles. The Chorus must have proven particularly vexing to Jonson, who throughout his career as dramatist and masque-maker restlessly toyed with various kinds of choruses. Never, though, did he try in his dramatic works to acknowledge and overcome mimetic constraints through his choruses, as Shakespeare does here. The problem posed by Shakespeare's Chorus was that even as it exposes the fictionality of theatrical representation in its repeated reminders of the limited capabilities of the Elizabethan stage, it invites the audience to accept and participate in the making of this fiction. The Chorus thereby anticipates the very criticism of rusty swords and tiring house wounds that Jonson levels in the opening lines of the Prologue by acknowledging them but then goes beyond this to assert a new kind of mimetic possibility. It is a brilliant strategy because it precludes parody by admitting and then making a virtue of its own mimetic limitations.

Jonson is left to insist, a little weakly, that Shakespeare's self-conscious dramaturgy nevertheless violates the natural actions and language of men. The use in *King Lear* and elsewhere of artificial stage properties and noises to simulate natural phenomena is particularly faulty. Audiences, accordingly, need neither the

rolled bullet heard
To say, it thunders; nor tempestuous drum
Rumbles, to tell you when the storm doth come.

(H&S 3:303)

Above all, it is Shakespeare's recent romances, a return to the genre of comedy that Jonson had dominated since the outset of James's reign, that most unsettled Jonson. Again, the attack is directed at Shakespeare's mimetic practice. Jonson shows little patience for plays like *Pericles* (the "mouldy tale" singled out specifically in the Ode appended to *The New Inn* [1632]) that

> make a child, now swaddled, to proceed
> Man, and then shoot up, in one beard, and weed,
> Past threescore years.

(H&S 3:303)[37]

The Tempest, too, comes under attack for its unnaturalness, especially in its depiction of Caliban, whom Jonson alludes to in the closing line of the Prologue when requesting that: "You, who have so graced monsters, may like men" (H&S 3:303).

Here, in the opening Preface to the Folio, before we are invited to enter the world of Jonson's drama, the critical position that emerged only in the years between the initial staging and the re-publication of *Every Man in* is articulated. The most decisive claim concerns mimesis itself, the need for "deeds, and language, such as men do use:/ And persons, such as Comedy would choose" (H&S 3:303). The argument is a timeworn one, insofar as writers have long tried to displace rivals and predecessors by claiming that their own art represents reality more accurately. As with parody, in order to promote the "realism" of one's own work, the mimetic limitations, the "untruthfulness" of one's rivals must be exposed. It gets tricky, however, because in making such an assertion Jonson must lay claim to "art" (since his principles are carefully considered and reworked) and at the same time must pass his work off as true to life and therefore "natural." At the same time, his rival's work must be re-presented as one that consists of artificial deeds, language, and persons and yet is somehow artless. Shakespeare is thus condemned both for lacking art and for employing too much of it when he offers us the unnatural "monsters" of the *Tempest* or what Jonson construes as the feeble attempt at verisimilitude in the battle scenes of his history plays. We need to be cautious about accepting dichotomies like "art" and "nature" (such as Jonson's claim that "Shakespeare wanted art"); neither the one nor the other is the province of Shakespeare or Jonson; rather they offer handy terms in the struggle for mimetic superiority.

It is worth repeating that Jonson's critical revaluation of Shakespeare begins only after Shakespeare has stopped writing plays and has retired as playwright (and, for that matter, shortly before Jonson would turn away from writing stage plays, though he would return to them a decade later). The prefaces to *Volpone* and *The Alchemist,* which have been construed as critiques of Shakespeare's dramatic practice, carefully steer just clear of any direct allusion to Shakespeare or his works. In the former, Jonson focuses instead on offering himself up to the university communities as one who "shall raise the despised head of poetry again, and stripping her out of those rotten and base rags, wherewith the times have adulterated her form" (H&S 5:21). And in the latter Jonson's attack also remains unspecific; he condemns those plays "wherein, now, the concupiscence of dances and antics so raigneth, as to run away from Nature, and be afraid of her, is the only point of art that tickles the spectators." While some critics have read his subsequent critique of Shakespeare's copiousness in the *Discoveries* back into the warning in the Preface to the *Alchemist*— "that there is a great difference between those that (to gain the opinion of copy) utter all they can, how ever unfitly; and those that use election and a mean" (H&S 5:291)—the object of the attack remains sufficiently vague, and, it should be noted, the Preface is omitted in the Folio.[38]

In 1614 or so, around the time that the Prologue to *Every Man in* was composed, the Induction to *Bartholomew Fair* restates the case. Once again, Jonson begins at the beginning, going so far as to exaggerate the datedness of his Shakespeare's early work. Thus, in the Induction, the Bookholder asks the Scriviner to read the "certain articles" drawn up between author and audience, and included in this contract is the proviso that "He that will swear *Jeronimo,* or *Andronicus* are the best plays, yet, shall pass unexcepted at, here, as a man whose judgement shows it is constant, and hath stood still, these five and twenty, or thirty years" (H&S 6:16). The generosity of this claim (which makes *Titus Andronicus* considerably more ancient than it was) is belied by what immediately follows: the spectator is urged "neither to look back to the sword-and-buckler age of Smithfield, but content himself with the present." Jonson's own play offers a new and improved kind of drama and repudiates the principles of plays at the rival Globe that currently capture the popular imagination:

> If there be never a servant-monster i'th fair; who can help it? He
> says; nor a nest of anticks? He is loath to make Nature afraid in his

plays, like those that beget *Tales, Tempests,* and such like *Drolleries,* to mix his head with other men's heels. (H&S 6:16).

What had been a veiled attack in *The Alchemist* is in 1614 given a local habitation and a name: *The Winter's Tale* and *The Tempest.* Jonson's drama also represents monstrous vices, but his bestiary is a legitimate one, composed of London's "Bartholomew birds," not the fantastic servant monster Shakespeare had set onstage (Caliban is called "servant monster" repeatedly in *The Tempest,* three times in the opening lines of Act 3, scene 2). Similarly, Jonson's practice excludes the "nest of anticks"—identified by Herford and Simpson and subsequent editors as the scene in *The Winter's Tale* where "twelve Rusticks" enter, "presenting Satyrs" (4.4.334)[39] The Oxford editors go on to argue that *The Tempest* is also implicated in Jonson's attack on the masque-like elements in Shakespeare's romances in the allusion to "Drolleries" and note that the " 'several strange shapes' who bring in the banquet in *The Tempest* III.iii.19, are called by Sebastian 'A living drollery' " (H&S 10:177).

This Induction, probably composed after the Preface to *Every Man in,* was performed before its publication, though published after it. A number of features are peculiar to it and are worth noting. First, the Induction appears in the first play for the public stage that Jonson did not write for the Chamberlain's Men in close to a decade. Since it was written for Elizabeth's Men at "the Hope on the Bankside," Jonson avoids the problem of writing against Shakespeare in a play performed by the King's Men (we have already seen how he gets around this through changes in the published texts of *Every Man out*). Moreover, the object of his attack has already retired, and the Globe itself has recently burned down. More interesting still is the intertextual space Jonson has claimed. Rather than limit himself to a formal dedicatory epistle or prologue, the Induction is both within and outside the formal boundaries of the play—onstage and in print. Shakespeare's recent and not-so-recent work is recalled before the action begins and helps generate the kind of expectations—by negative example—Jonson would seek to overturn or reshape. The allusions are thus intertextual to the extent that they are contained within, and thereby rendered vulnerable by, the "host" text. As with any parody, it is a risky venture. But it is one that Jonson must employ, in part because it is easy not to keep in mind a Shakespearean dramatic universe when paying to see a Jonsonian one. But the meaning of Jonson's play is contingent upon such a comparison, a comparison (or more formally, an intertextual recollection) that is nonetheless displaced to the margins of the play. Parody depends upon our simultaneous exposure to two artistic styles; it does not work unless audiences can keep both in mind at the same time. Jonson accomplishes much the same thing in places like the Induction to *Bartholomew Fair* by reminding his audience of Shakespeare's practice and inviting us to keep it in mind when evaluating his own dramatic style in relation to it in its capacity to represent the "language that men do use" and the "reality" of our everyday experience of the world.

This practice could not be more different than Shakespeare's, whose "anticks" and "drolleries" in the late plays only obliquely call to mind Jonson's practice in the court masques. Where Shakespeare appropriates elements of Jonson's court spectacle and relocates them within the heart of the pastoral visions of romances performed on the public stage, Jonson's parodic response to Shakespeare is guarded and delegated to the margins of a text that takes on Marlowe and other native authors much more directly. In the Induction to *Bartholomew Fair* Jonson depends upon Shakespeare's art to complete the meaning of his own, no less than he would depend upon "Shakespeare" to complete his reputation and legacy in the poems he wrote to pay tribute to his rival in 1623. Needless to say, we can only speculate (although we rarely do) about Shakespeare's response to Jonson's 1616 Folio: did Jonson or the publishers invite him to contribute a dedicatory poem? After all, he had worked alongside Jonson for many years and had acted in some of these plays. Did Shakespeare acquire (or was he sent) a copy of the volume? Was he jealous that his rival's works were so sumptuously preserved, while his were only partially available, often in defective quartos? Once again, how telling was Shakespeare's silence?

☙

In contrast, reading Shakespeare's collected plays in preparation for the 1623 Folio seems to have had a profound impact on Jonson's sense of Shakespeare and on his own work in relationship to what Shakespeare had produced.[40] Again, we can only imagine how Jonson reacted to the news that his silent rival, who had not bothered to see his plays into print, was now posthumously achieving the very thing that Jonson had struggled so hard to achieve: a literary monument that promised to ensure his reputation for posterity.

We do not know the full extent of Jonson's participation in Heminges and Condell's project, though some scholars have speculated that

Jonson had a significant role in the production of the volume. What we do know for sure is that Jonson contributed verses to the collection and that his two poems ("To the Reader" and "To the Memory of My Beloved, William Shakespeare") take pride of place in the Folio. Less well known is the fact that the latter poem was increasingly displaced in the successive Folios, even during Jonson's lifetime. Sharply reduced in size and no longer predominant, "To the Memory of Shakespeare" became just one among many glowing accolades. By the early eighteenth century Jonson no longer stood as Shakespeare's presenter or, in Heminges and Condell's phrase, the first of Shakespeare's "[f]riends, whom if you need, can be your guides."

Purchasers of the first Folio of Shakespeare's work in 1623, though, might have been a bit surprised that the portrait of the artist did not appear on the left hand page as they opened the expensive volume; in a departure from standard Renaissance practice, Shakespeare's portrait was displaced to the facing page. In its place, in large print, was the following ten-line poem, by Ben Jonson:

> This figure, that thou seest put,
> It was for gentle Shakespeare cut,
> Wherein the graver had a strife
> With Nature, to outdo the life;
> Oh, could he but have drawn his wit
> As well in brass, as he hath hit
> His face; the print would then surpass
> All, that was ever writ in brass.
> But since he cannot, reader, look
> Not on his picture, but his book.

(H&S 8:390)

The argument of the poem is a peculiar one: instead of praising the likeness of the Droeshout portrait, the poem insists upon the mimetic failure of the artist to render Shakespeare's "wit" (presumably something that Jonson knew well enough). The effect of the poem runs counter to its ostensible purpose: if this is not Shakespeare, how are we to discover who, or what he is? For Leah Marcus, the critic most attentive to the poem's teasing complexities, "Jonson's poem undermines the visual power of the portrait by insisting on it as something constructed and 'put' there."[41] In so doing, it "sets readers off on a treasure hunt for the author: where is the 'real' author to be found?"[42] The ambiguities and deflections of the poem, I suggest, go even further. Is the "figure" of the opening line Shakespeare himself, his representation in a reversed brass engraving, or perhaps, the rhetorical figuration of the printed poem itself? To what extent does the second line—which specifies that the figure was cut "for" Shakespeare—sustain this ambiguity? The problems persist: Why does the engraver strive with Nature, rather than try to imitate her? What, for that matter, can it mean to "outdo the life"?[43] Why does the poem signal a possible conflation of engraving and writing in the shift from that which is "drawn" to that which is "writ in brass"? And why, finally, are we urged to *not* look on "his picture," the ostensible subject of the poem, "but his book"? The twists in "his" in the closing line do little to resolve the pattern of ambiguous pronoun references to "he" and "his" throughout the poem (e.g., does "his picture" in the closing line refer to Shakespeare or the engraver?)

Part of the strangeness of this short poem derives from the relationship *between* artists imagined by Jonson. The portrait is deemed a double failure: the artist who strives with Nature is outdone by her; moreover, the artist likewise fails to surpass all that ever writ in brass because he cannot draw "his wit." The artist's effort, because of the mimetic limitations, is to be passed over, in favor of Shakespeare's own.

Jonson's address to the readers offers, in condensed and inchoate form, a number of his characteristic strategies. Rather than directly addressing Shakespeare (which he reserves for the longer poem "To the Memory of Shakespeare" that follows) he speaks of his art indirectly, through the mediation of a third artist, in this case no poetaster, but, curiously, a rival with Nature herself in "imitating" Shakespeare. The poem is rife with Jonson's sense of literary engagement in contestatory terms: it is about striving, outdoing, and surpassing, even as Shakespeare himself is imagined as "gentle," a passive figure in all this emulative strife.

If Shakespeare is listed in Jonson's Folio as first among the actors who performed in Jonson's plays, then Jonson (obsessed with the role of the Induction in his own plays) here appropriates that role of Induction to Shakespeare's. There is even a trace in Jonson's poem of the opening Prologue to *Henry V,* which begins by acknowledging the mimetic limitations of certain artistic endeavors and insists that we go beyond the always inadequate visual representation in favor of the imaginative power and wit afforded by language itself. No doubt the irony was lost on Jonson. Regardless, the poem signals Jonson's extreme uncomfortableness with his role of mediator—or in Heminges and Condell's description of the poets writing commendatory verse to the Folio, the roles of 'friend' and 'guide.' At the same time it indicates Jonson's recognition that it is a role he cannot avoid, as Shakespeare had avoided, when he either passed over or was never asked to perform a similar role, eight years before, and already in retirement, for Jonson's *Works*. The poem also includes the outrageous claim that to compass Shakespeare's wit is to surpass all that was ever writ in brass, figuratively, to outdo immortal verse. The ambition to do so is not an engraver's, however, but Jonson's own. And in the long companion poem "To the Memory of Shakespeare" that follows, Jonson undertakes precisely what the artist had failed to do: bring Shakespeare to life, draw his wit, explain not just the face but the nature of the achievement. In doing so, he moves from a trope of figuring to the trope of envy, from "he" to "I."

In the final lines of the Epilogue to *The New Inn* Jonson returned to a lifelong concern with the tension between the death of a writer and the life of his works, when he asserts that "When e're the carcass dies, this art will live" (H&S 6:490). The lines hearken back to those he had translated from Marlowe's version of Ovid's *Elegies* a quarter of a century before in his *Poetaster:*

> Envy the living, not the dead, doth bite:
> For after death all men receive their right.
> Then when this body falls in funeral fire,
> My name shall live, and my best part aspire.

> (H&S 4:208)

In one of the few significant departures from Marlowe's version, Jonson had altered Marlowe's closing couplet ("Then though death rakes my bones in funeral fire,/ I'll live, and as he pulls me down mount higher" [*Poems,* 135]), replacing Marlowe's emphasis on overreaching with one that celebrates the writer's name, and aspiration, as he defeats envy and achieves immortality.[44]

In "To the Memory of Shakespeare" Jonson returns to this Ovidian model and set of concerns:

> To draw no envy (Shakespeare) on thy name,
> Am I thus ample to thy book, and fame:
> While I confess thy writings to be such,
> As neither man, nor muse, can praise too much.
>
> (H&S 8:390)

Any estimation of Shakespeare is predicated on a similar valuation of Jonson himself, so that the the first section of the poem is spent establishing Jonson's credentials, his 'ampleness' to undertake such a task—and suggesting the inadequacy of others who would attempt this praise.

One of the mildly unnerving things about this poem is Jonson's habit of redirecting attention back towards himself at the very moment when he insists that he will finally account for Shakespeare's greatness:

> For if I thought my judgement were of years,
> I should commit thee surely with thy peers,
> And tell, how far thou did'st our Lyly outshine,
> Or sporting Kyd, or Marlowe's mighty line,
>
> (H&S 8:391)

Is it Shakespeare or Jonson that we are asked to compare with Lyly, Kyd, and Marlowe? Or with "Aeschylus, Euripides, and Sophocles"? Or yet another trio, Chaucer, Spenser, and Beaumont?

Sara Van Den Berg, who finds that in "the first half of the poem [Jonson] subdues his own norms to those of Shakespeare,' argues that before Jonson "can write of 'my gentle *Shakespeare*' . . . Jonson must become in some sense Shakespeare's Jonson."[45] I see it in the exact opposite way: before Jonson can write of "my gentle Shakespeare" Shakespeare must become in some sense Jonson's Shakespeare, or, as he himself put it in the *Discoveries, "De Shakespeare nostrat"* (H&S 8:538). It is precisely because Shakespeare is reimagined in Jonsonian terms that Jonson is able to call him, imperiously, "our Shakespeare." For Lawrence Lipking, "Jonson reconstructs Shakespeare in his own image." He does so by "metamorphosing him into, if not a Son, then a Brother of Ben."[46] I would qualify this to say that Jonson reconstructs Shakespeare in the image Jonson has carefully created for himself: one who is to be compared with classical antecedents, whose ends are admonitory, a guiding light to the stage, a reviser, and a born and made poet. As Lipking notes, there is not much of Shakespeare's character, personality, or even his plays that emerge in this poem; these are all either effaced or generalized, so that Shakespeare becomes an abstracted "example": "[d]istilled, perhaps denatured, Shakespeare changes into a humanist's ideal."[47] It is in the third section of the poem, which centers on the mimetic issues of art and nature, that this emerges most clearly:

> For though the poet's matter nature be,
> His art doth give the fashion. And that he
> Who casts to write a living line must sweat
> (Such as thine are) and strike the second heat
> Upon the muses' anvil: turn the same
> (And himself with it) that he thinks to frame;
> Or for the laurel he may gain a scorn:
> For a good poet's made, as well as born;
> And such wert thou. Look how the father's face
> Lives in his issue: even so, the race
> Of Shakespeare's mind and manners brightly shines
> In his well-turned and true-filed line:
> In each of which he seems to shake a lance,
> As brandished at the eyes of ignorance.

(H&S 8:392)

This is Shakespeare new forged on Jonson's anvil. It is a Shakespeare who, like Jonson, revises his work, sweats and reworks his material, aggressively attacking the ignorant, proud of his paternity.

Heminges and Condell inform Folio readers that what Shakespeare "thought, he uttered with that easiness, that we have scarce received from him a blot in his papers" (F1, Sig. A3ᵛ). In the Folio poem, however, Jonson reverses his position in the *Discoveries,* now portraying Shakespeare as reviser of well-turned lines who "must sweat . . . and strike the second heat/Upon the muses' anvil." The need for consistency is superseded by the larger demand of representing Shakespeare as both mirror image and opposite.[48]

Even more remarkably, Jonson imagines a Shakespeare as obsessed as he himself is with self-fashioning or framing, who in his acts of revision must "turn the same/ (And himself with it) that he thinks to frame" (H&S 8:392). Jonson here conflates poetic revision and poetic self-creation, reversing the old saying that a poet is born not made (in contrast to what he had once written in *Every Man in*); in Shakespeare's case the poet is "made, as well as born." But made by whom?

These thoughts upon the fashioning of the writer lead, not surprisingly, to thoughts of the laureateship. Here, though, the same impulse is projected onto Shakespeare who "for the laurel he may gain a scorn" (H&S 8:392). Shakespeare is reconceived as a claimant and competitor for the laureateship, and in extending this conception of literary success and succession he is also cast in the patriarchal terms by which Jonson, with his sons and tribe of Ben, imagined himself: "Look how the father's face/ Lives in his issue"(H&S:392).

Shakespeare is next imagined as a poet intent on moral reclamation. His very name signals this didactic impulse: reading Shakespeare's "well-turned and true-filed" lines, Jonson discovers a poet who, like himself, "seems to shake a lance,/ As brandished at the eyes of ignorance" (H&S 8:392). The "gentle" Shakespeare mentioned earlier in the poem has become an aggressive and armed one, cast once again in one of Jonson's characteristic (militaristic) images. Schoenbaum reminds us that "these lines apply more aptly to Jonson than they do to Shakespeare, who wages no campaign against ignorance. Self-congratulation is the sincerest form of compliment."[49]

And if, in the concluding lines of the poem, through Jonson's agency Shakespeare is metamorphosed into a constellation, a "star of poets," his new role remains Jonson's accustomed one: the "gentle" Shakespeare must "with rage/ Or influence chide or cheer the drooping stage" (H&S 8:392). In such a light, Dryden's stricture against Jonson's poem — that it was "an insolent, sparing, and invidious panegyric"[50] — misses the mark. The question is not whether Jonson is meanspirited or "loved the man and [did] honor his memory (on this side idolatry) as much as any" (H&S 8:584). In retrospect, it matters less what Jonson meant than in what terms he has introduced Shakespeare to us. And the "Shakespeare" he presents in this preface to what Shakespeare "Hath Left Us" — sounds a lot like the "Jonson" he would have wished to offer to posterity, a Jonson busily writing his own epitaph — even as this assertion is carefully hedged by the repeated qualifications that Shakespeare's dramatic practice is opposed to Jonson's.

◈

EPILOGUE

THE IMPACT OF Jonson's version of "Shakespeare" (and of "Jonson") would be considerable, not only on the reception of their work, but also on poetic self-representation and the making of the canon of English literature and criticism for the next two hundred years. To describe this legacy would require another (and considerably larger) volume.[51] A few key illustrations, though, give some indication of how the vocabulary through which this poetic rivalry was constructed became the basis for radically different poetic controversies and canonical disputes.

With John Dryden, in the late seventeenth century, we arrive at a crossroads. After Milton in his first published poem ("On Shakespeare," which first appeared in the 1632 Folio) had turned Jonson's own terminology against him in an epitaph to a Shakespeare whose "easy numbers flow" to "the shame of [Jonson's] slow-endeavoring art," Dryden helped harden these binary categories into fixed critical positions.[52] This is not to argue that Dryden's own relationship to Shakespeare and Jonson, any more than Milton's, was formulaic or reductive. A quick glance at his *All for Love,* his version of *Antony and Cleopatra* "written in imitation of Shakespeare's style," but no less deeply indebted to Jonsonian dramatic principles, indicates that for Dryden, it was not simply a matter of consciously choosing between the two.[53] And, as a practicing playwright, he had to confront Shakespeare's and Jonson's legacies not only as literary predecessors, but also as fierce competitors for the patronage of Restoration theatergoers.

While Dryden was clearly torn between the dramatic models that had come to be identified with Jonson and Shakespeare, the critical principles that Jonson espoused (though not necessarily followed himself) proved congenial to Dryden's defense of dramatic art:

> If I would compare [Jonson] with Shakespeare, I must acknowledge him the more correct poet, but Shakespeare the greater wit. Shakespeare was the Homer, or father of our dramatic poets; Jonson was the Virgil, the pattern of elaborate writing. I admire him, but I love Shakespeare.[54]

The passage is justly famous. What is often forgotten is the context of the remarks: Dryden's obligation in his *Essay of Dramatic Poesie* to defend modern against classical, English against French, and rhyme against blank verse. Jonson provides a handy (and almost complete) solution to Dryden's difficult task, insofar as his classicism at once solves the problem of ancients vs. moderns, and his strong sense of rules for composing plays signals an English victory over the French. For Dryden, Jonson

> has given us the most correct plays, so in the precepts which he has laid down in his *Discoveries*, we have as many and profitable rules for perfecting the stage as any wherewith the French can furnish us.[55]

Dryden must finesse the third part of his argument, since the play he analyzes at length to confirm his argument—Jonson's *Epicoene*—was written in prose (though as a comedy it happily stands outside the debate over the proper verse form for a serious play). Jonson's Roman tragedies, Dryden notes, "showed Ben no enemy to this way of writing" (i.e., rhymed couplets). It therefore served Dryden's immediate ends to represent Jonson as "the most learned and judicious writer which any theater ever had" and "deeply conversant in the Ancients." In making this claim, however, Dryden has to dismiss both the Caroline Jonson ("for his last plays were but his dotages") and the Elizabethan plays that he had written "unsuccessfully" before *Every Man in His Humour*. Dryden prefers, instead, to consider Jonson at the point in his career when "he was himself" [sic]. Shakespeare emerges as Jonson's foil: one who was "naturally learned" and drew the "images of nature . . . not laboriously, but luckily." Whereas in Jonson's labored art "you find little to retrench or alter," Shakespeare "is many times flat, insipid; his comic wit degenerating into clenches, his serious swelling into bombast."[56] The critical terms first offered by Jonson at the turn of the century proved elastic enough to resolve Dryden's critical dilemma in the Restoration.

A generation later Alexander Pope, perhaps less attuned to the specific critical demands that explain Dryden's willingness to accept the binary oppositions concerning "Jonson" and "Shakespeare" inherited from Jonson (and free from the anxieties of a practicing playwright), expresses considerable surprise at how these assertions about their difference had hardened into fact. In his edition of Shakespeare's *Works* in 1725 he asserts that these dichotomies are false and derive from partisan poetics. Pope's remarks are worth quoting at length:

> I am inclined to think, this opinion proceeded originally from the zeal of the partisans of our author and Ben Jonson; as they endeav-

oured to exalt the one at the expense of the other. It is ever the nature of parties to be in extremes; and nothing is so probable as that because Ben Jonson had the most learning, it was said on the one hand that Shakespeare had none at all; and because Shakespeare had much the most wit and fancy, it was retorted on the other, that Jonson wanted both. Because Shakespeare borrowed nothing, it was said that Ben Jonson borrowed everything. Because Jonson did not write extempore, he was reproached with being a year about every piece; and because Shakespeare wrote with ease and rapidity, they cried, he never once made a blot. Nay the spirit of opposition ran so high, that whatever those of the one side objected to the other, was taken at the rebound, and turned into praises; as injudiciously, as their antagonists before had made them objections. . . . But however this contention might be carried on by the partisans on either side, I cannot help thinking these two great poets were good friends, and lived on amiable terms and in offices of society with each other.[57]

As for the claim that Shakespeare never blotted out a line, Pope, who edited Shakespeare, knew that "in reality (however it has prevailed) there never was a more groundless report, or to the contrary of which there are more undeniable evidences."[58]

Nevertheless, while disabusing us of this truism, Pope reinforced others. For example, he turns Rowe's story about Shakespeare's early patronage of Jonson into "fact" and writes elsewhere of Shakespeare as imitator that: "If ever any author deserved the name of an original, it was Shakespeare. . . . The poetry of Shakespeare was inspiration indeed: he is not so much an imitator, as an instrument, of Nature."[59] He builds here on Rowe, who wrote that "Shakespeare, on the other hand, was beholding to nobody farther than the foundation of the tale, the incidents were often his own, and the writing entirely so."[60] Despite Pope's complaint, the image of the dramatists as mighty opposites was too convenient, the neat dichotomies too attractive to jettison. Reinforced by anecdotes recorded by Fuller and others, it continued to hold the field.

Samuel Johnson's immensely influential *Preface to Shakespeare* (1765) offers a more original, indeed radical, reappraisal of Shakespeare's worth, one that subsequent Romantic critics—including Coleridge, Hazlitt, and Schlegel—would feel compelled to challenge. G. F. Parker's recent *Johnson's Shakespeare* reveals just how vital Shakespeare was for Johnson's assertion of independence from the neoclassical dramatic theories of Dryden, Rapin, Gildon, Theobold, and Hurd and for clarifying his own sense of what it meant to be a poet of "nature."[61] Ironically, for Parker, Dr. Johnson's appropriation of the by now fixed critical vocabulary (e.g., that "Shakespeare is above all writers . . . the poet of nature," that his "drama is the mirror of life," and, in a reversal of Jonson's claim to speak of language of men, that "Addison speaks the language of poets, Shakespeare of men")[62] condemned Johnson to being misread, not only by the Romantics, but also by twentieth-century editors, who have recentered Johnson within the very tradition he had gone far towards repudiating in *The Preface*. Parker's study convincingly shows that the idea of "Nature" that Dr. Johnson speaks of had undergone a sea change in the century and a half since Ben Jonson had invoked the term in the 1623 Folio. Jonson's influential terminology would prove, once again, both a springboard to critical independence and a trap from which even the strongest of critical minds would find it difficult to escape (or escape misunderstanding).

By the early nineteenth century " 'Shakespeare' and 'Jonson' " would be reintroduced as surrogates in a confrontation between Coleridge and Wordsworth that helped shape the next great work of English literary criticism, the *Preface to Lyrical Ballads* (1802). In a remarkable piece of literary detective work, Anne Barton has shown how Wordsworth's exposure to Jonson in that year (through volume 4 of Robert Anderson's *British Poets* which contained an introduction that promoted the inherited view of Jonson and his relationship to Shakespeare) enabled him to clarify his own artistic endeavor, both in the poems and critical prose he was producing at this time. So that Wordsworth's revised *Preface to Lyrical Ballads* appropriates the Jonsonian claim to "a selection of language really used by men," recalling Jonson's earlier call for "language, such as men do use" in his own revised Prologue to *Every Man in.*[63]

Wordsworth and Coleridge fought on Friday, March 19, 1802. And Dorothy Wordsworth records the cause: "they disputed," she wrote, "about Ben Jonson."[64] Barton goes on to summarize how these crucial predecessors became the measure of the differences between their Romantic sucessors:

> There can be little doubt about the general lines along which such
> an argument between Wordsworth and Coleridge would have been
> conducted, or about the terms of the opposition: Jonson versus
> Shakespeare, matter of fact as opposed to symbolic poetry, short
> poems against long, a plain against a metaphoric style, poetry as

independent of metre versus poetry as something generically distinct from prose, a selection of the very language of men running full tilt against Coleridge's growing conviction that poetry ought itself to create new linguistic combinations and modes. Jonson must have served as a catalyst, polarizing the thinking of the two men, and bringing them to a painful understanding of how far they had grown apart since the Alfoxen days.[65]

Like his predecessors, Wordsworth chose from the pool of critical dichotomies selectively: in positioning himself against Coleridge he was the advocate of Jonsonian brevity, fact, and plain style (though when defining himself against Pope he would identify with the Shakespearean side of the equation, insisting on the naturalness of his artistic genius when juxtaposed with the highly artificial style of his neoclassical precursor). At the risk of offering a generalization that builds upon Barton's own generalized account of an unrecorded dispute, it seems clear that the set of oppositions Jonson invents—"Jonson" and "Shakespeare"—had become flexible enough to serve once more as the basis for emerging critical and poetic differences. Thus, to pick just one example, Jonson's opposition of "Nature" and "Art," for instance, would be quietly conflated by subsequent critics with the distinction between 'native' and 'classical.' This procedure enabled them to juxtapose such concepts as: borrowed learning vs. native genius, Latinate and vernacular style, and classical (as opposed to native) dramatic sources, structures, and genres. Although these opposing categories had little to do with their origins in the rivalry between Elizabethan dramatists, they nonetheless helped frame Restoration, Enlightenment, and Romantic critical debates that continued to provide a basis for the distinctions between writers and traditions through the nineteenth and twentieth centuries.

It would be a mistake to conclude by suggesting that our own critical age has been free of this kind of reductiveness. The portraits of Shakespeare and Jonson have not changed all that much since the days of Dryden, Johnson, and Wordsworth. We need to recognize the constructedness of both "Jonson" and "Shakespeare," and we also need to ask why we have chosen to accept traditional versions of their development as dramatists. When we think of the masque, or Rome, or Plautine form, or prose comedy, why is it that Jonson, and not Shakespeare, first comes to mind? Likewise, when the subject is romance comedy, bombast, revenge drama, or Richard Crookback, why is it that Shakespeare, and not Jonson, instinctively registers? Why do we hesitate to think of Jonson as the consummately native dramatist, steeped in the morality, romantic, and revenge traditions of early Elizabethan drama, and the great heir to Kyd and Marlowe; or as a masterful versifier (rather than simply the "master of prose comedy"), comfortable in every metrical form ranging from fourteeners to deflating rhymed couplets? And why do we hesitate to read Shakespeare as a dramatist who from the outset to the end of his career can be seen as deeply situated within a classical tradition, from his early Plautine and Terentian comedies and Ovidian and Senecan tragedy, through the *Tempest*'s flirtation with neoclassical dramatic rules? Or as a writer who would exhibit throughout his career an abiding concern with Roman history and politics? The lines dividing their artistic practice could easily be redrawn in any numbers of ways. The issue remains: if we are to break out of these constraining and constructed ways of thinking about their respective careers and dramatic output we also need to consider what purpose these divisions serve us institutionally, especially in relationship to the canon of authors that we teach, stage, and anthologize.

In the introductory chaper I argued, following critics like Margaret Rose and Linda Hutcheon, that parody is an encapsulated form of literary critical history, "an inscription of literary-historical continuity" and a "custodian of the artistic legacy."[66] In concluding, I wonder now if it is not the other way around. Insofar as literary critical history, when concerned with canon formation, proceeds by reducing a poet's art to a set of readily definable features that fit within a neat preexisting scheme of self-confirming and self-contained values, that criticism could be seen as simply a vastly expanded (and authorized) version of parody. What began in the interpersonal and inscrutable encounter between the minds and hearts of rival Elizabethan writers has resulted (through the workings of a literary history whose basis is belated, reductive, and ultimately parodic) in restrictive ways of thinking about their work that continue to frustrate our abilities to pluck out the heart of its mystery.

Marlowe, meanwhile, for a variety of reasons (including the processes by which the canon of dramatists was formed), disappeared from the equation. By the Restoration his plays were no longer staged and no longer published. He is ignored by Dryden, Pope, and Johnson. When in 1804 Wordsworth wrote to Charles Lamb in London about the availability of the works of Elizabethan dramatists Lamb noted that "Marlowe's plays and poems are totally vanished; only one edition of Dodsley retains one, and the other two, of his plays."[67] Marlowe was missing, too, from the portrait of Shakespeare, Jonson, and their fellow poets and dramatists, painted by John Faed and popularized in the subsequent engraving of his brother James Faed in the 1850s [see figure 1].[68] Faed's engraving reinforces the neat dichotomy that characterizes descriptions of the rival poets: seated across from each other at the Mermaid are the two giants of the period, Shakespeare and Jonson. Surrounding them are authors such as Dekker, Donne, Chapman, and Raleigh. Clearly, the ghost of Marlowe hovers about the room. It might help to think of the scene as the denouement of a murder mystery, "Who Killed Kit Marlowe?" All the possible perpetrators are gathered together. And it turns out that each had a hand, along with Faed and others who perpetuated in this canonizing portrait the myths that had hardened into poetic opposition and hierarchy. It is a static portrait, one that might lead us to forget that literary relations and especially the problem of influence are the kind of things critics try to systematize and categorize. But they remain messy, fluid, often inscrutable.

Missing from Faed's representation of these authors are the very features that made the interaction between their works so vital, as writers picked up what weapons come to hand in their attempts to surpass each other and clear enough space for themselves. Sometimes, these weapons were physical ones (as when Jonson beat Marston); more typically, they were verbal or visual parody, the imposition of poetasters, or attacks on another's personal or writing habits. The fantasy setting in the Mermaid tavern can help us forget the institutional forces in play in the late sixteenth and early seventeenth centuries, forces that shaped how writers sold their work, perished, or languished in debtor's prison (which is where Dekker probably was when this portrait would have been taken). Left out too are the dynamics created by the broader socioeconomic climate, especially the nascent capitalistic practices of the theater that mirror the changing economic landscape of early modern England. To its credit, Faed's portrait at least hints at the ways in which the personalities of authors mattered in the making of the canon and in the kind of influence that was practiced, though here too, we are offered visual equivalents of the critical reductiveness we have found elsewhere: the open, gentle Shakespeare, the anxious Jonson, the romantic Donne, etc.

In a recent study Robert S. Knapp asks why none of Marlowe's "plays begins a lineage" and why Marlowe's achievement "inspired so little repetition."[69] In challenging such critical assumptions in this study, I have tried to explain how Marlowe, whose works resisted easy imitation, ultimately proved more vulnerable to the more inclusive appropriations of Shakespeare and of Jonson. And yet as critics now ask new questions of Shakespeare's and Jonson's work—questions about genre, authority, sexuality, power, subjectivity, and violence—it is no surprise that it is to the trangressive and uneasy Marlovian aspects of their works to which they frequently turn.

Marlowe did not create a school, but the pressure of his influence continues to prove consequential. Jonson, who did everything in his power to establish a tribe of Ben, failed to realign English drama in his footsteps. Shakespeare, who neither resisted imitation nor sought to establish a literary dynasty, became the most influential, and yet peculiarly inimitable, of the three. The best that can be said with any confidence is that the issue of this complex exchange—the canon of English Renaissance drama currently anthologized, taught, and occasionally staged—is powerfully marked by the confrontation among three remarkable Elizabethan artists who measured their own and each other's accomplishments within a complex configuration of literary, personal, commercial, and historical relations. Rivals with each other, it is fair to say that they have not been rivaled since.

NOTES

1. INTRODUCTION

1. The best accounts of Marlowe's reputation are still Tucker Brooke, "The Reputation of Christopher Marlowe," *Transactions of the Connecticut Academy of Arts and Sciences* 25 (1922): 347–408; and F. S. Boas, *Christopher Marlowe: A Biographical and Critical Study* (Oxford: Clarendon Press, 1940), pp. 294–306. Also helpful are: Millar MacClure, ed., *Marlowe: The Critical Heritage 1588–1896* (London: Routledge & Kegan Paul, 1979); John T. Shawcross, "Signs of the Times: Christopher Marlowe's Decline in the Seventeenth Century"; and Lois Potter, "Marlowe in the Civil War and Commonwealth: Some Allusions and Parodies," the latter two in *"A Poet and a filthy Play-maker": New Essays on Christopher Marlowe,* Kenneth Friedenreich, Roma Gill, and Constance B. Kuriyama, eds. (New York: AMS Press, 1988), pp. 63–72 and 73–82, respectively.

2. Jonson's fantasy of setting fire to his rivals' works was ironically reversed some years later when his own library, including much unpublished work, went up in smoke. Jonson's account of this disaster in "An Execration upon Vulcan" turns on canonical concerns similar to those expressed in *Every Man in*. This time, however, he complains that Vulcan's ire was misdirected: unlike contemporary prose romances or trifling verse that merit destruction, Jonson's worthier efforts—except, he concedes, an unfinished play—should have been spared (H&S 8:202–12).

3. As quoted in E. K. Chambers, *William Shakespeare,* 2 vols. (Oxford: Clarendon Press, 1930), 2:188, from *A Groatsworth of Wit* (1592).

4. *The Compact Edition of the Oxford English Dictionary,* 2 vols. (Oxford: Oxford University Press, 1971), 2:2082.

5. Linda Hutcheon, *A Theory of Parody: The Teachings of Twentieth-Century Art Forms* (London: Methuen, 1985), p. 32.

6. Hutcheon, *Parody,* p. 109.

7. Hutcheon, *Parody,* p. 35.

8. Hutcheon, *Parody,* pp. 75 and 102.

9. The subtitle of Hutcheon's book—*The Teachings of Twentieth-Century Art Forms*—clearly signals her intention to define parody as a peculiarly modern strategy, ideally suited to contemporary artistic and critical concerns with ironic distance, self-reflexivity, and intertextuality. Other critics, like Margaret Rose, have also argued for parody as a modern phenomenon (see *Parody//Metafiction* (London: Croom Helm, 1979). For Rose parody is grounded in a Foucauldian "mode of discontinuity" that contrasts with Hutcheon's emphasis on what a culture passes on (Hutcheon, p. 20).

10. It is worthwhile at this point distinguishing my definition from that used by other scholars writing about "parody" in Elizabethan drama. For example, Joan Hartwig in *Shakespeare's Analogical Scene* (Lincoln: University of Nebraska Press, 1983) looks at the way that parody operates *within* rather than *between* plays. In an effort to refocus attention on the thematic relevance and resonance of so-called minor scenes, often cut in production, Hartwig argues that these scenes parody, sometimes proleptically, the major plots and themes of the play. I would prefer to restrict my definition of parody to intertextual allusions between the works of different authors. Yet I would not go so far as Robert Watson, who in his *Jonson's Parodic Strategy* (Cambridge: Harvard University Press, 1987), focuses primarily on Jonson's response to contemporary genres (e.g., romantic comedy, revenge tragedy), rather than on personal encounters with rival playwrights. The analyses that follow, while sensitive to the self-parody that interests Hartwig, and to the broader generic parody at the heart of Watson's work, focus on the ways that authors responded to personal rivals and specific plays.

11. *Hamlet* 3.2.1, ff. Also see David Bevington, *Action Is Eloquence: Shakespeare's Language of Gesture* (Cambridge, Mass.: Harvard University Press, 1984).

12. Among the most influential of these are Jonathan Dollimore, *Radical Tragedy* (Chicago: University of Chicago Press, 1984); Catherine Belsey, *The Subject of Tragedy* (New York: Methuen, 1985); Joseph Lowenstein, "The Script in the Marketplace," *Representations* 12 (1985):101–14; Stephen Greenblatt, *Renaissance Self-Fashioning* (Chicago: University of Chicago Press, 1980) and *Shakespearean Negotiations* (Berkeley and Los Angeles: University of California Press, 1988); and three collections: Patricia Parker and Geoffrey Hartman, eds., *Shakespeare and the Question of Theory* (New York: Methuen, 1985); Greenblatt, ed., *Representing the English Renaissance* (Berkeley and Los Angeles: University of California Press, 1988); and Dollimore and Alan Sinfield, eds., *Political Shakespeare* (Ithaca, N.Y.: Cornell University Press, 1985). For an early and still useful study of what Elizabethan writers themselves had to say about imitation, authorship, and literary property rights, see Harold Ogden White, *Plagiarism and Imitation During the English Renaissance* (Cambridge, Mass.: Harvard University Press, 1935; rpt. New York: Octagon Books, 1965).

13. See, for example, John Webster's preface to *The White Devil* (c. 1610–12), where he offers his "good opinion of other men's worthy labors, especially of that full and heightened style of Master Chapman, the labored and understanding works of Master Jonson; the no less worthy composures of the both worthily excellent master Beaumont, and Master Fletcher; and lastly . . . the right happy and copius industry of Master Shakespeare, Master Dekker, and Master Heywood, wishing what I write may be read by their light." Webster concludes his acknowledgments with a canonizing flourish: "*non norunt, haec monumenta mori*," 'these monuments do not know how to

die.' (As cited in John Russell Brown, ed., *The White Devil* [Cambridge, Mass.: Harvard University Press, 1960], p. 4).

14. For an account of the *Eastward Ho* incident, see H&S 1:38-39.

15. See G. E. Bentley, *The Profession of Dramatist in Shakespeare's Time* (Princeton, N.J.: Princeton University Press, 1971), p. 199.

16. Cited in MacClure, *Critical Heritage*, p. 35.

17. For an extended discussion of playhouse audiences see Andrew Gurr, *Playgoing in Shakespeare's London* (Cambridge, England: Cambridge University Press, 1987); Ann Jennalie Cook, *The Privileged Playgoers of Shakespeare's London* (Princeton, N.J.: Princeton University Press, 1981); and Martin Butler's reply to Cook, "Shakespeare's Unprivileged Playgoers," in *Theatre and Crisis 1632-42* (Cambridge, England: Cambridge University Press, 1984), pp. 293-306.

18. Drayton writes of Marlowe having "in him those brave translunary things/That the first Poets had." As cited in MacClure, *Critical Heritage*, p. 47, from "To my Most Dearly-Loved Friend Henry Reynolds, Esquire, of Poets and Poesie" (1627).

19. For an incisive consideration of Jacobean and Caroline nostalgia, see Anne Barton's chapter "Harking back to Elizabeth: Jonson and Caroline nostalgia," in *Ben Jonson, Dramatist* (Cambridge, England: Cambridge University Press, 1984), pp. 300-320; and Martin Butler, *Theatre and Crisis,* esp. the chapter on "The survival of the popular tradition," pp. 181-250.

20. Thomas M. Greene, *The Light in Troy* (New Haven, Conn.: Yale University Press, 1982), pp. 45-46. Also see G. W. Pigman III, "Imitation and the Renaissance Sense of the Past: the Reception of Erasmus' *Ciceronianus*," *Journal of Medieval and Renaissance Studies* 9 (1979):155-77; and "Versions of Imitation in the Renaissance," *Renaissance Quarterly* 33 (1980):1-32; David Quint, *Versions of the Source* (New Haven, Conn.: Yale University Press, 1983); and Howard Felperin, *Shakespearean Representation* (Princeton, N.J.: Princeton University Press, 1978).

21. Harold Bloom, *The Anxiety of Influence* (New York: Oxford University Press, 1973), pp. 11 and 27. Bloom is now at work on a project on Shakespeare and originality.

22. Nashe, *Works,* Ronald B. McKerrow, ed., 5 vols. (Oxford: Basil Blackwell, 1904-10; rpt., F. P. Wilson, ed., 1958), 1:319.

23. R. S. Forsythe, "'The Passionate Shepherd' and English Poetry," *PMLA* 40 (1925):692-742.

24. See Fredson Bowers, ed., *The Complete Works of Christopher Marlowe,* 2 vols. (Cambridge, England: Cambridge University Press, 1973), 2: 519-33; 536-37.

25. Bowers, ed., *Marlowe's Works,* 2:527.

26. Bowers, ed., *Marlowe's Works,* 2:536.

27. For a valuable account of how this is played out in terms of the dynamics of manneristic and baroque styles, see James V. Mirollo, "Three Versions of the Pastoral Invitation to Love," *Mannerism and Renaissance Poetry* (New Haven, Conn.: Yale University Press, 1984), pp. 160-178.

28. Bowers, ed., *Marlowe's Works,* 2:542.

29. While we have no firm date for the earliest version of "The Passionate Shepherd," the appearance of this parodic version as early as 1589 would point to a

very early dating of the poem, perhaps from Marlowe's Cambridge days. Additional evidence for the early dating of this lyric is another, less specific parodic recollection, where the invitation to love is replaced by an invitation to arms by Marlowe's militant shepherd in *Tamburlaine, Part Two:*

> Well done, my boy! Thou shalt have shield and lance,
> Armour of proof, horse, helm, and cuttle-axe,
> And I will teach thee how to charge the foe,
> And harmless run among the deadly pikes.
> If thou wilt love the wars and follow me,
> Thou shalt be made a king and reign with me,
> Keeping in iron cages emperors.
> If thou exceed thy elder brothers' worth,
> And shine in complete virtue more than they,
> Thou shalt be king before them, and thy seed
> Shall issue crowned from their mother's womb.

$$(1.4.45-55)$$

Shields, armor, and cuttle-axes have replaced slippers, gowns, and kirtles. It is not enough for his sons to go to war: they must "love the wars and follow me."

30. Ezra Pound, *ABC of Reading* (New York: New Directions, 1960), p. 72.

31. Brooke, "Reputation," p. 365.

32. Brooke, "Reputation," p. 362.

33. R. C. concludes: "You shall find also how studious he is to follow him in those many quick and short sentences at the close of his fancy, with which he everywhere doth adorn his writings" (As cited in Brooke, "Reputation," p. 362).

34. As cited in Brooke, "Reputation," p. 362.

35. C. S. Lewis, "'Hero and Leander,'" *Proceedings of the British Academy* 38 (1952):23–37; rpt. in Paul Alpers, ed. *Elizabethan Poetry: Modern Essays in Criticism* (New York: Oxford University Press, 1967), p. 240.

36. Bowers, ed., *Marlowe's Works,* 2:428, n. 2, italics mine.

37. In his address "To the Common Reader" in his translation of *The Divine Poem of Musaeus* (1616), as cited in Richard Hooper, ed., *Batrachomyomachia, Hymns and Epigrams. Hesiod's Works and Days. Musaeus' Hero and Leander. Juvenal's First Satire.* Trans. George Chapman (London: John Russell Smith, 1858), p. 213.

38. See Louis Martz, ed., *Hero and Leander* by Christopher Marlowe (New York: Johnson Reprint Co., and Washington D.C.: The Folger Shakespeare Library, 1972), pp. 1–14.

39. Cited from *The Selected Plays of Thomas Middleton,* David L. Frost, ed. (Cambridge, England: Cambridge University Press, 1978), 1.2.49–50.

40. All too little is known of Nashe's personal and professional dealings with Marlowe. The title page of *Dido, Queen of Carthage* indicates that sometime around 1590 they had collaborated, but the nature of that collaboration is unclear. Unfortunately, the poetic epitaph that Nashe is reported to have written on Marlowe is lost (see McKerrow's discussion in Nashe, *Works,* 2:335–37).

41. Nashe, *Works*, 3:195.

42. Nashe, *Works*, 3:195.

43. G. R. Hibbard, *Thomas Nashe* (Cambridge, Mass.: Harvard University Press, 1962), p. 245.

44. Nashe, *Works*, 3:196.

45. Nashe, *Works*, 3:201.

46. Peter Berek, "'Tamburlaine's Weak Sons': Imitation as Interpretation before 1593," *Renaissance Drama* n.s. 13 (1982):58.

47. J. S. Cunningham, ed., *Tamburlaine the Great* (Manchester: University of Manchester Press, 1981), p. 65.

48. See Cunningham, ed., *Tamburlaine*, p. 66.

49. Cunningham, ed., *Tamburlaine*, p. 65.

50. Roy W. Battenhouse, *Marlowe's "Tamburlaine"* (Nashville: Vanderbilt University Press, 1941; rpt. 1964), preface to second printing, p. xi.

51. Battenhouse, *Marlowe's "Tamburlaine"*, p. 253.

52. William Empson, *Faustus and the Censor: The English Faust-book and Marlowe's Doctor Faustus*, recovered and edited with an introduction and postscript by John Henry Jones (Oxford: Basil Blackwell, 1987).

53. As cited in MacClure, *Critical Heritage*, p. 29, from *Perimedes the Blacksmith* (1588).

54. Una Ellis-Fermor, "A Note on Their Relations as Dramatic Artists," in *Studies in Honor of T. W. Baldwin*, Don Cameron Allen, ed. (Urbana: University of Illinois Press, 1958), p. 138. Greene would later regain some lost ground in *Orlando Furioso* (c. 1591?), where he reveals a strong enough grasp of Marlowe's style to attempt a legitimate parody (though here too, it is not entirely clear what is merely derivative, what parodic).

55. Irving Ribner, "Greene's Attack on Marlowe: Some Light on *Alphonsus* and *Selimus*," *Studies in Philology* 52 (1955):162–71.

56. David Bevington even speculates that (if the play does echo *Tamburlaine*) "*Wounds* is a specific rejoinder to Marlowe's seductive heterodoxy," *Tudor Drama and Politics* (Cambridge, Mass.: Harvard University Press, 1968), p. 234.

57. Thomas Dekker, *A Knight's Conjuring* (1607) (Percy Society Reprints [London, 1842]), p. 76.

58. Brooke, "Reputation," p. 384.

59. As cited in Kennneth Muir, "Marlowe and Shakespeare," in *"A Poet and a filthy Play-maker,"* p. 1.

2. MARLOWE AND JONSON

1. T. S. Eliot, "Ben Jonson," *Selected Essays* (London: Faber and Faber, 1932), p. 154. It first appeared in 1919.

2. For a recent exception, see James A. Riddell's balanced account in "Ben Jonson and 'Marlowes mighty line,'" in *"A Poet and a filthy Play-maker,"* Kenneth Friendenreich, Roma Gill, and Constance Kuriyama, eds. (New York: AMS Press, 1988), pp. 37–48.

3. See, for example, Richard S. Peterson, *Imitation and Praise in the Poetry of Ben Jonson* (New Haven, Conn,: Yale University Press, 1981); Thomas M. Greene,

The Light in Troy (New Haven, Conn,: Yale University Press, 1982); Katherine Eisaman Maus, *Ben Jonson and the Roman Frame of Mind* (Princeton, N. J.: Princeton University Press, 1984); and Douglas Duncan, *Ben Jonson and the Lucianic Tradition* (Cambridge, England: Cambridge University Press, 1979).

4. Important exceptions, emphasizing Jonson's development in relation to native dramatic traditions, are offered by Alvin Kernan, Robert Watson, and especially Anne Barton, whose illuminating chapter on "Jonson and the Elizabethans" proved an important point of departure for this study (though Barton does not deal at any length with Jonson's debt to Marlowe). Kernan's foreword to *Two Renaissance Mythmakers: Christopher Marlowe and Ben Jonson, Selected Papers from the English Institute, 1975—76* (Baltimore: The Johns Hopkins University Press, 1977), in which he alludes to Marlowe and Jonson in terms of the succession of "a great tragic mythmaker" by "a great comic mythmaker," offers a suggestive link between Marlowe and Jonson studies. Robert Watson's *Jonson's Parodic Strategy* (Cambridge, Mass.: Harvard University Press, 1987) provides a valuable account of Jonson's parodic response to the generic styles of his Elizabethan predecessors in his comedies, though it does not address the issue of Marlowe's influence directly. For a useful account of Jonson's relationship to an earlier native tradition, see Robert C. Evans, "Ben Jonson's Chaucer," *ELR* 19 (1989):324—45.

5. For alternative and cogent readings of Jonson's development as a dramatist (but which often follow Jonson's own revisionist procedure), see W. David Kay, "The Shaping of Ben Jonson's Career," *Modern Philology* 67 (1970):224—37; Richard Helgerson, *Self-Crowned Laureates* (Berkeley and Los Angeles: University of California Press, 1983); George E. Rowe, *Distinguishing Jonson: Imitation, Rivalry, and the Direction of a Dramatic Career* (Lincoln: University Of Nebraska Press, 1988); and David Riggs, *Ben Jonson: A Life* (Cambridge, Mass.: Harvard University Press, 1989). For a revisionist view closer to my own position, see Douglas M. Lanier, "Brainchildren: Self-representation and Patriarchy in Ben Jonson's Early Works," in *Renaissance Papers, 1986*, Dale B. J. Randall and Joseph A. Porter, eds. (Durham, N. C.: The Southern Renaissance Conference, 1986), pp. 53—68.

6. Eliot, "Ben Jonson," p. 147.

7. So much so, that, for instance, when Jonson does mention a woman writer, he does so to question her authorship. Thus, for example: "Sir P. Sidney had translated some of the *Psalms,* which went abroad under the name of the Countess of Pembroke" (H&S 1:138).

8. See, for example, Joe Lee Davis, *The Sons of Ben* (Detroit: Wayne State University Press, 1967); and Claude J. Summers and Ted-Larry Pebworth, *Classic and Cavalier: Essays on Jonson and the Sons of Ben* (Pittsburgh: Pittsburgh University Press, 1982).

9. Sigmund Freud, *The Standard Edition of the Complete Works,* trans. James Strachey, et al., 24 vols. (London: Hogarth, 1953—74), 11:247.

10. Jesse Franklin Bradley and Joseph Quincy Adams, *The Jonson Allusion Book* (New Haven, Conn.: Yale University Press, 1922), p. 6.

11. Anne Barton, *Ben Jonson, Dramatist* (Cambridge, England: Cambridge University Press, 1984), p. 18.

12. Barton, *Ben Jonson,* pp. 18—28.

13. F. S. Boas, ed., *The Works of Thomas Kyd* (Oxford: Clarendon Press, 1901), pp. 95–96.

14. Subsequently expanded to "He died, and left it unfinished." See the discussion in H&S, 7:53–54.

15. Henslowe records a payment for two "suits . . . for the play of *Mortimer*" [i.e., *Edward II*], in R. A. Foakes and R. T. Rickert, eds. *Henslowe's Diary* (Cambridge, England: Cambridge University Press, 1961), p. 205.

16. A dissenting view is offered by Barton (*Ben Jonson,* pp. 338–40), who dismisses the Oxford editors' assertion that "it is clearly early work" (H&S 7:53) and follows an earlier tradition that considered it "the last draught of Jonson's quill."

17. Take, for example, the simple exchange in which Caius Silius and Titus Sabinus "Hail" each other in the play's opening line. Jonson's note in the right-hand margin of the 1605 Quarto accompanying this greeting reads:

a De Caio	b **De Titio**
Silio. vid.	Sabino. vid
Tacit. Lips.	Tac. **lib. 4.**
edit. 4⁰.	pag. 79.
Anna. lib. I	
pag. II. lib.	
2. pag. 28.	
& 33.	(H&S 4:472)

Aware of his departure from classical strictures, Jonson acknowledges in his address "To the Readers" that the play does not observe "the strict laws of time" and lacks a "proper chorus" (H&S 4:350). He might have added that Silius' vivid suicide onstage also fails to satisfy the demands of classical decorum.

18. Barton, *Ben Jonson,* p. 99.

19. Barton, *Ben Jonson,* pp. 105–6.

20. Harold Bloom, *A Map of Misreading* (New York: Oxford University Press, 1975), p. 19.

21. Margaret Rose, *Parody//Metafiction* (London: Croom Helm, 1979), p 17.

22. Freud, *Works,* 8:201.

23. Gabriele Bernhard Jackson, ed., *Every Man in His Humor,* by Ben Jonson (New Haven, Conn.: Yale University Press, 1969), pp. 221–39.

24. Jonas Barish, *Ben Jonson and the Language of Prose Comedy* (Cambridge, Mass.: Harvard University Press, 1960), p. 87.

25. The problem of Jonson as Marlowe's poetic heir cannot be separated from Jonson's general ambivalence to paternal authority. Psychological speculation may perhaps cast some light on the case of Jonson's difficulties with authority—political, poetic, and paternal. See, in this regard, Ian Donaldson, "Jonson and Anger," *Yearbook of English Studies,* 14, (1984), 56–71; Roger B. Rollin, "The Anxiety of Identification: Jonson and the Rival Poets," in *Classic and Cavalier,* Summers and Pebworth, eds., pp. 139–56; and E. Pearlman, "Ben Jonson: An Anatomy," *ELR* 9 (1979):363–94. Pearlman's illuminating essay shows how Jonson, in his life and

work, reiterated a concern with (and a struggle against) authority. In seeking to fill the void created by the death of a natural father he never knew, Jonson repeatedly sought his replacement—in the Scottish grandfather mentioned in *Discoveries,* his schoolmaster Camden, the priest who converted this son of a Protestant clergyman to Catholicism, and his bricklayer stepfather. Pearlman concludes that all "that can be said with certainty is that Jonson wants and needs to acknowledge parental figures," that "again and again he returns in his work to just such a theme," and that a "common subject in his plays is the relation of father to son" (p. 371). For the most up-to-date biographical acount of Jonson and his personal relationships, see David Riggs, *Ben Jonson: A Life.*

26. Terrance Dunford, "Consumption of the World: Reading, Eating, and Imitation in *Every Man out of His Humour,*" *ELR* 14 (1984):147.

27. Barton, *Ben Jonson,* p. 73.

28. Dunford, "Consumption," p. 133.

29. Dunford, "Consumption," p. 147.

30. M. C. Bradbrook, "Shakespeare's Recollections of Marlowe," in *Shakespeare's Styles,* Philip Edwards, Inga-Stina Ewbank, and G. K. Hunter, eds. (Cambridge, England: Cambridge University Press, 1980), pp. 191–93.

31. James Riddell notes the tradition, beginning with Gifford's *Works of Ben Jonson* (2:397n.-398n.), that Jonson wrote *both* versions. This argument has recently been supported by Joan Carr in "Jonson and the Classics: The Ovid-Plot in *Poetaster,*" *ELR* 8, (1978):298. Along with Riddell I reject the claim that Jonson could not have "stooped to using someone else's translation" (47, n. 10), though I would not go so far as Riddell in identifying Jonson's response to Marlowe with Horace's response in the play to Ovid (Riddell, "Ben Jonson and 'Marlowes mighty line,' " p. 41).

32. J. B. Steane, *Marlowe: A Critical Study* (Cambridge, England: Cambridge University Press, 1964), pp. 280–301.

33. Steane, *Marlowe,* p. 282.

34. Barton, *Ben Jonson,* pp. 113ff.

35. See *Conversations,* (H&S 1:143–4). He uses the term in another (perhaps Aristophanic) sense in the Induction to *Every Man out* where Cordatus speaks of Asper's "strange" play as "somewhat like *Vetus Comoedia*" (H&S 3:436). Jonson was not unique in calling the native interlude tradition Old Comedy. See, for instance, *The Return of Pasquill,* where Thomas Nashe speaks of "*Vetus Comaedia* [that] began to prick him at London in the right vein, when she brought forth Divinity with a scratcht face. . . . " (Nashe, *Works,* 1:92). Cf. Edmund's remark in *King Lear:* "pat he comes like the catastrophe of the old comedy" (1.2.137–38).

36. David Bevington, *From "Mankind" to Marlowe* (Cambridge, Mass.: Harvard University Press, 1962); and Bernard Spivack, *Shakespeare and the Allegory of Evil* (New York: Columbia University Press, 1958).

37. See Greene, *Light in Troy,* pp. 43–48.

38. Eliot, "Ben Jonson," p. 154.

39. Eliot, "Ben Jonson," p. 157.

40. For production and printing histories, see John Jump, ed., *Doctor Faustus* (London: Methuen, 1964), p. xxvi and ff.

41. Barton, *Ben Jonson,* p. 140.

42. Freson Bowers, ed., *The Complete Works of Christopher Marlowe*, 2. vols. (Cambridge, England: Cambridge University Press, 1973), 2:542.

43. From "To Ben Jonson upon occasion of his Ode to Himself," as cited in H&S 11:335–36.

44. See Barton, *Ben Jonson,* pp. 194–218; see also Watson, *Jonson's Parodic Strategy,* pp. 139–71; and Rowe, *Distinguishing Jonson,* pp. 138–59.

45. Edmund Wilson, *The Triple Thinkers* (London: John Lehmann, 1952), p. 217.

46. Jonas Barish, *"Bartholomew Fair* and Its Puppets," *Modern Language Quarterly* 20 (1959):13, 13n.

47. Eliot, "Ben Jonson," p. 159.

48. See Barton, *Ben Jonson,* pp. 258–84; and Michael Hattaway, ed., *The New Inn,* by Ben Jonson (Manchester: Manchester University Press, 1984), pp. 6–7.

3. SHAKESPEARE AND MARLOWE

1. Woody Allen, "But Soft, Too Soft," in *Without Feathers* (New York: Ballantine Books, 1983), p. 196. I am grateful to Matthew Miller for this reference.

2. Archie Webster, "Was Marlowe the Man?" in *National Review* 82 (1923):81–86.

3. For a helpful account of these conspiracy theories see Kenneth Friedenreich, "Marlowe's Endings," in *"A Poet & a filthy Play-maker: New Essays on Christopher Marlowe,"* Friedenreich, et al. eds. (New York: AMS Press, 1988), pp. 361–68.

4. As quoted in E. K. Chambers, *William Shakespeare,* 2 vols. (Oxford: Clarendon Press, 1930), 2:188, from Greene's *A Groatsworth of Wit* (1592).

5. For an in-depth account of the controversy over this passage see D. Allen Carroll, "Greene's 'Upstart Crow' Passage: A Survey of Commentary," *Research Opportunities in Renaissance Drama* 28 (1985):111–27.

6. Chambers, *William Shakespeare,* 2:189.

7. In *Palladis Tamia,* as cited in G. Gregory Smith, ed., *Elizabethan Critical Essays,* 2 vols. (Oxford: Oxford University Press, 1904), 2:319.

8. F. P. Wilson, *Marlowe and the Early Shakespeare* (Oxford: Clarendon Press, 1953), p. 105.

9. John Bakeless, *The Tragicall History of Christopher Marlowe,* 2 vols. (Cambridge, Mass.: Harvard University Press, 1942).

10. Nicholas Brooke, "Marlowe as Provocative Agent in Shakespeare's Early Plays," *Shakespeare Survey* 14 (1961):34–44.

11. Brooke, "Provocative Agent," p. 39.

12. Brooke, "Provocative Agent," p. 40.

13. Brooke, "Provocative Agent," p. 44.

14. Marjorie Garber, "Marlovian Vision/ Shakespearean Revision," *Research Opportunities in Renaissance Drama* 22 (1979):3.

15. Garber, "Marlovian Vision," p. 7.

16. Garber, "Marlovian Vision," p. 3.

17. Harold F. Brooks, "Marlowe and Early Shakespeare," in *Christopher Marlowe,* Brian Morris, ed. (London: Ernest Benn, 1968), p. 72.

18. M. C. Bradbrook, "Shakespeare's Recollections of Marlowe," in *Shake-*

speare's Styles, Philip Edwards, Inga-Stina Ewbank, and G. K. Hunter, eds. (Cambridge, England: Cambridge University Press, 1980), p. 203.

19. M. C. Bradbrook, "Greene's *Groats-Worth of Wit* and the Social Response of *Venus and Adonis,*" *Shakespeare Survey* 15 (1962):62—72.

20. Bradbrook, "Recollections," p. 202.

21. Joseph Porter, "Marlowe, Shakespeare, and the Canonization of Heterodoxy," *South Atlantic Quarterly* 88 (1989):132. See, too, Porter's recent *Shakespeare's Mercutio* (Chapel Hill, N.C.: University of North Carolina Press, 1989), for a provocative account of Shakespeare's response to Marlowe in *Romeo and Juliet.*

22. Porter, "Heterodoxy," p. 138.

23. Porter, "Heterodoxy," p. 132.

24. Porter, "Heterodoxy," p. 138.

25. Porter, *Shakespeare's Mercutio,* p. 162.

26. Harold Bloom, *The Anxiety of Influence* (New York: Oxford University Press, 1973), p 11.

27. David Bevington, in *Tudor Drama and Politics* (Cambridge, Mass.: Harvard University Press, 1968), observes that "in the years of the Armada, dramatists preferred to invoke memories of Crécy and Agincourt rather than deal face-to-face with the Armada victory itself. Such avoidance of literalism helped created the dramatic genre that most forcefully represents the culmination of Tudor political drama: the English history play" (p. 301).

28. Anne Barton, "The King Disguised: Shakespeare's *Henry V* and the Comical History," in *The Triple Bond,* Joseph G. Price, ed. (University Park, PA.: Pennsylvania State University Press, 1975), p. 100. For an extended discussion of this pastiche see James C. Bulman, *The Heroic Idiom of Shakespeare's Tragedy* (Newark: University of Delaware, Press, 1985), pp. 74—75; and Eugene Waith, *Ideas of Greatness: Heroic Drama in England* (London: Routledge and Kegan Paul, 1971), pp. 96—97.

29. See Winston Graham, *The Spanish Armadas* (London: Collins, 1972).

30. *Calendar of State Papers, Domestic Series, of the Reign of Elizabeth, Preserved in the Public Record Office,* vol. 5, 1598—1601, M. A. Everett Green, ed. (London, 1869), pp. 239—40.

31. For an extended textual account of this view, see the arguments advanced in Stanley Wells and Gary Taylor, with John Jowett and William Montgomery, *William Shakespeare: A Textual Companion* (Oxford: Oxford University Press, 1987), pp. 175—208 and 217—27.

32. Cf. David Riggs, *Shakespeare's Heroical Histories* (Cambridge, Mass.: Harvard University Press, 1971) pp. 100ff.

33. Andrew S. Cairncross, ed., *The First Part of King Henry VI* (London: Methuen, 1962), p. 6. In his note to line 45 Cairncross, for whom the presence of the hearse is intolerable, insists that it "is inconceivable dramatically that this 'funeral' should remain motionless there throughout the rest of the scene," though this is analogous to what contemporary audiences witnessed with the omnipresent hearse of Zenocrate in *Tamburlaine, Part Two.*

34. Riggs, *Heroical,* p. 21.

35. I would disagree, then, with Bulman's argument that for Shakespeare

chivalric heroism and duty to one's king "cannot be divorced" (*Heroic Idiom*, p. 30); Mervyn James argues compellingly in *Society, Politics, and Culture: Studies in Early Modern England* (Cambridge, England: Cambridge University Press, 1986) against this position: "The political culture of the world of honor was essentially pluralistic. There was little room for the concept of sovereignty, or of unconditional obedience, and such other *etatiste* notions whose acceptance rose and declined in the course of the century before 1640" (p. 327).

36. Both Riggs and Bulman see in Joan Pucell a parody of Tamburlaine. I am not persuaded.

37. See Clifford Leech, "The Two-Part Play: Marlowe and the Early Shakespeare," *Shakespeare Jahrbuch* 94 (1958):90–106.

38. See, for example, Bakeless, *Tragicall History*, 2:221–41.

39. Howard Howarth, *The Tiger's Heart* (London: Oxford University Press, 1970), pp. 32–33.

40. Curiously, Marlowe does not respond directly to *1 Henry VI* in *Edward II*. One possible explanation is that the play was first staged in 1591, after he had begun writing his late history. Alternatively, since, like *Edward II*, both *2* and *3 Henry VI* were Pembroke plays, Marlowe may have had a greater familiarity with the plays that were in repertory with his latest effort.

41. Barton, "The Disguised King," p. 116.

42. Note that the line is absent from *The Contention* and that Marlowe must have gotten it from a version closer to Shakesepeare's original.

43. See James Shapiro, "Marlowe's Metrical Style: Infinite Riches in a Little Room," dissertation, Univ of Chicago, 1982, pp. 223–86.

44. See Wilbur Sanders, *The Dramatist and the Received Idea: Studies in the Plays of Marlowe and Shakespeare* (Cambridge, England: Cambridge University Press, 1968); and Walter Cohen, *Drama of a Nation: Public Theater in Renaissance England and Spain* (Ithaca, N.Y.: Cornell University Press, 1985).

45. Andrew S. Cairncross, ed., *The Second Part of King Henry VI* (London: Methuen, 1957), pp. xxv-xxix. In their *Textual Companion* (Oxford: Clarendon Press, 1987) to the Oxford edition of Shakespeare's *Works*, Stanley Wells and Gary Taylor consider Cairncross's claims about censorship and conclude that while "he may be right," the "arguments he adduces . . . are not very strong." They concede that the Folio editors may have "lightly censored the manuscript," or perhaps that some censorship occurred when the play was resubmitted for licensing in the late 1590s (p. 176). Alternatively, these changes may be explained by the Quarto "reporters' interpolations from other plays they knew" (p. 175). In the example quoted above, some form of censorship seems to me the most reasonable explanation for the differences between the Quarto and Folio texts.

46. In none of the the four (possibly five) printings in the late sixteenth and early seventeenth centuries (1593?, 1594, 1598, 1612, 1622) were passages from *Edward II* suppressed. Stephen Orgel wonders that had "Richard II been presented as a sodomite, would the authorities have found it necessary to censor the deposition scene? Maybe Edward's sexuality is a way of protecting the play, a way of keeping what it says about power intact." In "'Nobody's Perfect': Or Why Did the English Stage Take Boys for Women?," *South Atlantic Quarterly* 88 (1989):25.

47. For an early discussion of this borrowing see William Dinsmore Briggs, ed., *Edward II,* by Christopher Marlowe (London: David Nutt, 1914), pp. 141–42.

48. Geoffrey Bullough, *Narrative and Dramatic Sources of Shakespeare,* 8 vols. (New York: Columbia University Press, 1957–75), 3:90.

49. Cohen writes, for example, that Marlowe was "wrong to conclude that the struggles over the state in the late Middle Ages and in the Renaissance, and particularly the use of absolutism, were of no importance either to the aristocracy or the English people as a whole" (*Drama of a Nation,* p. 239). Wilbur Sanders's disappointment at the non-Shakespearean turn of Marlowe's play results in a similar condemnation: "Perhaps the most remarkable thing about Marlowe's *Edward II* is the fact that, although it has every appearance of being a play on a national and political theme, a play about kingship, it is yet an intensely personal play in which the public issues hardly arise" (*The Dramatist and the Received Idea,* p. 121).

50. Philip Edwards, *Threshold of a Nation* (Cambridge, England: Cambridge University Press, 1979), pp. 54–65.

51. This may also explain why, though writing such different kinds of drama, both playwrights have been seen as advocates of, alternatively, the truly radical and subversive on the one hand, and the truly conservative and orthodox on the other.

52. See, for example, Nicholas Brooke, *Shakespeare's Early Tragedies* (London: Methuen, 1968).

53. *HMC, Calender of the MSS of the Most Honourable the Marquis of Salisbury, K.G., Preserved at Hatfield House* (London, 1902), 9:262.

54. I. A. A. Thomson, "The Impact of War," in Peter Clark, ed. *The European Crisis of the 1590s* (London: George Allen & Unwin, 1985), p. 286.

55. M. J. Power in "London and the Control of the 'Crisis' of the 1590s," *History* 70 (1985), describes a bizarrely Tamburlainian scene in London by the mid-1590s, when, as a "deterrent to the unruly and the rogue . . . street cages [were set up] as temporary prisons" (p. 380). One can only wonder if they resembled the one that Tamburlaine used to imprison Bajazeth.

56. For an alternative view, which sees London weathering the crisis better than most historians have acknowledged, see Steve Rappaport, *Worlds within Worlds: Structures of Life in Sixteenth-Century London* (Cambridge, England: Cambridge University Press, 1989), esp. pp. 6–22.

57. Peter Clark, "A Crisis Contained? The Condition of English Towns in the 1590s," in Clark, ed., *The European Crisis,* p. 275.

58. I. A. A. Thompson, "The Impact of War," p. 276.

59. A recent, typical example is Jasper Ridley, *Elizabeth I* (London: Constable, 1987).

60. *Calendar of State Papers Domestic,* 5:257.

61. John Stow, *Annales* (London, 1615), p. 788.

62. Reported in a letter from G. Coppin to Cecil, *HMC Salisbury,* 9:282–3.

63. Stow, *Annales,* p. 788.

64. *The Letters of John Chamberlain,* Norman E. McClure, ed., 2 vols. (Philadelphia: The American Philosophical Association), 1939), 1:78.

65. Chamberlain, *Letters,* 1:83.

66. Chamberlain, *Letters,* 1:78.

67. Thomas Cartelli has suggested to me that given this historical context, Laurence Olivier's film version of *Henry V* as an Armada play (which was conceived in 1943 and first shown in 1944, as Allied forces congregated around England's south coast in anticipation of the Normandy landings) was truer to the original conditions of performance as an "Armada" play than is ordinarily acknowledged.

68. "The principal note of her reign will be that she ruled much by factions and parties, which she herself both made, upheld, and weakened as her own great judgment advised" (from Sir Robert Naunton, *Fragmenta Regalia or Observations on Queen Elizabeth, Her Times & Favories* (1638), John S. Cerovski, ed. (Washington, DC: Folger Shakespeare Library, 1985), p. 41.

69. The military burden placed on London was increasingly severe: M. J. Power notes in "London and the Control of the 'Crisis' of the 1590s," that in November 1596, "the Lord Mayor, ordered to have 3,000 men ready to be despatched to Kent and Essex to meet the threatened Spanish invasion, asked the privy council to remember that even in the Armada year, 1588, the city sent only 1,000 men to Tilbury" (p. 383, quoting from the *Analytical Index to the Remembrancia,* H. C. and W. H. Overall, eds. [London, 1878], p. 224). From all accounts, the demands on Londoners to provide ships and men in 1599 were even greater.

70. For a discussion of how Dekker's play addresses contemporary economic, military, and social problems, see David S. Kastan, "Workshop and/as Playhouse: Comedy and Commerce in *The Shoemakers' Holiday," Studies in Philology* 84 (1987):324–37.

71. From a letter to Robert Sidney, October 28, 1599. *HMC Report on the MSS of Lord De L'Isle and Dudley Preserved at Penshurst Place* (London, 1934), 2:408.

72. For an important discussion of the relation of *Henry V* to comical history written at this time, see Anne Barton, "The King Disguised," esp. pp. 107–17.

73. Nashe, *Works,* Ronald. B. McKerrow, ed. 5 vols. (Oxford: Basil Blackwell, 1904–10; rpt. F. P. Wilson, ed., 1958), 1:213.

74. Irving Ribner, *The English History Play in the Age of Shakespeare* (Princeton, N. J.: Princeton University Press, 1957); Robert Egan, "A Muse of Fire: Henry V in the Light of Tamburlaine," *Modern Language Quarterly* 29 (1968):15–28. See, too, Roy Battenhouse, "The Relation of Henry V to Tamburlaine," *Shakespeare Survey* 27 (1974), p. 76 ff. This is the most extended treatment of the links between the plays, identifying a half-dozen major correspondences that "add up to a rather widespread network of analogy."

75. This Tamburlainian identification is underscored in the Olivier film version of *Henry V,* where Pistol, parting from Mistress Quickley on his way to the wars in France, exits reciting an interpolated version of Marlowe's lines:

Farewell, farewell divine Zenocrate—
Is it not passing brave to be a King
And ride in triumph through Persepolis!

See Laurence Oliver, *Henry V,* Classic Film Scripts (London: Lorrimer Publishing Ltd., 1984), p. 28. I am indebted to Tom Berger for this reference.

76. As cited in Barton, "The King Disguised," p. 100.

77. See Gary Taylor's Oxford edition of *Henry V*, which retains this line (p. 243). For Taylor, who rejects the modern editorial tradition that sees this line as a textual interpolation, this is "Pistol's moment of choice, and his moment of greatness" (p. 65).

78. *The New Variorum "As You Like It"*, Richard Knowles, ed. (New York: MLA, 1977), p. 213.

79. See Millar MacClure, *Marlowe: The Critical Heritage, 1588–1896* (London: Routledge & Kegan Paul, 1979), pp. 41–42; 45–46.

80. The rivalry as lyric poets extended to the pursuit of literary patronage as well, and Marlowe, on the basis of surviving evidence, seems to have been the more successful up to 1593. He appears to have cultivated the support of Roger Manwood, Chief Baron of the Queen's Exchequer, whose Latin epitaph he wrote; he dedicated *Amintae Gaudia* to Mary, Countess of Pembroke; knew Thomas and probably also Sir Francis Walsingham, to whom "Hero and Leander" was dedicated by Blount and to whose estate messengers in search of Marlowe were sent by the Privy Council in May 1593. To this list of potential patrons we can add the unidentified "lordship" (perhaps the Lord Admiral?) Kyd alludes to in his torture-extracted deposition on Marlowe. Shakespeare apparently pursued a different source of patronage at this time, most notably the young Earl of Southampton, to whom he dedicated both *Venus and Adonis* and *The Rape of Lucrece*.

81. T. S. Eliot, "Christopher Marlowe," in *Selected Essays* (London: Faber and Faber, 1932), p. 123.

82. John Russell Brown, ed., *The Merchant of Venice* (London: Methuen, 1955), p. lviii; and C. L. Barber, *Shakespeare's Festive Comedy* (Princeton: Princeton University Press, 1959), p. 190.

83. René Girard, "'To Entrap the Wisest': A Reading of *The Merchant of Venice*," in *Literature and Society, Selected Papers from the English Institute*, n.s. 3, Edward W. Said, ed. (Baltimore: The Johns Hopkins University Press, 1980), pp. 100–119.

84. See Northrop Frye, "The Argument of Comedy," in *English Institute Essays 1948*, D. A. Robertson, ed. (New York: Columbia University Press, 1949), pp. 58–83.

85. See Bradbrook, "Recollections," p. 191.

86. Brooke, "Provocative Agent," p. 42.

87. See Maurice Charney, "Jessica's Turquoise Ring and Abigail's Poisoned Porridge: Shakespeare and Marlowe as Rivals and Imitators," *Renaissance Drama* n.s. 10 (1979):33–44.

88. For a representative version of the Gratiano's dirty joke, see the story of Hans Carvel and his fear of losing his wife's "ring" in book 3, chapter 28 of Rabelais's *Gargantua and Pantagruel*, J. M. Cohen, trans. (Middlesex: Penguin Books, 1955), p. 368.

89. Brooke, "Provocative Agent," p. 34. Shakespeare responds to Marlowe's version, not to the Ovidian original, where Endymion is vaguely rendered as "iuvenis" and which reads:

> *aspice quot somnos iuveni donarit amato*
> *Luna.*

(AMORUM, book 1, 13, ll. 43–44).

90. These early editions of the *Elegies* exercised a powerful influence on contemporary poets and dramatists, including both Jonson and Donne. Shakespeare, who had quoted from one of the Ovidian Elegies (1.15) on the title page of "Venus and Adonis," was undoubtedly familiar with Marlowe's notorious and recently published translation.

91. See *Henslowe's Diary*, R. A. Foakes and R. T. Rickert, eds. (Cambridge, England: Cambridge University Press, 1961) pp. 16–47. The competition extends to the players as well: the two great actors of the rival companies, Edward Alleyn and Richard Burbage, offering alternative versions of the stage Jew.

92. Bernard Beckerman, "Philip Henslowe," in *The Theatrical Manager in England and America*, Joseph W. Donohue, Jr., ed. (Princeton, N. J.: Princeton University Press, 1971), pp. 19–62. Thus, for example, by 1615 "Articles of Grievance" and "Articles of Oppression" were brought by the players against Henslowe. He was charged with, among other things, "manipulation of hired personnel," maintaining "control over the players by keeping them in debt," and "requiring exorbitant bonds." It would be a mistake simply to castigate Henslowe as a villainous, Shylock-like usurer. Times had changed, and with them the financial demands of running a successful company. By 1615 Henslowe was bonding, not just individuals, but an entire company of players.

93. See Chambers, *William Shakespeare*, 2:18–101.

94. David Thomas, ed., *Shakespeare in the Public Record* (London: Her Majesty's Stationery Office, 1985), pp. 2–3.

95. H. J. Oliver, ed., *The Merry Wives of Windsor*, by William Shakespeare (London: Methuen, 1971), p. 70.

96. Ralph Berry, "The Revenger's Comedy," in *Shakespeare's Comedies: Explorations in Form* (Princeton, N. J.: Princeton University Press, 1972).

97. David Scott Kastan, "*All's Well that Ends Well* and the Limits of Comedy," *ELH* 52 (1985):575–89.

98. Anne Richter, *Shakespeare and the Idea of Play* (London: Chatto & Windus, 1962), p. 155.

99. O. W. F. Lodge, *Times Literary Supplement* (May 14, 1925).

100. See, for example, Eugene Waith, "The Metamorphosis of Violence in *Titus Andronicus*," *Shakespeare Survey* 10 (1957):39–49.

101. Nashe, *Works*, 3:315.

102. For a detailed account of this production, see Alan Dessen's study of *Titus Andronicus* in performance (Manchester: Manchester University Press, 1990).

103. Brian Cox, in conversation with Alan Dessen, who, in turn, related the conversation to me. If we accept Eugene Waith's suggestion that in Elizabethan productions Titus appears in a chariot in the opening scene (since he refers to one at 1.1.249) the original staging of the opening scene may have been meant to recall Marlowe's play by reusing the very prop (since *Titus* was performed by Derby's, Pembroke's, and Sussex's Men) made famous by Tamburlaine's unforgettable entrance.

104. See Eugene Waith, ed., *Titus Andronicus* (Oxford: Oxford University Press, 1984), where the stage direction at 1.1.70 has bracketed "enter Titus Andronicus [in a chariot]." Waith argues strongly for the centrality of this prop in the play.

105. Bradbrook, "Recollections," p. 194.

106. J. M. Robertson was the first to claim that Marlowe (perhaps along with

Kyd) wrote a Caesar play in three parts early in the 1590s. To compound matters, he further argued that Jonson revised Shakespeare's subsequent share. William Wells and E. H. C. Oliphant would subsequently maintain the tradition that Shakespeare began with an "old and apparently good Marlowe play" (as cited in T. S. Dorsch, ed., *Julius Caesar* (London: Methuen, 1955), p. xxii.

107. An alternative theory is that the bad quarto of *The Massacre* was produced as late as 1602, allowing for the possibility that the actors involved in this memorially reconstructed text worked in bits of Shakespeare's recent play rather than vice versa. W. W. Greg dates the quarto 1594, Oliver in 1602. Bowers, reviewing the evidence, finds the argument for the late date unpersuasive and argues himself for a date around 1594 (*Complete Works of Christopher Marlowe* 1:355–60). I would agree.

108. See *Henslowe's Diary*, pp. 86, 319, 320, 323.

109. H. J. Oliver, ed., *Dido Queen of Carthage* and *The Massacre at Paris*, by Christopher Marlowe (Cambridge, Mass.: Harvard University Press, 1968), p. xxxiii.

110. From the *Preface to "Troilus and Cressida,"* as cited in the *Variorum Hamlet,"* H.G. Furness, ed. (Philadelphia: J. P. Lippincott), 1:189.

111. Maximillian E. Novak, ed., *The Works of John Dryden* (Berkeley and Los Angeles: University of California Press, 1984), 13:244.

112. As cited in the *Variorum "Hamlet,"* 1:184.

113. C. W. Wallace, "The Swan Theatre and the Earl of Pembroke's Servants" *Englische Studien* (1910–11):378.

114. As cited in Harold Jenkins, ed., *Hamlet* (London: Methuen, 1982), p. 479.

115. *Variorum "Hamlet",* 1:180. Coleridge would have none of it and rejects the possibility of parody in favor of Shakspeare striving towards epic: "This admirable substitution of the epic or the dramatic diction of Shakespeare's own dialogue, and authorized, too, by the actual style of the tragedies before his time (*Porrex & Ferrex, Tit. And.,* etc.) is well worthy of notice. The fancy that a burlesque was intended sinks below criticism; the lines, as epic narrative, are superb" (1:183).

116. *Variorum "Hamlet",* p. 1:182.

117. Bullough, *Sources of Shakespeare,* 7:37.

118. *Variorum "Hamlet",* 1:184.

119. See Harry Levin, *The Question of Hamlet* (New York: Oxford University Press, 1959), pp. 163–64.

4. JONSON AND SHAKESPEARE

1. This version of the anecdote appears in the Bodleian Ashmole MS. 38, p. 181, and is reprinted in H&S 1:186. Stanley Wells and Gary Taylor note that the "epitaph survives in at least four seventeenth century manuscripts" and print the variants (*William Shakespeare: A Textual Companion* (Oxford: Oxford University Press, 1987, pp. 457–58).

2. What are we to make of the appearance of the following lines in the commonplace book of Sir Francis Fane, dated c. 1629, well before Jonson's death in 1637:

Here lieth Ben Jonson
Who was once one:

In his life a slow thing
And now he is dead nothing.

Cited in G. E. Bentley, *Shakespeare and Jonson: Their Reputations in the Seventeenth Century Compared*, 2 vols. (Chicago: University of Chicago Press, 1945), 2:37.

3. His *Conversations with Drummond* reads as a catalogue of such judgments. See H&S 1:128–78.

4. As quoted in Joseph Quincy Adams, "The Bones of Ben Jonson," *Studies in Philology* 16, (1919):293, from Peter Cunningham, *Hand-book of London* (London: J. Murray, 1850).

5. Adams, "Bones," p. 294.

6. Adams, "Bones," p. 301.

7. Adams, "Bones," p. 289.

8. E. K. Chambers, *William Shakespeare*, 2. vols. (Oxford: Clarendon Press, 1930), 2:259.

9. Chambers, *William Shakespeare*, 2:181.

10. Adams, "Bones," p. 289.

11. For discussions of their relative reputation in the early seventeenth century see G. E. Bentley, *Shakespeare and Jonson;* and John Freehaven, "Leonard Digges, Ben Jonson, and the Beginning of Shakespeare Idolatry," *Shakespeare Quarterly* 21 (1970):63–75.

12. See Mary Edmond, "Pembroke's Men," *Review of English Studies* n.s. 25 (1974):129–36.

13. The following is Rowe's influential account. Note that he never specifies that the play Shakespeare saved was *Every Man in:*

> His acquaintance with Ben Jonson began with a remarkable piece of humanity and good nature. Mr. Jonson, who was at that time altogether unknown to the world, had offered one of his plays to the players, in order to have it acted. And the persons into whose hands it was put, after having turned it carelessly and superciliously over, were just upon returning it to him with an ill-natured answer, that it would be of no service to their company, when Shakespeare luckily cast his eye upon it, and found something so well in it as to engage him first to read it through, and afterwards to recommend Mr. Jonson and his writings to the public. After this they were professed friends, though I don't know whether the other ever made him an equal return of gentleness and sincerity.

From *The Works of Mr. William Shakespeare* (London, 1709), 1:xii-xiv. By the time we get to Pope this has hardened into fact: "It is an acknowledged fact, that Ben Jonson was introduced upon the stage, and his first works encouraged, by Shakespeare" (Alexander Pope, ed., *The Works of Shakespeare*, 6 vols. (London: 1723–25), 1:xii).

14. In addition to the books by Russ McDonald, Anne Barton, E. A. J. Honigman, George Rowe, and Robert Watson (all of which deal with the relationship of Jonson and Shakespeare) there has been a wealth of other studies that compare the two, including, to list but a representative sampling not mentioned elsewhere in this

chapter: John G. Sweeney, III, *Jonson and the Psychology of Public Theater* (Princeton: Princeton University Press, 1985); Robert Ornstein, "Shakespearian and Jonsonian Comedy," *Shakespeare Survey* 22 (1969):43–46; Maurice Charney, "Shakespeare—and the Others," *Shakespeare Quarterly* 30 (1979):325–42; Ian Donaldson's collection of essays, *Jonson and Shakespeare* (Totowa, N.J.: Barnes and Noble, 1983), especially those by D. H. Craig, "The Idea of the Play in *A Midsummer Night's Dream* and *Bartholomew Fair*," pp. 89–100; F. H. Mares, "Comic Procedures in Shakespeare and Jonson: *Much Ado About Nothing* and *The Alchemist*," pp. 101–118; Ann Blake, "Sportful Malice: Duping in the Comedies of Jonson and Shakespeare," pp. 119–34; and Anthony Miller, "The Roman State in *Julius Caesar* and *Sejanus*," pp. 179–201; Nancy Leonard, "Shakespeare and Jonson Again: The Comic Forms," *Renaissance Drama* n.s. 10 (1979):45–69. G. K. Hunter, "Poem and Context in *Love's Labor's Lost*," in *Shakespeare's Styles*, Philip Edwards, Inga-Stina Ewbank, and G. K. Hunter, eds. (Cambridge: Cambridge University Press, 1980), pp. 25–38; Samuel Schoenbaum, "Shakespeare and Jonson: Fact and Myth," in *Shakespeare and Others* (Washington, D.C.: Folger Books, 1985), pp. 171–85; T. J. B. Spencer, "Ben Jonson on his Beloved, the Author Mr. William Shakespeare." *The Elizabethan Theatre* 4, pp. 22–40; and R. A. Foakes, "The Descent of Iago: Satire, Ben Jonson, and Shakespeare's *Othello*" and "*Julius Caesar* and *Sejanus*: Roman Politics, Inner Selves and the Powers of the Theatre," both in *Shakespeare and His Contemporaries*, E. A. J. Honigmann, ed. (Manchester: Manchester University Press, 1986), pp. 16–30 and 60–78, respectively. Few studies of Jonson omit at least a passing comparison to Shakespeare. Obviously, there is a thin line between comparisons and studies of mutual influence; I have tried hard in this chapter to avoid the former and concentrate as closely as possible on the latter.

15. See Stephen Orgel's valuable discussion of Shakespeare and the Jacobean masque in his edition of *The Tempest* (Oxford: Oxford University Press, 1987), pp. 43–50.

16. George E. Rowe, *Distinguishing Jonson: Imitation, Rivalry, and the Direction of a Dramatic Career* (Lincoln, Univ. of Nebraska Press, 1988), goes so far as to argue that Shakespeare—"who seems to have had relatively little interest in continually distinguishing himself from other English dramatists"—only enters the Poets' War in *Troilus and Cressida* in order to expose the "causes, characteristics, and ultimate futility of the theatrical quarrel itself" (pp. 173–74). Accordingly, for Rowe, the play reveals that with the erasure of difference between rivals, Shakespeare indicates that "no reputation is lasting and that all victors become victims" in a world in which even Homer and Chaucer are subject to 'envious and calumnating Time' (p. 176).

17. Herbert Howarth, in "Shakespeare's Gentleness," *Shakespeare Survey* 14 (1969):95, makes a strong case for seeing Shakespeare's gentleness as a "mask." For Howarth, Jonson (who uses this term in his poem in praise of Shakespeare) "intended 'gentle' to recall Shakespeare's struggle to establish his father's gentle rank; to endorse the grant of the patent by the College of Arms; to recall the civil demeanor with which he attempted to impress his gentility on his acquaintance; and to record how the gentle style had first distinguished his writing from his rivals', and had remained his most supple strength" (p. 90). While I would distance myself from some of the biographical-critical speculation Howarth subsequently engages in, I would agree that

Shakespeare carefully develops this gentleness as a strategy and as part of his dramatic self-presentation. Howarth's essay is important for showing how Shakespeare himself cultivated this image. It is also worth exploring Howarth's suggestion that Shakespeare appropriates this "mask of gentleness" from Chaucer. A number of recent critics have illuminated the silence in Shakespeare, and this perspective has some bearing too on Shakespeare's understanding of the power of silence. See Harvey Rovine, *Silence in Shakespeare* (Ann Arbor, Mich.: UMI Research Press, 1987), and Philip McGuire, *Speechless Dialect: Shakespeare's Open Silences* (Berkeley and Los Angeles: University of California Press, 1985).

18. E. A. J. Honigmann, *Shakespeare's Impact on His Contemporaries* (Totowa, N. J.: Barnes and Noble, 1982), pp. 104–7. Anne Barton writes in *Ben Jonson, Dramatist* (Cambridge: Cambridge University Press, 1984), p. 354, note 13, that she has "arrived independently at a similar conviction that there was what Honigmann calls an 'obsessive element' in Jonson's concern with Shakespeare's rival art at this stage in his life, and at a similar view of the impact on Jonson of the Shakespeare First Folio." I do not see evidence of obsession occurring until considerably later than the early years of the seventeenth century, and I see it resulting less from Shakespeare's impact on Jonson than from Jonson's increasing recognition that the meaning of his drama (and his literary reputation) were inescapably intertwined with Shakespeare's powerful art.

19. Barton, *Ben Jonson,* pp. 50–51. The jealous Thorello has also been suggested as a prototype for Othello (whose name sounds similar). See J. W. Lever's introduction to his edition of *Every Man in His Humour* (Lincoln: University of Nebraska Press, 1971); and Russ McDonald, "Othello, Thorello, and the Problem of the Foolish Hero," *Shakespeare Quarterly* 30 (1979):51–67.

20. Barton, *Ben Jonson,* p. 35.

21. Honigmann, *Shakespeare's Impact,* p. 102.

22. Honigmann, *Shakespeare's Impact,* p. 101.

23. Though see the provocative essay of James Bednarz, "Shakespeare's Purge of Jonson: the Literary Context of *Troilus and Cressida*" (forthcoming in *Shakespeare Studies* 21), part of a forthcoming book that traces evidence of Shakespeare's participation in this topical and personal debate. For additional support for the view that Shakspeare engaged in the Poets' War, see William Elton, "Shakespeare's Portrait of Ajax in *Troilus and Cressida,*" *PMLA* 63 (1948):744–48.

24. Barton, *Ben Jonson,* p. 84.

25. For Barton, it "seems clear that Jonson was remembering the mock-combat between Viola and Andrew Aguecheek in *Twelfth Night* when he devised the encounter between Daw and La-Foole in Act Four, each one falsely persuaded through the malice of a third party of the fury and terrifying swordsmanship of his adversary" (*Ben Jonson,* p. 125). This kind of claim comes dangerously close to what Richard Levin has called Fluellenism, because of the Welshman's habit of finding "figures in all things": "'tis all one, 'tis alike as my fingers is to my fingers" (*Henry V,* 4.7.29–30). Again, there is a thin line between analogy and a line of influence. The issue recurs when Barton links the Winwife/ Palamon subplot in *Bartholomew Fair* to the main plot of Shakespeare and Fletcher's *The Two Noble Kinsmen* (1613), likening the triangle of Winwife, Quarlous, and Grace to that of Palamon, Arcite, and Emilia in

Shakespeare's plot (p. 212), because the thematic interest in love and friendship recur in Jonson's play, and because Winwife chooses the name "Palemon" in his rivalry with Quarlous (who picks the nonShakespearean name "Argalus"). It may be that Jonson is hearkening back in this scene to a Chaucerian model. If he is responding to *The Two Noble Kinsmen* the response is not especially sustained and the point of the recollection is unclear, especially when compared to his treatment of Marlowe's "Hero and Leander" in the same play. I am made nervous when the possible allusion to *The Two Noble Kinsmen* becomes the basis for including Shakespeare in the claim that "only with the help of Chaucer, Edwards, Sidney, Marlowe, Fletcher and Shakespeare that Jonson has been able to look with steadiness at the whole disorderly panorama of Smithfield" (p. 218). Robert Watson's study notes several more possible allusions, including: the "clear echoes of Shakespeare's *King John*" (3.3.19–58) in "Kitely's dithering speech in *Every Man In*" (3.3.47–53), (p. 37); the Epilogue to *The Devil Is an Ass* as a "clear (and clearly parodic) allusion to the opening of Shakespeare's great Epilogue [in *The Tempest*] . . . suggesting a comparison between Shakespeare's theatrical magic and Merecraft's impressive but absurd scams" (206–7); and a brief echo of *Macbeth*'s witches in the line "A practice foul/ For one so fair" (*Devil Is an Ass* 5.8.53–54).

26. Anne Barton, "Jonson and Shakespeare," in *Shakespeare, Man of the Theater*, Kenneth Muir, Jay Halio, and D. J. Palmer, eds. (Newark: University of Deleware, Press, 1983), p. 160. Thus, for Barton, the attempts of Kitely, Zeal of the Land Busy, and Sordido "to transform themselves in a positive [*sic*], Shakespearean manner" reflect a "Jonsonian desire to experiment with the rival mode, coupled with a weird failure of conviction at the crucial moment" (p. 161). It seems unfair first to claim that Jonson imitates Shakespeare, then loses his will in the very act of imitation, since there is no evidence to suggest that he sets out in the first place to imitate Shakespeare in his handling of these characters, nor is it entirely fair to attribute to Shakespeare features that characterize a genre that Jonson explored in the mid-1590s (he told Drummond that half his comedies were not in print) and to which he returned at the end of his career.

27. Harry Levin, "Two Magian Comedies: *The Tempest* and *The Alchemist*," *Shakespeare Survey* 22 (1969), 47–58; and Thomas Cartelli, "*Bartholomew Fair* as Urban Arcadia: Jonson Responds to Shakespeare," *Renaissance Drama*, n.s. 14 (1983):151–72. Cartelli's claim has been accepted and extended by subsequent critics, esp. Rowe, *Distinguishing Jonson*, pp. 139–58.

28. Russ McDonald, "Skeptical Visions," *Shakespeare Survey* 34 (1981):135. For an extended discussion see McDonald's *Shakespeare & Jonson/Jonson & Shakespeare* (Lincoln: University of Nebraska Press, 1988), pp. 97–136.

29. McDonald's account of the deep resemblances between Shakespeare's major tragedies and Jonson's major comedies identifies Marlovian language as a common denominator:

> The connection of Volpone and Faustus [in regard to the "sumptuous language spoken by Jonson's great imaginative figures"] is relevant to Shakespeare as well, who must have noted the connections between language and vision in the plays of Christopher Marlowe. Most efforts to locate specific

Marlovian echoes center upon Shakespeare's earliest productions, but it seems likely that at the height of his career the wish to develop an appropriate tragic idiom led Shakespeare to recall not only the sounds he had heard at the Rose in the early 1590s but also the principles underlying them. The most fundamental of these is Tamburlaine's identification of language with power: the aspiring mind expresses itself in soaring speech (p. 104).

McDonald's claim dovetails with my larger suggestion that Jonson and Shakespeare appropriated the defining features of Marlowe's style, ultimately subordinating it to each one's own artistic vision, and rendering it anachronistic.

30. Honigmann, *Shakespeare's Impact,* p. 118.

31. Barton, *Ben Jonson,* pp. 258–59.

32. Barton, *Ben Jonson,* p. 284.

33. Michael Hattaway, ed., *The New Inn,* by Ben Jonson (Manchester, England: Manchester University PRess, 1984), pp. 6–7.

34. Honigmann, *Shakespeare's Impact,* pp. 111–120.

35. As cited in Samuel Schoenbaum, "Shakespeare and Jonson: Fact and Myth," *Shakespeare and Others* (Washington, D.C.: Folger Books, 1985), p. 174.

36. James Riddell's forthcoming investigation of the compositional features of the 1616 Folio leads to the surprising conclusion that *Every Man in,* though it appears first in the volume, was the last play to be typeset, and there is a strong possibility that Jonson's revisions of the play took the problem of constraints on the number of pages reserved for the *Every Man in* into account. It would also seem to suggest that Jonson was taking special care in presenting the revised play, and perhaps its aggressive Prologue, as well.

37. Cf. his comment in "On *The New Inn:* Ode To Himself":

> No doubt some mouldy tale
> Like *Pericles,* and stale
> As the shrieve's crusts, and nasty as his fish-
>   scraps out of every dish,
> Thrown forth, and raked into the common tub,
>   May keep up the play club.

(H&S 6:492–3)

38. This is all the more striking in view of the argument that *The Alchemist* is a critique of Shakespeare's late work that in turn provoked *The Tempest,* which, the argument runs, generated Jonson's couter-riposte in *Bartholomew Fair.*

39. Cf. the less specific allusion in Jonson's address "To the Reader" of the quarto of *The Alchemist:*

> . . . thou were never more fair in the way to be cozened (than in this age) in poetry, especially in plays: wherein now, the concupiscence of dances, and anticks so raigneth, as to run away from Nature, and be afraid of her, is the only point of art that tickles the spectators" (H&S 5:291).

40. See Barton, *Ben Jonson*, p. 258ff.

41. Leah Marcus, *Puzzling Shakespeare: Local Readings and Its Discontents* (Berkeley and Los Angeles: University of California Press, 1988), p. 18.

42. Marcus, *Puzzling Shakespeare*, p. 19.

43. Is Jonson recalling here Shakespeare's own lines on this Renaissance commonplace in "Venus and Adonis"?:

> Look when a painter would surpass the life
> In limming out a well-proportioned steed,
> His art with nature's workmanship at strife,
> As if the dead the living should exceed . . .
>
> (lines 289–92)

The threat that Jonson struggles to come to terms with in his epitaph is made explicit in Shakespeare's lines: what if "the dead the living should exceed."

44. Ovid's tamer version says only that: "I shall live, and the great part of me survive my death."

45. Van Den Berg, "'The Paths I Meant unto Thy Praise': Jonson's Poem for Shakespeare," *Shakespeare Studies* 11 (1978):209.

46. Lawrence Lipking, *The Life of the Poet: Beginning and Ending Poetic Careers* (Chicago: University of Chicago Press, 1981), p. 144.

47. Lipking, *Life of the Poet*, p. 145.

48. The *Discoveries*, compiled (according to Herford and the Simpsons) sometime between the mid-1620 and 30s, appear to be yet another example of Jonson's obsession with defining his own art in relationship to Shakespeare's. We do not know the compositional genetics of the *Discoveries* (how much was put into the current order by Jonson, how much patched together posthumously by his editors), but it appears that the long digression on Shakespeare—"*De Shakespeare nostrat*"—(H&S 8:583) are triggered by Jonson's frustration with the misvaluing of his own kind of art in favor of those who produce more popular spectacle:

> Indeed, the multitude commend writers, as they do fencers, wrestlers; who if they come in robustiously, and put for it, with a deal of violence, are received for the braver-fellows. . . . But in these things, the unskilfull are naturally deceived, and judging wholly by the bulk, think rude things greater than polished; and scattered more numerous, than composed (H&S 8:583).

We also do not know in what manner Jonson intended these literary observations to come into print. His account of Shakespeare in its pages does seem to conform to the general lines of my argument that late in his life Jonson recognized how inextricably bound his own reputation was to Shakespeare's, and by presenting the reception of Shakespeare's art (implicit in the quotation above) he was passing judgment on his own as well.

49. Schoenbaum, "Shakespeare and Jonson," p. 173.

50. *Discourse Concerning the Original and Progress of Satire* (1692), as cited in Schoenbaum, "Shakespeare and Jonson," p. 176.

51. For the best recent account of these canonical developments, see Jonathan Bate, *Shakespeare and the English Romantic Imagination* (Oxford: Clarendon Press, 1986) and *Shakespearean Constitutions: Politics, Theatre, Criticism 1730–1830* (Oxford: Clarendon Press, 1989).

52. The issue of Milton's response to both Shakespeare and Jonson is too vast a subject to explore here at any length, though see Jonathan Goldberg, "Milton's Warning Voice," in *Voice, Terminal, Echo* (New York and London: Methuen, 1986), pp. 124–58; John Guillory, *Poetic Authority: Spenser, Milton, and Literary History* (New York: Columbia University Press, 1983), esp. pp. 75–93; and Paul Stevens, "Subversion and Wonder in Milton's Epitaph "On Shakespeare," *ELR* 19 (1989):375–388. In addressing Wordsworth's self-positioning in response to Milton, Paul de Man notes in "Autobiography as De-Facement" [rpt. in *The Rhetoric of Romanticism* (New York: Columbia University Press, 1984], pp. 67–81), that Wordsworth omits lines 9–14 (italicized below) when quoting Milton's epitaph on Shakespeare in his *Essays Upon Epitaphs:*

> What need my Shakespeare for his honored bones,
> The labour of an age in piled stones,
> Or that his hallowed relics should be hid
> Under a star-ypointing pyramid?
> Dear son of memory, great heir of fame,
> What needs't thou such dull witness of thy name?
> Thou in our wonder and astonishment
> Hast built thyself a lasting monument.
> *For whilst to the shame of slow-endeavouring art,*
> *Thy easy numbers flow, and that each heart*
> *Hath from the leaves of thy unvalued book,*
> *Those Delphic lines with deep impression took,*
> *Then thou our fancy of herself bereaving,*
> *Dost make us marble with too much conceiving;*
> And so sepulchred in such pomp dost lie,
> That kings for such a tomb would wish to die.

> (1632 folio)

According to de Man, as Paul Stevens observes, Wordsworth omits these lines because they "make him aware that the trope he recognizes as the dominant figure of epitaphic discourse, prosopopeia, 'the fiction of the voice-from-beyond-the-grave' or the death that speaks, subverts its own consoling or restorative function"; instead, the belated poet is turned into stone, made marble (Stevens, p. 378). I would press beyond de Man's deconstructive reading to suggest that Wordsworth's omission has as much to do with his own ambivalence over the alternatives embodied in "Jonson" and "Shakespeare"; his identification with Jonson may well have caused him to omit Milton's dig at Jonson's "slow-endeavouring art." Milton's early poem, which succeeds Jonson's in the 1632 Folio, thus becomes a site of intergenerational struggle, not only between Milton and both Jonson and Shakespeare, but also between Wordsworth and Milton (rather than Pope) and between Wordsworth and Jonson and Shakespeare through the mediation of Milton, in each instance hearkening back to Jonson's initial monumentalizing effort to "enhearse" Shakespeare.

53. For an extended discussion of this subject, see William Myers, "Dryden's Shakespeare," in *Augustan Worlds*, J. C. Hilson, M. M. B. Jones, and J. R. Watson, eds. (New York: Harper and Row, 1978), pp. 15–27.

54. *An Essay of Dramatick Poesie,* in *The Works of John Dryden,* Samuel Holt Monk, ed. (Berkeley and Los Angeles: University of California Press, 1971), 17:58.

55. Dryden, *Works,* 17:58.

56. Dryden, *Works,* 17:54–57.

57. Pope, ed., *Shakespeare's Works,* 1:xi-xii.

58. Pope, ed., *Shakespeare's Works,* 1:viii.

59. Pope, ed., *Shakespeare's Works,* 1:ii.

60. Rowe, ed., *Shakespeare's Works* (London, 1709), 1:xv.

61. G. F. Parker, *Johnson's Shakespeare* (Oxford: Clarendon Press, 1989), pp. 3–4.

62. Quotations are cited from volume 7 of the Yale edition of Johnson's *Works: Johnson on Shakespeare,* Arthur Sherbo, ed. (New Haven, Conn.: Yale University Press, 1968).

63. Anne Barton, "The Road from Penshurst: Wordsworth, Ben Jonson and Coleridge in 1802," *Essays in Criticism* 37 (1987):209–33. For an illuminating account of Wordsworth and the problem of literary progenitors, see Robert J. Griffin, "Wordsworth's Pope: The Language of His Former Heart," *ELH* 54 (1987):695–715.

64. Barton, "The Road from Penshurst," p. 227.

65. Barton, "The Road from Penshurst," pp. 227–28.

66. Linda Hutcheon, *A Theory of Parody: The Teachings of Twentieth-Century Art Forms* (London: Methuen, 1985), pp. 35 and 75.

67. Cited in T. J. B. Spenser, "Shakespeare vs. the Rest: The Old Controversy," *Shakespeare Survey* 14 (1969):76–89. William Hazlitt's "Lectures Chiefly on the Dramatic Literature of the Age of Elizabeth," which, along with Lamb's *Specimens of English Dramatic Poets,* did much to rehabilitate Marlowe standing, gives some sense of the reputation of Marlowe and other "minor" Elizabethan and Jacobean playwrights in the early nineteenth century:

Their works and their names, 'poor, poor dumb names,' are all that remains of such men as Webster, Dekker, Marston, Marlowe, Chapman, Heywood, Middleton, and Rowley! 'How loved, how honored once, avails them not': though they were the friends and fellow-laborers of Shakespeare, sharing his fame and fortunes with him, the rivals of Jonson, and the masters of Beaumont and Fletcher's well-sung woes! They went out one by one unnoticed, like evening lights. . . . Marlowe is a name that stands high, and almost first in this list of dramatic worthies.

(As quoted in Millar MacClure, *Marlowe: The Critical Heritage 1588–1896* [London: Routledge & Kegan Paul], p. 78).

68. See Mary McKerrow, *The Faeds* (Edinburgh: Canongate, 1982), pp. 34–35.

69. Robert S. Knapp, *Shakespeare—The Theater and the Book* (Princeton, N. J.: Princeton University Press, 1989), pp. 160–61.

INDEX